Philosophical Skepticism
and
Ordinary-Language Analysis

Philosophical Skepticism
and
Ordinary-Language Analysis

GARRETT L. VANDER VEER

THE REGENTS PRESS OF KANSAS
Lawrence

5-8-80 ₁₂G

Library of Congress Cataloging in Publication Data
Vander Veer, Garrett L   1934-
Philosophical skepticism and ordinary-language
analysis.
Includes bibliographical references and index.
1. Ordinary-language philosophy. 2. Skepticism.
3. Wittgenstein, Ludwig, 1889-1951. I. Title.
B828.36.V36   149'.73   78-1940
ISBN 0-7006-0174-0

TO DELMA

For her encouragement, criticism, and common sense

Contents

ACKNOWLEDGMENTS

The first draft of this book was written during 1973–74 when I was the beneficiary of a sabbatical leave from Vassar College. Professor Steven Cahn of the University of Vermont read that draft and made several helpful suggestions which have resulted in a better work. Mrs. Norma Mausolf typed the manuscript quite perfectly, and my wife, Delma, prepared the index. I have tried to express my greater debt to the latter on the dedication page of this book.

INTRODUCTION

The purpose of this book is to provide a means of evaluating that style of philosophizing called Ordinary-Language Analysis. The influence of this style in the United States has now receded from its high-water mark reached some fifteen years ago, although it seems to retain much of its power in England today. In any case, the pervasive impact of ordinary-language methods on philosophers of very differing persuasions over twenty-five years or more is an obvious fact and by itself justifies the close scrutiny that this work embodies.

Since philosophers of this persuasion have directed much of their energy to exposing the inadequacies and confusions of Cartesian and Humean skepticism, it seems appropriate to think of this area as providing a test case for the viability of approaching philosophical issues in the ordinary-language manner. If it can be shown, as I hope to do, that Ordinary-Language Philosophers have not succeeded in explaining away epistemological skepticism, then there will no longer be a strong case from that direction for the exclusion of other problems and their solutions from the domain of philosophy. One may still consider a concern for our ordinary forms of speech as a legitimate interest of philosophers, but a prime reason for thinking that philosophers should not have other, more central, concerns will have been eliminated. My claim, then, is that the philosophical importance of Ordinary-Language Analysis hinges very largely on its success with skepticism, and that failure in this area moves the study of "what we say" to the edges of philosophical interest.

Modest claims for the study of "what we should say when" will not be affected by the results of this study. For example, Austin says nothing that I would wish to quarrel with when he says that words are one's tools and that "as a minimum, we should use clean tools," or when he says: "Ordinary language is *not* the last word: in principle it can everywhere be supplemented and improved upon and superseded. Only remember, it *is* the *first* word."[1] Nor do I wish to quarrel with him when he stresses that one must look to facts as well as to words in doing philosophy. But as we shall see, the practice of most philosophers has had more of a cutting edge than Austin's "linguistic phenomenology" seems to indicate.[2] For example, when Wittgenstein tells one that philosophers "must do away with all *explanation*, and description alone must take its place,"[3] one is being restricted in one's investigations to "looking into the workings of our language." And in the resolution of philosophical perplexity this does seem to make ordinary language the last word. Or to take another example, when Malcolm states that philosophical theses that imply that one is using incorrect language when one makes ordinary claims in ordinary circumstances are absurd because "ordinary language *is* correct language,"[4] he seems to give ordinary language an absolute veto over the proposals of revisionist philosophers generally.

If skepticism is not laid to rest by ordinary-language therapy, then I think the latter claims above are severely, if not fatally, undermined. For, while I cannot agree with Malcolm that revisionist and skeptical philosophers are saying or even implying that ordinary speech is incorrect for ordinary purposes, I do think that they wish to claim that there are genuine theoretical reasons that prompt one to revise one's conceptions of, and (philosophical) speech about, the world in order to obtain a more viable theoretical account of the way things are. And this claim does entail that one's ordinary use of words not be the standard by which one judges the adequacy of these proposals. Neither, however, are such proposals viewed as merely the introduction of a new technical vocabularly which hovers above ordinary speech and in no way at all corrects it. For the revisionist insists that the picture of the world embedded in ordinary speech does need criticism, even if it be adequate for our day-to-day transactions. He does want to insist that there is a standard in terms of which ordinary conceptions fall short.

If the revisionist is correct in this belief, then appeals to what we say cannot be used as bases from which one can definitively reject metaphysical proposals. Such appeals can highlight the extent to which these proposals depart from one's ordinary way of talking and can, thereby, accent the need to justify these departures; however, they cannot be used to deflate such theories and, in the process, to bring one back to one's home base. Theoretical speculation of the revisionist variety will remain a viable enterprise whose success will have to be judged by an examination of the details of any such theory, rather than by a wholesale rejection of any instance of this kind of activity. If skeptical doubts can be shown to remain real doubts even after they have been treated by the ordinary-language therapist, then there will no longer be good reasons either for restricting philosophical activity to the description of ordinary language mentioned by Wittgenstein or for regarding ordinary language as correct language in any sense that need bother the skeptic or revisionist.

The objection might be raised at this point that I am mistaken in my apparent assumption that there is a single school of Ordinary-Language Analysis whose doctrines can be revealed and refuted en masse. It is true, I think, that philosophers of this persuasion do not hold to an explicit doctrinal text, for although their spiritual inspiration comes from Wittgenstein, his own approach to philosophy is by suggestion, analogy, description, and, in general, the avoiding of theoretical commitments. Whether he is consistent in this practice is a subject for later discussion. But my claim is that there are unstated, common philosophical commitments that support and make reasonable the approach to philosophical issues that is an obvious feature of the practice of many British and American philosophers. And, we shall see that Wittgenstein's attempt to avoid doing philosophy in the traditional sense has often been paid the merest lip service by those who follow him. Suggestions harden into arguments which then become part of the assumed truths of our current era. Interestingly, there is, on reflection, often surprisingly little agreement as to the basis, meaning, and import of these arguments. In brief, many contemporary philosophers have reverted to the very type of philosophical argument that Wittgenstein opposed, all the while basing their arguments on statements gleaned from the *Investigations*.

My reaction to the above criticism is then twofold. There is no single text, such as *Language, Truth, and Logic* was for Positivism in the eyes of the English-speaking public, to which one can refer for *the* doctrines of Ordinary-Language Analysis. On the other hand, common arguments and positions surface often enough in the work of many philosophers so that one can uncover claims that are characteristic of this movement. At least in his unguarded, more traditional moments, this seems to me to be true of Wittgenstein himself. Together, these reactions suggest the following approach: Make no attempt to define who should fall within the bounds of such a study. Rather, rely on a vague sense of what kind of philosophical moves are relevant to the topic, taken in the broadest sense. Err on the side of over-inclusion. Consider each argument on its own merits and not as a representative of some explicit position. But second, do not despair that there are no arguments at all that one can consider. For while in the writings of some major philosophers it is extremely difficult to know how much emphasis is to be given to a point or how universally one is to take a certain claim, in the writings of others there is a direct attack on skeptical claims.

This approach cannot pretend to have covered all the possible variations on a common theme. But if none of the currently fashionable variations work, it is reasonable to conclude, however tentatively, that the theme remains questionable. And if one can conclude that basic errors pervade these variations, one can offer a stern, though not definitive, rebuke to this way of philosophizing. In what follows I consider several topics that are of prime concern to present-day analysts, with the hope of demonstrating the vitality of skepticism in these areas despite the attempts of some philosophers to dissolve such perplexities. By casting a wide net over a variety of both philosophers and topics, I hope to include most of the material that is relevant to an evaluation of the treatment of skepticism from the perspective of post-Wittgensteinian philosophy.

1

A Preliminary Survey
of Skepticism and Its Critics

The striking feature about philosophical skepticism is that once one is in its grasp, one's most unquestioned certainties appear to be shaky and without justification. It has this result, not because it finds that particular judgments have not been fulfilling accepted standards, but because it finds a weakness in those standards themselves. And the weaknesses it finds are so judged, not because they have led to erroneous judgments, but because they do not meet other, stricter, standards, ones that often seem incapable of realization. The result is that entire areas of knowledge claims become relegated to the realm of opinion and guesswork.

Certainly the development of the scientific conception of nature played an important role in the development of Cartesian skepticism. If nature was as different from the common-sense view as scientific theory suggested, then an explanation of how and why one had mistaken the appearance for the reality was in order. And once this new picture of nature was developed, there seemed to be other areas in which the same sort of argument applied. The haunting result was that philosophers seemed to be burdened with doubts that the ordinary man ignored, that had no effect on even the philosopher's behavior, and that could not be settled by any kind of appeal to experience. As Ayer points out, what was in question was how to interpret experience, and in this case, experience is of no help.[1]

But I think that the new science simply promoted an idea that had historical roots and that would have found its way into philosophy eventually. I refer to the idea of a "gap" between what is presented to one and the ultimate subject of one's judgment. Under the guidance of this idea, the former becomes evidence, and the latter becomes a conclusion reached on the basis of that evidence. In some cases this gap seems undoubtedly to be there, as in the case of induction; at other times it is difficult to verify, as in the case of sensations and the external world. Generally, the skeptic thinks that what functions as evidence is a different kind of thing from that of which it is evidence, but the case of induction would be an exception to this rule. And in some cases, that which functions as the subject of judgment—say the external world as the inference from our ideas or sensations —can function as a datum: for example, in inferences to the past based on observations of physical objects, or in treating the ordinary world as Idea or Representation of the real world.

But these differences make no important difference in the pattern of argument that the skeptic applies in each case: Admit that we normally cross the gap unthinkably and with no sense of risk. How can this move be shown to be reasonable? Can one uncover principles of inference that will justify one's knowledge claims in these areas and restore one's confidence in ordinary attitudes? Of course, the skeptic claims that once these "gaps" are discovered, there is no way back to the naïve security of common sense. One may well continue to find that one's beliefs are of immense practical value, and one may never doubt them in one's nonphilosophical moments, but one will have to admit that they are theoretically unjustified. And there seems to be nothing that one can do to produce such a justification. As Ayer says: "He wants to maintain both that a certain sort of evidence is in the circumstances the best that we could possibly have, and also that it is not good enough. It thus becomes for him a necessary fact that we have no sufficient guarantee of truth."[2]

Often this point is put in terms of a proposed "strict" sense of some term such as "know" or "identical," in contrast to which our ordinary use of such terms seems sloppy and misleading. Ordinary cases are not real cases of identity or knowledge. And I think it is not difficult to see why the skeptic insists on the strict sense as being the genuine sense. (Alternative accounts will be explored below.) Once the evidence-conclusion model is accepted as the correct analysis of our ordinary judgments, and once one accepts the existence of the gap that this picture suggests, one feels as if one were on one side of a door, wondering from clues what is going on in the other room. One then feels a need to get to the other side of that door, since one had previously not been aware of any such barrier. Under the influence of this picture, the only way to reinstate one's former relation to one's object is to demand direct contact with that object. However, now the new notion of "direct contact" is contrasted with the former, "indirect contact." One's former state can be called "direct contact" only in retrospect, for the notion of "direct" obtains a meaning only as a part of the evidence-conclusion model. Of course, this denigrates one's former state and makes it appear that true knowledge is dependent on direct contact with the object of knowledge. Hence, one is led to embrace the strict sense of 'know'. In order to make his case, the skeptic must convince us of at least three propositions: (1) that there are such gaps between evidence and object; (2) that if there are, they are harmful; (3) that knowledge by acquaintance is a meaningful alternative to knowledge by inference (for if it is not, there is no contrast by which the latter may seem to fall short of the standard set by the former).

Philosophers have tried to attack skepticism in almost every possible manner. One method is to deny that there is any gap by denying that the object transcends the evidence. Thus arise realism, phenomenalism, behaviorism, operationalism. And if one can conceive of statements about the past as concealed predictions about the future, there will be no unbridgeable gap between evidence and object even in this case. On the other hand, some philosophers are content to accept this gap but insist that it makes no difference in knowledge claims. For example, Moore says that he does not know the proposition that the earth existed for many years before his birth directly, nor does he know what the evidence for this proposition is with any exactness. Yet, he claims, these facts do not provide a good reason for denying that he knows the proposition to be true.[3]

The ordinary-language approach admits the gap but tries to reveal the deep-seated incoherence of the skeptic's attempt to turn this into a problem for the knower. The demands of our linguistic or conceptual scheme are such that there is no coherent way in which our claims about the past, other minds, inductions, and so forth, could be shown to be systematically unfounded. Once the concepts that one uses are fully understood, one will no longer feel that there is any problem in one's ordinary claims, and one will be able to show how these claims actually work successfully. As we shall see, philosophers who attack skepticism in this manner try to find some way of crossing the gap which will be stronger than that provided by ordinary, empirically verified correlations, while falling short of deductive conclusiveness. The problem of other minds provides a case in point. No one claims that it follows deductively that if a person is in physical state X, he is in mental state Y; yet, one wants there to be some kind of necessity in the connection of the two. The notion of a criterion plays a crucial role in finding this kind of necessity.

Last, there are those philosophers who admit the gap that the skeptic insists upon, but who do not feel the need of any special means of crossing the gap. Such philosophers simply do not feel disturbed by the revelations of the skeptic and, therefore, are content to treat them with more conventional means. So, induction is said to be justified inductively: the Argument from Analogy is proposed as an adequate means of justifying one's beliefs about other minds, and inferences to physical objects are said to provide the best explanation of the appearance of our immediate data. The analogy here is with testing scientific theories and with providing the best possible explanation. Therefore, justification takes the form of the greatest coherence that can be brought to one's experiences, and probability is all that is promised. But why should one want more than that if the scientist is satisfied with as much?

Circularities have been alleged in both the reductionist's answer to the skeptic and in that of the empiricist. And if it can be shown that attempts to construct physical objects out of sense

10

data, or to think of selves as bundles of particulars, or to justify induction inductively, presuppose the very notions that are supposed to be satisfactorily reduced or explained, then these methods fail. However, as a preliminary remark to such a discussion one can say that neither approach seems to provide a promising answer to the skeptic. Neither provides the means by which one might recapture one's preskeptical beliefs and their characteristic aura of confidence.

The reductionist move fails because it does not leave us with a recognizable object. To escape this charge, reductionists are apt to argue that they are really not performing a reductive act at all. Rather, they insist that they are only analyzing the beliefs that we have, clearing the ground of unwanted philosophical complications and confusions, and exposing the bare bones of our common-sense commitments. Thus they hope to avoid the charge that they are as much revisionary metaphysicians as their opponents are.

But this reply seems questionable for several reasons. First, the origin of, say, Berkeley's conception of a physical object lies in Locke's philosophical theory of matter, which theory opens the door to skepticism. But it is unlikely that the reply to a philosophical claim can be anything but another philosophical claim whose main purpose is to defeat a philosophical opponent rather than to simply expose what we believed all along. In any case, Berkeley makes no detailed attempt to unpack common sense, and the view that he suggests is in many aspects obviously in conflict with common sense: for example, over the connection of physical objects with the perception of *anyone*; the question of the identity of physical objects; and so forth.[4]

The second reason is that the relation between philosophy, science, and common sense is not as clear as this reply presupposes. Thus, in sweeping away the objectionable metaphysical theory, one throws out those elements of common sense which that theory has built on and, perhaps, has distorted. No philosophy is without its ties to common sense, and there is much in common sense that is simply an alternative philosophical outlook. For example, Cartesianism and common sense are not separable at all points. Therefore, when Ryle tries to relieve one of the burden of the former in the interest of revealing the latter,

11

it is obvious that one ends up with another reconstruction of common sense for philosophical purposes. And one might add, the claim that nothing is lost in the new analysis is belied by the biased origin of the analysis. The Verificationist or the Behaviorist is so concerned about the progress of science that he is willing to promote a concept of meaningfulness or of mind that seems to be beyond doubt revisionary.

Third, the unclarity of the notion of analysis muddies the contrast between analysis and reduction. For if an analysis is only supposed to present an alternative concept that for *some* purposes is equivalent to the deposed concept—for example, that can do the same job as well or better than the latter—then the analysis seems to be a technical exercise that is irrelevant to the skeptic's charge. If the two concepts are extensionally equivalent, the charge of reductionism will still be valid, for the analyzed concept will not present one with the beliefs that were expressed in the meaning of the discarded concept.

Fourth, on the other hand, if the analysis is supposed to give one the meaning of the analyzed thing, it is obvious that it often fails to do so. Humeans, Ryleans, Phenomenalists, Behaviorists—all present one with objects that one knows are not what one meant, and one knows this even if one cannot say precisely what that meaning is or how the preferred analysis has altered it. Often the standards of meaningfulness or of clarity or of adequacy that are held by the analyst turn out to be much stricter than those implicit in common sense. The result is that the analyzed concept seems alien and reductive. My conclusion is that most cases of analysis really are cases of reduction, and that reduction, by eliminating the transcendent object that one intended all along, fails as an answer to skepticism. One wants transcendence of some variety without the skepticism that comes in its wake, and one refuses to escape from skepticism by being told that, for example, one really was referring to the future in one's assertions about the past or that all one meant, or could have meant, by another's pain was his behavior or his disposition to behave.

However, if one accepts the gap that skepticism feeds on and tries to treat it with ordinary minimal means, the results do not seem to be any more promising. For example, if one admits to any doubts about the reasonableness of induction—and one seems to do so if one feels the need to justify it—then it is hard to see how talk about the success that results from following inductive procedures will help. The difficulty or flaw that prompted this response will surely reappear at the level of justification, for it is a flaw that is endemic to the procedure wherever it is applied. And to take another case, the Argument from Analogy does not justify one's beliefs in other minds in a satisfactory manner. Even assuming that this argument is logically coherent, the inescapable conclusion is that if *this* is one's best means of justification in this area, then one's ordinary conviction is much too strong and unqualified. For since one cannot verify the analogy in even a single case, all that one can appeal to are notions of probability and coherence, notions that are not ingredients of our ordinary attitude.[5]

But even if the Argument from Analogy is not strong enough to recapture one's original innocence, one can take something positive from it. Our tentative conclusion from the failure of reductionism was that any method that successfully deals with skepticism must preserve the transcendent reference on which skepticism feeds. Here our tentative conclusion is that a successful answer to skepticism must show that this gap is harmless, that it does not provide the opportunity for skepticism that the skeptic believes it does. Both the Moorean and the Ordinary-Language replies to skepticism try to work this middle ground.

There is one more approach to skepticism that we should mention in this preliminary survey. One might argue that skeptical doubt is illegitimate because it is not doubt at all. According to this line of thought, practical doubt (taking 'practical' in a very wide sense) constitutes legitimate doubt, and purely theoretical doubt is what Peirce called "paper doubt." Peirce's position is that doubt originates in moments of real or feigned uncertainty, and it "stimulates to action until it is destroyed."[6] As he states, "The irritation of doubt causes a struggle to attain a state of belief" (p. 99). Whereas belief is a "habit of mind," doubt is "the privation of a habit" (p. 189). The *sole* function of thought or inquiry is to produce belief or habits of action (pp. 119, 123). Given this conception of thought and doubt, one is not surprised when he says that it is "make-believe" to think that one doubts something merely because one puts the matter in the form of a question. Inquiry can start only from a "real and living" doubt (p. 100), and without such a start, "discussion is idle" (see also p. 188).

The issues raised by Peirce are far-reaching and cannot be dealt with adequately here. However, a few remarks are in order. Unless one accepts the doctrine that all thought has a practical outcome as its goal ("The *final* upshot of thinking is the exercise of volition," p. 121), there seems to be no reason to think that all that doubt does is to stimulate thinking toward the establishment of rules for action. Presumably, thought "appeases the irritation of doubt" (p. 121) by resolving the questions that doubt raises. Despite the suggestion of Peirce's causal language here, thought can succeed only by fulfilling the purpose that is brought into view by the doubting process, an end that is usually called truth but is called belief by Peirce. And the question is, What reason is there for thinking that the end to be achieved always is a practical one? Why must all one's doubts be about what one should do?

One point should be clarified immediately. I take it that when Peirce says that "thought is essentially an action" (p. 121), he does not mean to reduce his theory to one that is merely verbally different from that of the Cartesian. For if thought be an action and if the end of thinking be the production of habits of action, it would follow that a readiness about what one might think of certain ideas if they were presented could be construed not only as the end of thinking but also as practical. For Peirce's view to be interesting, he must maintain a distinction between practical and theoretical actions, and while he can postpone to some hypothetical point in the future the practical action that is the final result of thinking, he must hold that such a result is the sole end that thought ultimately seeks. Otherwise, there is nothing in what he says that could not be accepted happily by the Cartesian, despite the appearance of a substantive difference between them. Peirce can stretch the term 'practical' only so far before his doctrine becomes empty, without a significant contrast, which is suggested, nevertheless, by his language (see p. 123). The same remarks apply when Peirce says that belief *is* a rule of action (p. 121) and that belief, not truth, is the end of thought or inquiry (p. 100).

The problem for Peirce is to convince us that he is not merely being arbitrary in limiting 'thought' to 'inquiry', where the latter entails actually doing something in the world. For example, when he says, "If there be a unity among our sensations which has no reference to how we shall act on a given occasion, as when we listen to a piece of music, why, we do not call that thinking" (p. 123), this seems merely arbitrary. If the "we" be native speakers of a language, then he must mean only that we *ought* not to call it thinking, and at once he is making a proposal rather than recording a fact of usage. I say this because one can surely *concentrate* on a piece of music, *recognize* themes, *notice* unusual features, *discriminate* various parts, and the like. Yet, this seems to be the vocabulary of thought, for to recognize something at least implies that one applies a concept to the thing in question; and this is enough to make the experience a thinking one. But even if one limits thinking to reflection, requiring an overt activity as a sign of thought, it seems difficult to justify the claim that thinking is ultimately practical.

If one considers what one is trying to accomplish when one thinks in science, mathematics, or philosophy, and one does so apart from any precommitment to a philosophical view about what one *must* be doing, I believe that the natural answer is that one seeks the truth, or in some cases the truth insofar as it is useful. To deny the existence of the disinterested pursuit of truth is to turn one's back on the experience of thinking and to confuse what we in fact often accept (beliefs that we could, but do not, question further) with the end that we seek. Peirce is an acute psychologist of thinking, but the fact that one settles for less than the ideal does not mean that one seeks only the lesser end. I claim, then, that one's experience of thinking does not disclose that one seeks and can only seek to institute habits for action.

Further, if one counters by saying that although one tells oneself that one is disinterested in one's theorizing, in fact all that one achieves are rules for action, it does not seem that the facts will bear out even this reduced claim. For the more abstract an idea is, the harder it is to say convincingly that it *commits* one to any specific action or type of action. Consider a Bradleyan metaphysics, for example. What actions am I *committed* to by the mere fact of assenting to the doctrine that relations are unreal? Perhaps one can think of actions that seem to be suggested by such ideas, but (1) these actions will tend to be things I would *say* or *think* under certain conditions, thus blurring the distinction between theoretical and practical, mentioned above, and (2) these actions or tendencies to act will be one thing and the ideas another.

That is, to be consistent, one may have to behave on given occasions in certain ways if one holds certain ideas, but to say this much is to say that the ideas and the actions are different but connected entities. This means that the actions or tendencies to act cannot be the *meaning* of the ideas. Instead they turn out to be something that may go along with the ideas but that are not constitutive of them. Each thing is what it is, and not another thing, as the saying goes. Speculations about the nature of matter or of goodness are just that; they are not concealed plans of what one would do under certain circumstances.

If one accepts this, there is no reason to limit doubt and the reflection that ensues to the realm of the practical. It may still be true that such doubt "has nothing to do with any serious business" (p. 188), but it will be doubt nonetheless; and the discussion that it engenders may be "idle" (p. 100), but discussion it will be for all that.

I conclude that Peirce has failed to show that skepticism has misconceived the nature of doubt and of thinking. He has not justified his decision to call doubt only that irritation which looks toward a practical issue. The result is that whether one treats his suggestion as an arbitrary limitation of the meaning of a word or as a proposal to limit the range of its legitimate use, there is nothing he says that prevents the skeptic from continuing to regard his doubts as genuine, though theoretical.

Looking ahead, the ordinary-language movement represents the attempt to locate the basic incoherence of skepticism in its refusal to acknowledge certain general principles which form necessary prerequisites for linguistic mastery and communication. The result is that philosophical skepticism cannot be part of a language, for it unknowingly subverts the very ground that makes meaningful utterances possible. By comparison with this "deep" move against the skeptic, the Peircean attempt to limit meaningful doubt and thought to the realm of the practical seems superficial and arbitrary.

There is a second side to Peirce's thought, however, which might seem at first to provide a better means of dismissing philosophical skepticism. He states that the primary way of clarifying our thoughts is to follow this rule: "Consider what effects, which might conceivably have practical bearings, we conceive the object of our conception to have. Then our conception of these effects is the whole of our conception of the object" (p. 124). Such a criterion—a version of the reductionist argument discussed above —would make philosophical skepticism either senseless or harmless. For if one takes "practical bearings" to refer to a change in one's behavior other than thought or speech, it is clear that the skeptical doubts of philosophers have no such effects and thus are meaningless. If, on the other hand, "practical bearings" extends over speech and thought, skepticism reduces to the claim that one's utterances would be different in certain philosophical settings. And this claim is both harmless and testable.

The problem with this criterion is that it is too strict to be plausible, for it requires that Operationalism be the only meaningful conception of scientific theories, that references to other minds be construed as references to what a person says, does, and so forth. And as Peirce states, in his view, "The rational meaning of every proposition lies in the future" (p. 194). Or, "A belief that Christopher Columbus discovered America really refers to the future" (p. 222). None of these substitutions of a testable object for the apparent object of one's concern carries conviction, for one ordinarily has no trouble in referring to transcendent objects, and one is quite able to spell out the meaning of one's claims in terms that are not reducible to those which refer to future or perceptible objects. Thus, once again Peirce's restrictions on meaning are found to seem arbitrarily narrow.

Perhaps the problem is not with the principle lying behind Peirce's criterion but with the strict interpretation that he gives to it. Then it would be a promising move against skepticism to loosen the requirements for meaningfulness while restricting them enough so that skeptical doubts remain meaningless. Let us

17

say that a statement is meaningful if it is weakly verifiable, the latter phrase requiring only that some evidence be relevant to the truth or falsity of the claim. But surely, evidence is relevant, in some sense, to skeptical or metaphysical claims. If someone doubts that one can know that there are other minds or that induction is rational, it is relevant, though not decisive, to point to the ordinary uses of 'know' and 'rational'. These provide at least prima facie evidence against the skeptic.

If one then retreats to some concept of strict verifiability, it is clear that skepticism cannot meet this test; but then, neither can scientific or common-sense claims. I conclude that the attempt to allow reference to transcendent objects, but only in those cases in which evidence is either relevant or decisive to the outcome, fails for lack of a concept of 'verifiable' that is neither too strict nor too generous. Enough attempts have been made at such a formulation that it is reasonable to believe that the fault lies, not with limited philosophical ingenuity, but with the very idea of such a program. Skepticism seems to be immune from attack in this direction.

We shall have to discuss the relation between the Positivist's move against skepticism and that of the ordinary-language philosopher, for many statements of the latter—those about criteria or beetles in boxes—*seem* to rest on some version of the Verifiability Principle. For the moment I only wish to point out one important difference in approach. The Positivist tries to impose a standard of meaningfulness on the skeptic, a standard that seems foreign and arbitrary both to the skeptic and to ordinary common sense. The natural result is that this standard seems arbitrarily devised to suit certain special interests. The ordinary-language philosopher, on the other hand, claims to uncover an incoherence which the skeptic will have to recognize because it is drawn from his own desire to say something. Since the skeptic is confident that his assertions are legitimate linguistic items, this approach has the promise of being both relevant to the skeptic and definitive against him; and a proof that his position undermines the conditions that make expressions in a language possible is bound to seem relevant to him. We now turn to the question of to what extent this promise is genuine and has been fulfilled in the writings of ordinary-language philosophers.

The Ordinary-Language Approach
to Philosophical Perplexity:
Some Examples

In this chapter I plan to examine the ordinary-language treatment of four traditional philosophical problems: (1) the nature of time, (2) the nature of self-identity, (3) the nature of free will, and (4) the nature of universals. Strawson has described this method of philosophizing as follows: "It consists in the attempt to describe the complex patterns of logical behaviour which the concepts of daily life exhibit. It is not a matter of prescribing the model conduct of model words, but of describing the actual conduct of actual words; not a matter of making rules, but of noting customs."[1] One can pursue this type of investigation for its own sake or with the conviction that such knowledge may be of some philosophical help. But those philosophers with whom we are concerned wish to use it as a means of revealing to the philosopher those linguistic confusions which are the origin of his perplexity. As Strawson says:

> The producer of philosophical paradox, or the sufferer from philosophical perplexity, is temporally dominated by one logical mode of operation of expressions, or by one way of using language, or by one logical type or category of objects, or by one sort of explanation, or by one set of cases of the application of a given concept;

and attempts to see, to explain, something which is different, in terms of, or on analogy with, his favoured model. [P. 515]

Strawson further characterizes this state of mind as a "temporary one-sidedness of vision, a kind of selective blindness which cuts out most of the field, but leaves one part of it standing out with a peculiar brilliance" (p. 515).

A similar position is taken by Norman Malcolm. To point out the ordinary usage of a term to one who has already been drawn to a line of reasoning whose conclusion conflicts with that usage may well prove unhelpful. Therefore, to free the person from the apparently conclusive line of reasoning which dominates his thinking, it is required, "first, that this reasoning and these analogies be sympathetically and accurately *reconstructed*; and, second, that they be examined in detail to find at what point the analogies deceive him and exactly where the reasoning is mistaken."[2]

Putting the two views together, one arrives at something like the following: philosophical perplexity can best be dealt with by (1) revealing the ordinary use of the term or terms in question, (2) showing how this use differs from the use preferred by the perplexed, and (3) explaining why this particular model has the attraction it has. Presumably, the result is that the attraction of the model will vanish and, with it, the perplexity that it generated.

However, as stated, there seems to be a gap between the ends to be reached and the means that are to achieve them. How will confronting the perplexed with the ordinary use of a term and contrasting that use with the use that one philosophically prefers convince one that one's reasoning is "mistaken" or that one's use is "distorted" or that certain analogies have "deceived" one? Unless these terms are to be either empty (mere synonyms for the difference between his usage and the ordinary one) or question-begging (the difference here is just *assumed* to imply a mistake), it must be shown (or be obvious) how the evidence in question should produce the desired conclusion. And there seems to be only one way in which it could: if the perplexed were trying to make explicit the ordinary use of a term and if it could be shown that he failed to do so *because* of the hold a use had on his attempted reconstruction, then both his failure and the reason for the failure would be apparent. We shall see in the next chapter that Malcolm interprets the claims of G. E. Moore in just this fashion; but for the moment, a few remarks are in order.

Let us agree that the philosopher in question does not know the ordinary use of a certain term in the sense that while he can use the term as any native speaker can, he is not able to spell out explicitly the different senses that the term has in different contexts. Stage one of the ordinary-language attack may well tell him something that he does not know. But this news will not be relevant to his proposal, unless the proposal was *about* ordinary usage. And since it is very likely that the perplexed will regard his proposed usage to be about the "real" sense of the term (that which is important for philosophical purposes), there is little reason to think that he will acknowledge the relevance of the proferred evidence to what he is doing. And the proposer has a prima facie claim to know what he is doing.

It seems, then, that the ordinary-language philosopher must find some way of showing that attempts to do something other than give the ordinary sense of a term are fundamentally incoherent. Either one is trying to present that usage (in which case one has failed to do so), or one is trying to call that usage into question (in which case one has done nothing at all). There is a third alternative, that of promoting the use of a special, technical use of a term, but that is philosophically harmless and easily allowable by the ordinary-language philosopher. As we shall see, both moves have been made against the philosophical skeptic, and if one is not convinced by these moves, it seems reasonable to say that the ordinary-language method described by Strawson and Malcolm will be without a justification. Let us turn now to our examples of the ordinary-language treatment of philosophical problems.

TIME

According to J. N. Findlay, the striking fact about philosophical problems concerning time is that time should seem problematic in this way when it is so familiar and so easily dealt with in ordinary situations. There is nothing troublesome about temporal expressions to native speakers of a language. A second peculiarity about philosophers' questions here, which he notes, is that they cannot be answered by an appeal to experience, "For he *has* all the kinds of experience that could throw light on his problem, and yet he is puzzled."[3] Findlay's conclusion is that these problems have no answer and are based on nothing "genuinely problematic" in one's experience. They arise because one finds something unsatisfactory in the ways that we speak about time, and they find their "answer" accordingly in the discovery of why one finds language inadequate in philosophical moments and "by deliberately adopting ways of talking that provide appeasement for those needs" (p. 146).

It is worth pointing out that everything will hinge on the precise reasons one gives for finding difficulties with ordinary language about time. For if one can show that one finds language inadequate because there are properties of time that, although familiar, are also causes of conceptual difficulty, one will not be willing to accept Findlay's sharp division between the experiential and the linguistic sources of philosophical perplexity. There seems to be no reason to think that when one uses ordinary temporal terminology, one is aware of the implications or questions that the use of such terminology creates; therefore, perplexity about the familiar loses some of its strangeness. And one can 'have' the experience of time without understanding that experience; therefore, one's perplexity can be grounded in the very experience that ordinarily seems unproblematic. Nor is it obvious that questions that cannot be answered by an appeal to experience cannot be drawn from experience. If one wonders about pervasive features of time, rather than about specific dates, then there is no reason to think that one ought to be able to answer such questions by methods that are normally appropriate to more specific problems. What methods are appropriate to solving philosophical problems remains an open question, but Findlay has not shown that the methods must be linguistic.

Findlay locates the specific source of confusion about time in a process by which one is gradually persuaded to use familiar expressions in both a wider and a narrower sense than is usual. This is possible because some words naturally widen and others naturally narrow, and because, in general, distinctions of right and wrong usage are unclear. Such changes in usage may result in a "temporary disorientation," which leads to philosophical confusion. Thus, one opens the way for trouble when in the name of *strictness* one insists that a term have only its narrowest possible meaning, or when in the name of *consistency* one insists that a term that has a use in one context should have the same use in an analogous context. For example, one may claim that 'present' or 'now' can mean in all strictness only a point-instant or that (assuming that there are such things as momentary presents) adding units of time together must be construed on the model of a pile of money being built up out of coins (p. 153). Both moves lead to the Augustinian problem of how there could be any length to time or how we could measure this length if it existed. Talk of things happening, taking time, and so forth, becomes of no use, or at least one becomes unsure that one uses such expressions properly.

But Findlay asks, Why apply "linguistic principles" to events of short duration which one normally applies only to long events? (Again, the answer is, Consistency.) Why not simply decide to say that some short events have no parts in the future or past, or that they can be present while some of their parts are future or past? Or recognizing the disanalogy between moments of time and parts of a whole, one could simply "rule" that events that take time can be said to be composed of events that take no time at all. As Findlay says, "It does not, in fact, matter, in all this choice of diction, *what* we say, provided only that we truly please ourselves: the facts are there, we can see and show them, and it is for us to talk of them in ways which will neither perplex nor embarrass us" (p. 153).[4]

Zeno's paradoxes of motion similarly yield to a refusal to accept the application of 'divisibility' to all happenings, however small, or to a recasting of Zeno's terms into ordinary ones or by noting that it is only to his technical terms that infinite divisibility applies. Last, McTaggart's claim that time is a self-contradictory concept can be shown to arise out of the understandable but regretable and avoidable conflation of two tendencies: that of our ordinary tensed language to describe events that happen at different times, and that of a de-tensed language, which might improve communication by ignoring the "local colouration" that tenses give to our statements. McTaggart's difficulties arise when one illicitly combines these two languages in a single conception of time.

Let us begin by agreeing that philosophical difficulties about time arise either because philosophers use key terms in narrow or strict ways or because one applies notions such as 'whole' or 'continuous' with an unusual consistency and in different contexts, and even that one allows oneself to follow what seem to be the natural implication of terms that one applies to time (p. 156). Certainly this explains why such problems do not occur to the ordinary man, but does it give one grounds for treating such philosophic moves as mistakes, to be cured by references to ordinary language? I think not.

Findlay makes no attempt to argue that the perplexities of Augustine and Zeno are meaningless, although he does assert that the notion that events come into being part by part has "no plain empirical meaning," there being a limit to the divisions that man and his machines can perform. However, this claim rests on an exploded version of the Verifiability Theory of Meaning—namely, that meaning can be limited to what one can in fact verify—and so one need not concern oneself with it. But if the perplexities are meaningful, then the fact of possible replies does not count against the perplexity or for the reply. The reasons behind the contending positions will have to be evaluated before one is judged preferable to the other. It will not do to say that one is free to say what one wishes about the existence of the past (p. 155) or of the infinite divisibility of time segments. Nor will one be "free" to disentangle the two dimensions of time that are found in McTaggart's argument for time's unreality if McTaggart can show that there are good reasons for characterizing time in this way. And above all, one cannot *assume* that such good reasons cannot be forthcoming.

Findlay might reply that (1) the disanalogy between the ordinary use of 'part' and 'whole' and the application of these terms to time allows us to reject the consequences that would follow from taking these terms in their ordinary sense in this new context and (2) in cases in which the perplexity arises because one has introduced a technical term (e.g., 'infinite happening') and then taken it for a normal term, one is free to give it any meaning one wishes which obviates the paradox. This move makes it clear that nothing that conflicts with common sense has actually been said. Thus, one can say that an infinite number of "happenings" must be completed before any act can be completed, but this does not mean, as it suggests, that an infinite number of ordinary happenings must occur.

But merely because the philosopher's argument rests on an analogy (thereby admitting a disanalogy) or because his use of terms is more strict than is usual or because he speaks of happenings that we cannot "see and show," Findlay is not given unrestricted freedom to so define his concepts that no problems arise. In all of these cases the philosopher is extending the use of a term in some sense beyond its normal range, but his argument is that this extension is appropriate because the nature of the subject matter demands it. He does not think of himself as introducing a technical vocabulary whose words he can define at will; rather, he claims to be continuing the characterization of time that one finds in ordinary speech because such speech has not pushed its characterization as far as the nature of time requires. If this requires one to say things that sound absurd, it is because the greater analytic power of the philosopher reveals difficulties that were hidden by the lesser characterization of one's ordinary vocabulary.

Nothing I have said shows that the philosopher is justified in these claims, and we will come to powerful arguments designed to show that he cannot be right. My only point here is that Findlay's method presupposes rather than shows that the philosopher's moves are mistakes and that redirection of the meaning of terms is a proper way to deal with his proposals. That is, Findlay's descriptions of what the philosopher does and how that differs from common use do not make an argument against the philosopher, and his method of "resolving" philosophical perplexity works only if he can first establish the arbitrary character of the philosopher's use of terms.

But his attempts to do this are very weak indeed. The fact that "no one has witnessed a lapse of time being built up out of instants, as he can witness a pile of money being built up out of coins" (p. 154), merely points out a disanalogy between the notion of 'whole' as applied in both cases. By itself, this does not show that the analogy is not a sound one; it merely points out the fact that it is an analogy. In general, one has no reason to accept Findlay's reconstruction of philosophical perplexity until he can show that the philosopher's extended use of terms is either illegitimate or at least not required by the subject matter. And he makes no attempt to do this.

Findlay's discussion of the nothingness of the past is a good case in point. He says that we are not "compelled to say that the past is nothing: we may, if we like, credit it with existence or subsistence or any other suitable status" (p. 155). He reasons as follows: (1) we think of the nothingness of the past as preventing one from learning about the past on an analogy with the way that the nothingness of a bachelor's children would prevent one from learning about them; (2) one sees that this analogy is absurd when one realizes that there are established ways of finding out what has happened in the past; (3) therefore, one has no good reason for saying that the past is nothing and can credit it with whatever form of existence is helpful and not misleading.

However, the evidence presented in (2) will not lead to the conclusion in (3), for there is nothing in the philosopher's claim that implies that there are not recognized ways of learning the facts about the past. He can fully accept the standards of historical scholarships that differentiate well-made and poorly made conclusions, questioning only the framework assumption that there is a past, which makes our statements about it true or false. Thus, the philosopher would reject the analogy with a bachelor's children. Within the ordinary meaning of the phrase, 'bachelor's children' expresses a self-contradiction; therefore, there are no ordinary methods for determining the facts about such beings. But since the philosopher's doubts about the reality of the past do not occur within one's ordinary concerns, there is no reason to expect that such doubts will deny or have an impact on the existence of historical methods. Once again, Findlay does not correctly characterize the nature of the philosopher's claim.

SELF-IDENTITY

Hume's discussion of self-identity is perhaps the best known in philosophical literature, and the impact of his views on subsequent discussion has been enormous. In outline, his argument is simple and apparently devastating. Introspection reveals that there is no simple, unchanging thing in the self; if there were, it would be a candidate for the essential, identical self. Instead, introspection shows that the parts of the self change with extreme rapidity. But such all-consuming change makes the self different at each moment; the whole is a different whole to the extent that the parts are different parts. In fact, Hume continues, the notion of identity is a confused blend of unity at one moment and diversity or difference over many moments. A simple thing such as an impression is self-same during any one brief segment of time (Hume does not tell us what the life span of an impression is), and a complex thing has diversity and difference over a larger segment of time. But to be identical a thing would have to be both one and many, and this is a self-contradictory combination of two exclusive notions. One's imagination helps one to ignore this difficulty, but one's reason discloses that self-identity (or any identity for that matter) is an illusion. Normally, of course, one does not treat change or difference as opposed to identify; one can change and yet be the same person for all that. Nevertheless, Hume insists that sameness and difference are opposed, and that one's ordinary view to the contrary is a fiction.

Thus we see that Hume's skepticism is built on taking 'identity' in a strict sense, a sense that excludes change and that, therefore, makes it impossible for anything to be identical. A self lacks true unity because it is composed of many parts; it has no true identity because it is different from moment to moment. As Augustine narrowed the scope of 'present', so Hume narrowed the scope of 'same', and the result is that things lack the identity that they are normally assumed to have. One overlooks this fact because the change is so rapid and often minimal that one's imagination treats the new, different thing as if it were the same as the thing it replaced, except for moments when the change is so obvious that one has to bring in the notion of a substratum, which is supposed to be unchanged, to guarantee the identity of the thing whose lack of identity is now obvious.

Hume tries to enhance the plausibility of this thesis, as Penelhum points out, by presenting a series of cases in which he assumes that it is clear that there is no identity but in which, nevertheless, one claims identity because one is able to ignore the change in each case. If one feigns identity in these cases, then it is not so hard to believe that one could feign it as well in the case of the self.

Penelhum finds, fairly enough, the key notion in Hume's skepticism about identity to lie in his strict limitation of 'same' to an object that suffers no change at all. For then it would be a contradiction to say that something that was different was also the same. Penelhum finds "it hard to believe that a mistake lies at the root of so much of our language, especially since Hume has claimed to reveal it by a piece of linguistic analysis."[5] And he offers the following counter to Hume's argument:

> The rejoinder to Hume, then, consists simply in saying that the pairs of expressions, (a) "numerically the same" and "containing many parts" and (b) "numerically the same" and "changed," are not pairs of contradictories. So we have not made a mistake in saying that a succession of related objects may form a unit of a certain kind, or that the same thing may undergo radical changes. [P. 581]

According to Penelhum, Hume is involved in two sorts of muddles. He thinks that something cannot be one if it is composed of many—and particularly successive—parts, and he thinks that something cannot be the same unless it remains unchanged over a given segment of time. The former error is easily exposed by noting that our language works in such a way that one can always treat the many, successive parts as parts of a whole. Thus: "A succession of notes is one theme. A succession of words is one sentence. If the succession does not form a theme or sentence, it is still a *succession* or series" (p. 580). Whether one kind of thing can have many parts "depends entirely on what sort of thing it is."

Hume's second error rests on a confusion between specific and numerical identity. When one speaks of something remaining unchanged, one is speaking of sameness in the "specific" sense, but there is nothing about numerical identity that requires this kind of sameness. In fact, not only can one be numerically the same while being specifically different, but one cannot be said to have *changed* unless one remains numerically the same (see p. 580). Penelhum points out that there are some special kinds of things that are numerically different if they change specifically—for example, a musical note; and the kinds of change that a thing can endure before becoming another thing depends on the kind of thing that it is. Nonetheless, it is, in general, true that our language allows or requires one to speak of something as numerically the same even when it has undergone specific change.

If questions about identity are to be answered by reference to the kind of thing in question and not by an analysis of 'same' and 'different', then we can reinterpret Hume's examples of feigning identity as discoveries of the identity criteria that are appropriate to a variety of things despite their undergoing more or less radical changes. There is nothing improper about saying that a church is the same church, despite the fact that it has been rebuilt, if its relation to its parishioners remains unchanged.

Hume thinks otherwise, because he is mesmerized by the idea that there is only a single standard of identity, that of invariance. By the standard of "strict" identity, other uses of that term are loose or improper, but then that is an imposition of one standard of identity on the plurality of ordinary standards. Penelhum concludes that Hume is guilty of a "linguistic error, of a misdescription of the way in which certain words in the language are in fact used" (p. 586), and he insists that there is no paradox about identity. As he says, "the ordinary language-user is quite innocent" (p. 588). The fact that substance philosophies are attractive to philosophical newcomers does not show that they are solutions to problems that are felt by the ordinary man. Rather, this is a sign of one's limited experience in philosophy. The issue was not felt before one became linguistically confused upon entering philosophy.

Now there is much in Hume's reflections about the self that is highly questionable. His attempt to find the identity of a self or mind rather than of a person, his treatment of the self's "parts" as being capable of existence and identification apart from reference to the self whose parts they are, and, as Chisholm points out, his introspective report, which seems to presuppose the very self that the report claims is not to be found: each of these needs

29

more defense than Hume provides.[6] My question here is whether Penelhum has employed a method that exposes a basic error in Hume, one without which his skepticism could never be generated.

I have no quarrel with Penelhum's description of the difference between Hume's use of 'identity' and one's ordinary use of that term. My question is, Why does this form a decisive objection to Hume's theory? It will not do, for example, to say that Hume has muddled the notions of specific and numerical identity (which Penelhum himself admits Hume distinguishes) unless one can show that his failure to grant this common-sense distinction shows that he has overlooked a real distinction. One would have thought that, on the contrary, the burden of Hume's argument is that this distinction proves to have no justification when it is examined with an eye to philosophical accuracy. Merely to point out that this distinction is embedded in ordinary language, or to say that 'same' and 'changed' are not ordinarily considered contradictories, will not constitute any kind of a rejoinder to Hume unless one has a conclusive argument that shows that departures from ordinary usage are always mistakes or that can show that the philosopher was trying to capture the nuances of ordinary talk.

In fact, Penelhum charges Hume with this latter goal when he says that Hume's belief in a contradiction between 'same' and 'different' results from his misdescription of the ordinary uses that certain words have. But since Hume is clearly opposing one's normal attitudes when he exposes the above contradiction, what reason is there for thinking that his main goal is to describe the ordinary working of certain terms? He may make such a description in order to have something to refute, but Penelhum's claim is that his treatment of these terms amounts to a misdescription. I can see no justification for this, and Penelhum offers none; but I suspect that it represents a rather desperate attempt to make the linguistic portion of his paper seem relevant to Hume's thesis. Lacking an argument that Hume cannot legitimately be doing what he seems to be doing, the natural maneuver would be to reconceive what he is doing so that it becomes amenable to linguistic treatment.

Nor will it help in criticizing Hume to point out that any

succession of different entities can be considered under some general title. Hume knew that one does this all the time, as his examples of feigning show, but he implicitly pushed a distinction between real and fictitious identity. Hume of course knew that one could treat the elements of a self as one; his term 'bundle' signifies this sense of unity. He only insists that this identity is fictitious, that it has no justifiable basis outside of one's common ways of speaking or one's special classifications, and that this does not constitute justification. I see no reason, then, why Hume could not happily admit unities of the harmless kind that Penelhum mentions.

More importantly, it would not further the case of one who believes in self-identity to accept any such weak sense of identity. One needs and wants an identity that will guarantee responsibility, that will explain the possibility of memory, self-awareness, and so forth. An identity that is merely the result of the way we speak of things will not carry with it the desired implications. Thus, I think that Hume was correct to look into the self for some bond that would really make the self one through change.

His answer to Penelhum is that there is no contradiction in saying that a plurality is one or that a succession is the same (a melody can be said to develop, implying that it is the same melody before and after the development), *if* one is willing to settle for fictitious identity. But if one requires real identity, then one will be contradicting oneself *unless* one can show how one and many, sameness and difference, can be combined in a single object. That is, one must make this combination intelligible so that one can comprehend the identity. Otherwise, one has nothing to fall back on, when attacked by Hume, but the fact that one does not ordinarily treat 'same' and 'different' as contradictories. Then one will be faced with the question, But if there is nothing that remains unchanged, what justification is there for saying that the thing is the same? The force of this question rests on one's adoption of the strict view of identity when one presses identity questions for philosophic purposes. The fact that this is not our only standard of identity in our pre- or nonphilosophical moments shows only that the puzzles that lie hidden in the notion of identity make only a token appearance in common sense.

The sharp division between common sense and philosophy that is suggested by Penelhum seems to me equally without foundation. Revisionary philosophers do not impose completely new standards on our common convictions. Rather, they develop and enlarge standards that are present in common sense. Because of their emphasis on theory over practice, they develop tendencies that are latent in ordinary speech and draw the conclusions that follow from their stricter use of terms. Thus, to say that the layman is not philosophically perplexed qua layman is not to say that he need regard such perplexity as completely foreign to common sense or that one need regard him, now that he is perplexed, as a "philosophical novice" rather than as a layman. I see no reason to think that he cannot recognize his new difficulties as ones which, qua layman, he would have felt if he had been more alert to the compromises and confusions that are latent in ordinary speech. He need not abandon common sense in order to enter philosophy, for common sense is inherently philosophical, and philosophy emerges from common sense. These remarks are not meant to urge an acceptance of Hume's particular theory; they are meant to suggest that one will tend to accept Penelhum's sharp division only if one is antecedently convinced that philosophical speculations are illegitimate. This division is the product of such thinking, not evidence for it.

FREE WILL

The ordinary-language approach to the problem of free will is nicely exemplified in Max Black's article "Making Something Happen." There Black announces as his general intention merely "to affirm something noncontroversial and hence acceptable in advance of any philosophical analysis or commitment."[7] To implement this intention he distinguishes clear cases of making something happen (lifting a glass) from cases that are not clear (leaving the room after hearing something a speaker says). In the latter case, but not in the former, it makes sense to investigate whether one did something or whether he was made to do it. This is because the former is a perfectly ordinary case of what we call "making something happen"; if one refuses to so accept it, no amount of evidence will convince one otherwise.

While lifting a glass in ordinary circumstances is to be distinguished from problematic cases, it is also to be distinguished from borderline cases, cases in which we do not know what to say since they allow of neither a right nor a wrong answer. But such instances of uncertainty about what to say do not make for uncertainty in the clear type of case already mentioned. The clear cases are paradigms or standards by means of which one decides the classification of doubtful cases; they cannot be evaluated, any more than one can ask whether a standard meter *is* a meter or whether a standard color *is* red. But if one is asked to do so, all one can say is "That's what I *call* 'making something happen'" (p. 34). In so doing, one is "repudiating the demand for a reason" rather than offering a genuine reason. These cases represent the termini of reason-giving; hesitation about them signifies a failure to understand one's linguistic conventions.

The conclusion is that there can be no doubt in such cases, no matter how extensively scientists may elaborate one's original description, provided only that such descriptions do not contradict the assumed normalcy of the original situation (p. 35). As Black says, "They could not do so, because the description of the paradigm case is complete" (p. 36).

It turns out, of course, that the very same situations that are clear cases of making something happen are also clear cases of doing something freely, for anything that caused one to say that someone was not acting freely would also provide a reason for saying that the same person was not doing anything at all but merely functioning as an "instrument or an intermediary between the true cause and its effects" (p. 38).

We will make a general evaluation of the argument from paradigm cases in chapter three. For the moment, let us look more closely at Black's analogy with the standard meter. Everyone would, I think, admit that it is silly to ask whether a standard meter is in fact really a meter. This is because (also, I take it, something noncontroversial) we have arbitrarily defined the concept of a meter in terms of the standard meter. Having done so, in all normal circumstances we use it as a standard and do not use other rulers as standards in relation to it.

Is the situation similar in the case of free will? As Black admits (p. 34), we have no formal definition of "making something happen." Rather, we have any number of standards, "any of which indifferently can serve to remind us of our linguistic conventions" (p. 35). But there are deeper, more important disanalogies. We do not want the concept of free will to rest on a linguistic convention, whereas this causes one no difficulty in the case of the notion of a meter. Too much rides with the way in which we take free will to leave it up to the way we speak, unless there is no other choice; and Black does not show that we must leave the matter in this unsatisfactory state.

Another way of stating this matter is to say that there is much in what Black does that is decidedly not uncontroversial. It is perhaps uncontroversial and prephilosophical to say that we ordinarily treat without question certain situations as paradigms of free acts and that, therefore, we would not ordinarily know how to go about questioning the validity of such instances. And in such ordinary circumstances, one would be thought not to know what 'free' means if one seemed hesitant about applying that word to the paradigmatic situation. But it is extremely controversial to assume that anything of philosophical interest follows from these facts. For example, it does not follow noncontroversially that there are no legitimate circumstances in which we might so change our conception of freedom that the old paradigms of free acts would cease to be paradigmatic.

Of course, as long as we accept them as paradigms, scientific explanations will seem irrelevant to their normal unquestioned role. But why may we not be led to jettison our allegiance to such paradigms in the interest of an evolving conception of freedom, one that emerges from our normal one but that pushes it beyond the point that is captured in our normal selection of paradigms of free acts? Presumably, such a conceptual development would take place in the interest of a better understanding of freedom. Merely knowing what kinds of things we normally and unthinkably take to be free acts does not constitute such an understanding, for these so-called paradigms may mislead one into thinking that they ostensively define freedom. In fact, they merely illustrate the vague sense that we normally have of what freedom is and what it entails.

There is much implied in what Black says that is far from innocent, for it packs a powerful philosophical wallop. But it seems to me there is an innocence in the idea that one can obtain philosophical leverage by citing the noncontroversial and the prephilosophical. Because this material is taken philosophically, it is thought to count against deterministic arguments that oppose free will. But then, to cite it is in reality to take a stand about the proper treatment of philosophical issues and to point in the direction of a particular resolution of the free-will issue.

In general it seems that Black's approach to the free-will issue could be warranted only if the illustrative examples that he calls paradigms fully embody the meaning of the concept that they illustrate. But only a philosophical investigation into the meaning of the concept could determine whether this is so. As long as the concept has other implications than those obviously present in the examples, the possibility remains that full development of these implications will result in a questioning of the appropriateness of the examples for philosophical purposes.

In the case of free will, one wants to know whether alternative modes of action were really possible when one lifted the glass to one's lips. If not, then the fact that this dimension of freedom is not highlighted in the paradigm, but emerges only upon reflection, in no way prevents one from taking the paradigms as less than fully adequate to our deeper understanding of freedom. Paradigms serve as standards in the settlement of ordinary disputes and doubts, but there is no reason why they must be viewed as cannonical from all points of view. At least, Black does nothing to show that they must in all cases be so regarded.

Given this perspective, his remarks correctly describe what we ordinarily take to be clear cases of free acts, but they do not show that we are right in taking things this way or that revisions of this attitude are unthinkable. Why *must* philosophers accept ordinary demarcations if they can highlight notions that are parts of our ordinary conceptions and that are ignored in our ordinary paradigms? The latter provide necessary but not sufficient conditions for free acts once we focus on choice as a component of freedom.

UNIVERSALS

In a recent paper, W. E. Kennick attempts to explain Wittgenstein's view that philosophical problems are in reality grammatical ones and to show that this general claim is justified as an interpretation of the dispute between Realists and Nominalists about the reality of universals. If this interpretation is sustained, then it will not be reasonable to look for a right answer to the question of whether there are universals. One will be free to say what one wishes to, as long as what one says does not cause needless problems.

Kennick begins by distinguishing two senses in which a proposition might be called 'grammatical':

> A proposition is explicitly grammatical if it mentions a word (or words) and says something about its (their) use; it is implicitly grammatical if it uses, but does not mention, a word (or words) but still expresses a rule, convention, or decision about verbal usage and imparts no information about the world.[8]

Empirical propositions, for Wittgenstein (according to Kennick), are about the world and are testable by an appeal to experience. Now, Kennick states that the dispute between Realists and Nominalists is not empirical, "despite occasional talk about observing recurrences, being closer to the facts, and the like" (p. 170). In his view of the dispute, the only relevant facts (such as the fact that fire engines are red) are those that are accepted by both sides. This means that "the disagreement is solely over the 'interpretation' or 'analysis' of such facts" (p. 170).

It follows, finally, that the dispute is grammatical. This conclusion, which forms the heart of Kennick's claim, perhaps needs a few words of explanation. It follows from steps 1 and 2 only if one includes a suppressed premise, 2a: The analysis or interpretation of the propositions expressing the known facts are not themselves testable by reference to nonlinguistic facts about the world. If they are, then they become empirical propositions of a sort; if they are not, then the claim that they are grammatical is a plausible one.

In Kennick's view, propositions about universals are not thought to be explicitly grammatical. The Realist does not intend to inform one of what kinds of things are properly referred to as 'same' and what ones as 'similar'. For one thing, neither term is ordinarily used as universally more fundamental than the other. Their relation is more complex than that. So both sides have done a bad job if they are attempting to report ordinary usage. For another, neither side debates the issue as if it were about usage; for example, no one proves his point by referring to that usage.

Thus, the philosophical propositions in this area are to be thought of as being implicitly grammatical. To say this much is to say that they embody "notational" innovations, proposals about how one *ought* to use words. One can then react to this suggestion either by objecting to it or merely by indicating that it is a linguistic suggestion and nothing more than that. In either case the issue seemingly raised by the proposition vanishes.

As above, I want to inquire whether Kennick's method is an effective way of justifying his claims. I want to argue that it is not, because his tendency is to analyze what Wittgenstein says, and then to act as if that were a sufficient defense of what he says, and because the foundations of the argument that he finds in Wittgenstein are not adequate to prove the point in question.

The problem lies in the word 'implicitly' in his phrase "implicitly grammatical." How will Kennick show that such propositions are properly thought to be implicitly grammatical when on the face of it he admits that they are not grammatical at all? The answer is disappointing. First, Kennick points out that with a proposition such as "the colours green and blue cannot be in the same place simultaneously," we cannot verify it as one can verify a normal empirical proposition; and second, he cannot imagine what it would be like for this proposition to be false (pp. 143–45). But surely these points are effective remarks in favor of the "grammar" thesis only if one can show that necessary propositions are not informative about nonlinguistic features of the world. If one assumes that this is so, then his case against the informative character of necessary propositions (and hence against the reality of the universals controversy) begs the question egregiously. Not only does Kennick not offer any such proof, but his points mentioned above obviously rest on a version of the old Positivist notion of the analyticity of necessary truth, a doctrine that has been effectively questioned by Rationalists such as Blanshard and Ewing.

Is one more sure that the above color statement is about green and blue rather than about 'green' and 'blue', or is one more sure of the theory that tells us that it *cannot* be about the former and so *must* be about the latter? The theory is so paradoxical that one wonders how it can appeal to intelligent men. Blanshard seems to me to have said it all:

> Assuming 'red' and 'green' to mean what they ordinarily do, the convention became what it is because no alternative was possible or conceivable. People could not if they tried make what was *meant* by red and green belong to the same surface at once. If they did not *apply* the names jointly, it was because they saw that the qualities could not *belong* jointly. They conformed their language to the structure of things, not the structure of things to their language.[9]

I do not see how an unbiased reading of what one means to say when one speaks of colors excluding one another from the same place at the same time can make out that one intends to speak of words and not of things. And no proof is forthcoming that despite what one knows oneself to be doing, one *must* be doing something else. Thus, one will believe in this "must" only if one is antecedently committed to a theory of knowledge that rules out the kind of knowledge claimed in necessary propositions. And, I suggest, such theories will themselves turn out to be founded on an antecedent adherence to science and a rejection of traditional, rationalist philosophy.

This brings me to the point about evidence. I see no reason whatever for denying that necessary propositions refer back to experience for their justification. The exclusion of colors quite obviously derives from one's experience of them and one's ability to capture pervasive, general features of that experience. Similarly, the Realist's belief in identities, and not just similarities, rests on his experience of two "identical" color shades, while the Resemblance theorist can point to the difficulty of finding anything more in two shades of a single color than resemblance. To be sure, in both cases, philosophers try to extend that evidential basis to include other areas, including the "facts" cited by their opponents. And they do so by arguments that move well away from any testing by experience, that are open to criticism, and that are found unconvincing by their opponents. But none of this points to the conclusion that the claims make no appeal to experience.

And there is no more reason to regard the analysis of propositions as being even implicitly about words. For example, Moore's discussion of the analysis of common-sense propositions in his "A Defense of Common Sense" makes this clear in two ways. First, the analysis requires prior understanding of the common-sense meaning of the proposition.[10] Presumably this is because one is to analyze the meaning, but then there seems to be no reason for speaking of the analysis as "grammatical." One does not analyze the words that express the meaning; one's analysis is about what the words mean. It is highly misleading to say that this analysis is "implicitly grammatical," for that suggests that it is about words and, since words are conventional, that it is consequently conventional. But Moore's analysis of "I see a hand" claims to be true, to give a correct picture of the state of affairs in question. There is nothing conventional or verbal in this, despite Kennick's easy transition from the analysis being about propositions to its being grammatical (see p. 170).[11]

And there is no reason for thinking that the Realist-Resemblance controversy over universals involves "stating a grammatical rule" (p. 171). Wittgenstein's claims (as reported by Kennick, pp. 164 and 170) that Realist assertions about colors amount to assertions that one uses the same color word in varying circumstances and that proposals about "same color" involve "stating grammatical rules" are equally implausible.[12] One has to torture one's clear understanding of what one is talking about—doing so in the name of a pre-commitment to a dubious analysis of the distinction between empirical and necessary propositions—in order to reach the conclusion that philosophical propositions are verbal. The evidence is that they are not verbal, even implicitly, and so far we have encountered nothing that can stand as a proof that they must be verbal.

The second way in which Moore's discussion of analysis suggests that analyses are not verbal is that he clearly intends to appeal to experience to support the validity of the analysis that he offers. He takes the existence of sense data to be established by experience (*PP*, pp. 53–54), and he appeals to the ways things look in varying conditions (e.g., under microscopes, *PP*, pp. 55–56) to show difficulties between alternative analyses. We shall see later that linguistic philosophers have in fact challenged the claim that sense data are known in experience; for the moment I only wish to make the point that one cannot *assume* that philosophical propositions are so detached from experience that they must be grammatical. Necessary truths cannot be mere generalizations from experience, but to assume that they are in no way drawn from experience and that they can make no appeal to experience is simply to assume the truth of the old Positivist conception of philosophy that is enshrined in the Verifiability Theory of Meaning and the Analytic Theory of Necessary Truth. Neither of these doctrines has found an adequate defense; therefore, to assume them is to substitute dogmatism for the rewards of honest toil.

In this light, Kennick's dismissal of appeals to experience in the Realist-Resemblance controversy, his conclusion that these claims are "obviously not empirical," and his claim that the only relevant facts are ordinary ones, not in dispute, such as "fire engines are red," are all gratuitous (p. 170). One can agree that this controversy has not been *settled* by an appeal to experience; but to conclude that this means that the controversy is simply nonempirical is so to limit the range of 'empirical' that the above linguistic characterization of philosophical propositions follows as a matter of definition. But if one looks at a discussion of universals, such as that found in Blanshard's *Reason and Analysis*, one finds a blend of argument and appeals to experience that defies classification by the 'either-or' of empirical or grammatical-necessary-analytic. I conclude that Kennick presents nothing even remotely definitive which should convince us that the problem of universals is a linguistic one.

The above brief dip into the linguistic treatment of philosophical issues prompts the following observation: One finds a surprising lack of argument for the crucial points in the linguistic case. Instead, one tends to find the application of already-accepted principles to specific cases. This suggests, of course, that these principles find their justification elsewhere, either in *The*

Philosophical Investigations or in the work of Wittgenstein's defenders. So far we have not found it in the latter source, but we now turn to explicit attempts to unearth and defend the principles that underlie the linguistic case against skepticism and that show such doubts to be only apparently genuine because they are based on confusions of a linguistic kind.

KNOWLEDGE AND CERTAINTY: PART 1

Obviously, two key concepts in the debate over the validity of skepticism are 'knowledge' and 'certainty'. To a large extent the skeptic's case against our knowledge of other minds, the past, the external world, and so on, rests on his commitment to a view about knowledge and certainty. Therefore, if the ordinary-language philosopher can show this view to be mistaken, he will have gone far toward undermining the appeal of skepticism. This chapter and the following one examine two related but different approaches to reinstating our ordinary sense that it is proper to speak of knowing a host of things that the skeptic seemingly thinks we do not know. First, I examine the discussions of Norman Malcolm and of Arthur Danto as prime examples of those who approach skepticism through the analysis of language. Second, I consider G. E. Moore's defense of common-sense knowledge against the skeptic. I conclude by examining the Dreaming Hypothesis to see if it is effective as a dramatic way of illustrating the possibility of systematic delusion.

THE LINGUISTIC TREATMENT
OF 'KNOW' AND 'CERTAIN'

In numerous articles, Norman Malcolm has been concerned with the claim, common in philosophy, that empirical propositions are not capable of complete or conclusive verification and that they are, therefore, not certain; they are the proper objects of belief, not knowledge. Against this skeptical position, Malcolm has tried to unearth mistakes on which that position rests, his intention being to restore one's normal orientation to knowledge about the world.

More particularly, he has claimed that such philosophical views are based on the philosopher's invention of an arbitrary meaning for phrases such as "know for certain" and "completely verify." This meaning makes it *self-contradictory* to say that empirical propositions can be known for certain or can be completely verified and *tautological* to say that they are at best probable or are capable of only partial verification.[1] Malcolm points out that 'know' and 'certain' have perfectly normal applications to empirical propositions, and he argues that since it is granted that 'verification' applies normally to empirical propositions, 'complete verification' must also apply to them (*CES*, p. 31). The same remarks hold, he claims, for the phrase "conclusive evidence" (*CES*, p. 44).[2]

One should then read skeptics' claims as follows:

> Their declaration that only *a priori* statements can be known with certainty is a disguised recommendation that the phrase "it is certain that" be applied to a statement if and only if the statement has a self-contradictory negative. It is a proposal to use the phrase "it is certain that *p*," so that it will be *equivalent* to the phrase "*p* has a self-contradictory negative." [*CES*, p. 34]

But this is a puzzling recommendation, for (1) there is nothing wrong or loose about ordinary usage,[3] and (2) as it stands, it is very misleading. By its standards, certainty about empirical matters is not merely difficult; it is a *self-contradictory* notion. Then, Malcolm asks, What sense is there in speaking of empirical statements as being merely probable, or in lamenting their failure to attain some higher state? (*CES*, p. 22). If for empirical statements there is no effective contrast to "probable," then that word ceases to convey any information, for it is essential to the meaning of that term that it be contrasted with 'certain' (*CES*, p. 38).[4]

It is also puzzling because it forces one to believe that ordinary claims to certainty about empirical matters are not just false but are self-contradictory. Not only is it a mistake to think that this is so of ordinary expressions, but it *could not* be the case. Malcolm argues as follows: (1) To be an ordinary expression means that the expression has a use, although it may not be used; (2) no self-contradictory expression could have any kind of descriptive use; (3) since ordinary expressions have such a descriptive use, they do in fact describe the situations in question. (4) Therefore, they cannot be self-contradictory. As Malcolm says, "We do not *call* an expression which has a descriptive use a self-contradictory expression" (*MOL*, p. 16).

Even more strongly, Malcolm claims that not only can such ordinary expressions not be self-contradictory but for certain types of such expressions, their use guarantees the existence of what they describe. In those cases in which one learns the meaning of the expression by being shown instances of its "true application" (as contrasted with expressions whose meaning is explained in terms of other words or phrases), one can be certain that there are kinds of things that the expression is used to describe. It follows that we can be certain that there are cases of empirical certainty (*MOL*, pp. 17–18). In contrast, a philosophical statement that is paradoxical is known to be false merely because it is paradoxical. This is because such a statement "asserts the impropriety of an ordinary form of speech" (*MOL*, p. 18) or "constitutes an offense against ordinary language" (*MOL*, p. 20). Thus one is able to rule out such claims as "all empirical statements are hypotheses" or "all matter is really animate" merely by noting that they do not use words in the ordinary manner.

Malcolm tries to bring out the "queerness" of the philosophical proposal regarding 'certain' in yet another way. He points out that 'certain' can be applied to sense statements, a priori statements, and empirical statements (*CES*, p. 32). The first two uses are "degenerate" in that one imparts no information whatsoever in saying that those kinds of statements are certain. To say this of them is to say nothing more than that they are the kinds of statements they are. On the other hand, to say that empirical statements are certain is to say something informative, namely, to describe the evidence in favor of the statement (*CES*,

p. 36). But then one finds it puzzling that anyone should want to eliminate the informative use of a word and retain only a use that is noninformative.

Malcolm tries to explain the reasons behind the philosopher's strange linguistic recommendation in several ways. One source lies in a confusion between logical and empirical possibility (*CES*, pp. 27 ff.). According to Malcolm, skeptics have argued that one cannot have knowledge of the past, of other minds, or whatever, because certain states of affairs are logically possible that would render all one's knowledge claims totally false. Malcolm admits that there is nothing self-contradictory about the states of affairs imagined by the skeptic, but he argues that it does not follow from this fact that there is *some* possibility that such states of affairs actually obtain. The latter notion, which expresses degree, applies only to empirical possibility, to cases in which the evidence indicates that a given result might happen, but in which the evidence is not strong enough to allow one to conclude that it will happen. It is simply irrelevant, Malcolm claims, to point out that "I am dreaming" is not self-contradictory if one is trying to assess the possibility that I might be dreaming, for it might be perfectly certain in a given situation that I am not dreaming and still might be a logical possibility that I am dreaming. An empirical statement could be completely verified even though the latter possibility remained. As he says, "It does not, in the least, follow from the fact that it is logically possible that you are mistaken, that you do not know with certainty that you are not mistaken" (*CES*, p. 45).

Another way of stating this point is to say that in the case of empirical propositions, asserting the possibility that p is false is merely to inform one of the kind of proposition that one faces. This fact "tells us *nothing* about the state of the evidence with respect to p" (*VA*, p. 34). The statement that p is not self-contradictory is *neutral* with regard to the question of whether one is certain that p is true. As Malcolm says, "Whether it is certain that c is true depends upon the state of the evidence with regard to c" (*VA*, p. 36).

In an important footnote, Malcolm concludes that while one's evidence for an empirical proposition never entails the truth of that proposition, the "state of the evidence" for such a proposition may be such that it is certain that the proposition is true (*VA*, p. 36 n). He adds that the only way to argue the point is to produce examples of when one would normally say that an empirical proposition was certain and yet would acknowledge that one's evidence did not entail the truth of the proposition.

Another source for the denial that empirical statements can be certain is the belief that the difference between 'probable' and 'certain' is one of degree only. This leads to the conclusion that 'certain', as applied to empirical statements, must really mean 'high probability' only (*CES*, p. 40). Malcolm agrees that the difference between certainty and probability in the empirical area rests on the number of favorable tests, and so it is correct to point out that this is a difference of degree. However, he argues that it is arbitrary to say that they are not also different in kind. As he says:

> To argue that, because the difference between "certain" and "probable" is only one of *degree*, therefore all empirical statements are probable only—is exactly analogous to arguing that, because the difference between "being bald" and "having a full head of hair" is only one of degree, therefore all men are really bald. [*CES*, pp. 41–42]

This line of thought represents a familiar move of the skeptic, the arbitrary limitation of 'kind' to the distinction between demonstrative and nondemonstrative proof and to the resulting recommendation (disguised though it be) that we refer only to a priori statements as certain.

There is a last argument for philosophical skepticism which Malcolm finds mistaken. It does not follow that because some people have been deceived into thinking that such and such *was* the case that one cannot now be certain that it *is* the case (see *VA*, p. 39). Nor does it follow that because veridical and nonveridical experiences lack an intrinsic difference, one can never have conclusive evidence one way or the other. If one has time to inspect one's surroundings, either before an experience occurs or while it is occurring, then there is no reason why one's evidence that the experience is veridical cannot be absolutely conclusive. Because there are a variety of circumstances in which we

46

want to make this determination, no blanket rule that absolutely prohibits such a determination is acceptable (*CES*, pp. 43–45). J. L. Austin made the same point with characteristic force when he said:

> I go into the next room, and certainly there's something there that looks exactly like a telephone. But is it a case perhaps of *trompe l'oeil* painting? I can soon settle that. Is it just a dummy perhaps, not really connected up and with no proper works? Well, I can take it to pieces a bit and find out, or actually use it for ringing somebody up —and perhaps get them to ring me up too, just to make sure. And of course, if I do all these things, I *do* make sure; what more could possibly be required? This object has already stood up to amply enough tests to establish that it really is a telephone; and it isn't just that, for everyday or practical or ordinary purposes, enough is *as good as* a telephone; what meets all these tests just *is* a telephone, no doubt about it.[5]

To probe more deeply into the mistakes that lie behind the skeptic's claims about empirical propositions, Malcolm conducts a detailed investigation of what he calls the Verification Argument. This is the argument that tries to show that we cannot absolutely verify any empirical proposition. We have already examined one of its premises, namely, that the consequences of the proposition *may* not occur, and we have seen that when we are no longer confusing logical and empirical possibility, we must mean that it is not *certain* that these consequences will occur. And the skeptic has no defense for this claim. In particular, he can offer no *evidence* for it in those cases in which the evidence allows us to claim certainty (*VA*, p. 49).

But Malcolm finds other errors in this argument. First, it assumes that if certain consequences fail to happen, then the relevant proposition could not have been absolutely verified at any earlier time. In Malcolm's words, "If at any time there are good grounds for believing that a given statement p is false then at no previous time was it known with certainty that p is true" (*VA*, p. 14). Since, Malcolm argues, it is clear that at a later time one may well have "good grounds" for doubting what was known earlier, the above assumption is false. He offers a reformulation, namely, that if at a later time it is "absolutely conclusive" that S is false, then it is not the case that at any earlier time it was "absolutely certain" that S was true (*VA*, p. 22). But one can see immediately that this proposition offers no help to skepticism of the all-inclusive variety, for it assumes that one *can* establish at least the absolute falsity of S.

A second error in the Verification Argument concerns what Malcolm calls "a misunderstanding of the ordinary usage of expressions such as 'verify,' 'establish,' 'make certain,' 'find out' " (*VA*, p. 53). Skeptics assume that while for practical purposes one may limit verification to a finite number of observations, in theory there is no limit to the number of possible verifications. In fact, Malcolm continues, there are many circumstances in which "there is nothing which we should *call* 'further verification' " (*VA*, p. 54). Further looking would not be further verification in cases in which one's past looks have left no doubt as to the truth of one's claim. Malcolm says, "The verification *comes to an end*" (*VA*, p. 54).

Third, Malcolm insists that skeptics make the mistake of identifying absolute with theoretical certainty, allowing empirical statements to attain only practical certainty. This is a mistake, because on their use of 'theoretical certainty' it would be a contradiction for any empirical proposition to be theoretically certain. But since we often say that empirical assertions are absolutely certain, this view would have us believe that we contradict ourselves on these occasions. Since this is absurd, the view that commits us to this conclusion is false.

Malcolm thinks that an examination of 'knowledge' and 'belief' supports the above view of the relation between certainty and empirical statements. He discerns a strong and a weak sense of the term 'know'. If one uses 'know' in the strong sense, one refuses to count anything that happens as evidence against the truth of p, while one makes no such implication if one uses 'know' in the weak sense.[6] Propositions that one says one knows in the strong sense need no proof or justification, for they depend on nothing, and one would find talk about their possibility unintelligible.

Malcolm adds several important explanatory remarks to these claims: (1) In stating what one is committed to by the use of 'know' in the strong sense, one does not *predict* what one would say under future conditions. Rather, one only reports one's *present attitude* toward possible future happenings (*KB*, p. 78). (2) The distinction between the strong and the weak use of 'know' applies within *both* empirical and a priori propositions. (3) The weak sense of 'know' is not the same as belief. (4) Can one be certain now not only that one uses 'know' in the strong sense but, in addition, that one also in fact knows something in the strong sense? Malcolm admits that it seems that merely because one would not *call* anything evidence against one's knowledge claim, it does not follow that the facts are as one claims them to be. Yet, he says that for a given person the thought is impossible that one might be wrong about one's strong knowledge claim. (One can think this about others.) And since this is a "logical," not a psychological," fact, he hesitates to conclude that knowledge and the strong use of 'know' are really distinct (*KB*, p. 81).

The upshot of the discussion is that empirical propositions can constitute knowledge in the strongest possible sense. Unlike 'certain', which has a different sense as applied to empirical and a priori propositions, the strong sense of 'know' applies equally and in the same sense to both. Thus Malcolm can conclude that the two kinds of propositions "possess the same logical character," by which he means that members of each may "lie beyond the reach of doubt" (*KB*, p. 79). In those cases in which the propositions in question form the foundation of one's reasoning and judging, one would bring chaos, not caution, into one's reasoning by undermining one's confidence in them. For this reason, one regards as unintelligible the possibility that they might be false. In a later reply to Richard Taylor, Malcolm makes it clear that he does not want to hold that the use of 'know' in the strong sense guarantees the truth of p, although it is a tautology to say that p follows from the truth of "X knows that p," whether 'knows' is used in the strong or weak sense. For while one's use of the strong sense of 'know' entails that one cannot accept anything as evidence against one's claim, there is always at least the possibility that others, differently placed than oneself, can regard something as evidence against one's claim.[7]

I wish to proceed with my discussion of Malcolm as follows.

First, I shall extract three kinds of argument employed by Malcolm, then examine their merits somewhat independently of his use of them. Second, I shall raise questions about several particular points that Malcolm raises. The three arguments I have in mind are (1) the Argument from Possibility; (2) the Argument from Meaningful Contrast; and (3) the Argument from Paradigm Cases.

The Argument from Possibility

I believe that Malcolm is correct, in his discussion of the distinction between logical and empirical possibility, to insist that the skeptic uses and needs the notion of logical possibility in order to make his case seem persuasive. One can cite many examples of this: Russell's claim that there is no "logical impossibility" in the view that the world "sprung into being five minutes ago";[8] Ewing's argument that the lack of an internal difference between dreams and waking experiences means that it is always (logically) possible that one confuses the two, which leads to the conclusion that one cannot in the strictest sense know that one is seeing a chair.[9] Also, Descartes's references to the Evil Demon surely are meant to dramatize the logical possibility of error, not to claim that one has detected some evidence in favor of this hypothesis. I think it is fair to conclude that if the move from logical possibility is invalid, then philosophical skepticism will be an indefensible position. Doubts about particular claims will remain, but there will be no reason to entertain a general, all-inclusive skepticism.

It is also worth pointing out that G. E. Moore found a similar confusion behind philosophical skepticism. In his *Commonplace Book*, Moore distinguishes three kinds of possibility: logical, causal, and epistemic.[10] Something can be epistemically impossible without being self-contradictory; something can be causally impossible without being self-contradictory; and something can be causally possible even though it is epistemically impossible. To know that something is not the case does not contradict the claim that it is (causally) possible. Moore makes an interesting linguistic point about logical and/or causal possibility, on the one hand, and epistemic impossibility, on the other (p. 184). When one says that something is impossible because

50

one knows that it is not the case, it remains possible, not that it *is* the case, but that it "should have been" the case or that it "could have been" or "might have been" the case.

Moore applies these distinctions to Russell's argument that one can be certain only of our momentary experience, because in dreams one sometimes seems to remember events that never happened. Moore claims that the conclusion that validity follows from the above premise is that it is possible for apparent memories of the kind that one is now having not to be veridical. This is true but harmless. But, Moore points out, the conclusion that the skeptic needs is that *this* present apparent memory may be invalid.[11] But to allege that because *some* memories are invalid, *this* one may be, is "precisely on a par with the following: It is possible for a human being to be of the female sex; (but) I am a human thing; *therefore* it is possible that I am of the female sex" (p. 216).

The point that Moore is making here is different from the one made by Malcolm when he distinguishes the two kinds of possibility or the one made by Moore when he distinguishes three kinds of possibility. Moore is saying that something does not become epistemically possible (i.e., cease being epistemically impossible) merely because *some* members of the group in question fall under a certain category. Thus, merely because one is deceived in some cases of perception, it does not follow that one is deceived in this one. (And certainly Descartes argues in precisely this way when he warns us against trusting our senses or our mathematical calculations on the grounds either that our senses have sometimes deceived us or that others are sometimes deceived about things they think they know best.)[12] One mistakenly thinks, Moore claims, that one's judgment of possibility means that *all* the members of a class *may* fall under this classification, when in fact all it means is that *some* members of the class *do* fall under the given classification.

The kernel of truth in what I have called the Argument from Possibility is that ordinarily one is not concerned about pointing out that this or that is logically possible. So many things are logically possible that this is an almost empty remark, and one is normally interested in pointing out those events for which or against which there is some (but not conclusive) evidence. When working with this notion of possibility, it is an intrusion to be told that so-and-so is not certain merely because something else is logically possible. This remark seems irrelevant, as Malcolm points out (*VA*, p. 34).

But Malcolm has not made out a good case that there are no legitimate contexts in which one should recognize that this remark is relevant, even if it is regarded as beside the point for normal purposes. In fact, I would argue, Malcolm has not even made out a bad case for his claim, for his assertions amount to no more than dogmatic claims which beg the question with the skeptic by taking one's ordinary standard of relevance as the norm by which irrelevance in general may be decided. Therefore, his position cries out for defense, and there seems to be no reason to accept it unless one is antecedently convinced, with Malcolm, that ordinary language is correct language.

For example, when Malcolm says that to say "p is false is logically possible" does not tell us about the "state of the evidence" regarding p, one can only agree (*VA*, p. 34). But then one wants to add that this does not mean that it is unrelated to the question of the certainty of p. This follows only if the certainty of p can be questioned in a single way, the ordinary, "evidential" way. Of course, the possibilities imagined by skeptics cannot be determined to be likely by producing evidence in their favor, for they are outside the entire process of gathering and weighing evidence. But if they are meaningful alternatives to one's ordinary assumptions (that one does know something; the question is only *what* one knows), then it is hard to see why they are not relevant to judging the certainty of one's ordinary claims. One says that one is certain about some things, but how can one be certain if there are alternatives in the field which suggest that one may be wrong? There is no ordinary way to disprove the skeptical alternatives; yet, if there be no past or other minds or physical world, how can one rest secure in one's judgment, which assumes that there certainly are such things?

One's normal investigations operate within a framework that presupposes the existence of the subject matter in question, and one tries to separate truth from falsity, or soundly based conclusion from unsoundly based conclusion, within the confines of that framework. Yet, these procedures and their standards of evidence stand in need of justification, for the assumptions on which they rest are theoretical postulates that are not self-justifying. (We shall see that this statement is challenged as we progress.) There are radically different viewpoints that challenge these foundational convictions, and unless these alternatives can be ruled out in some way, they will *indirectly* challenge the truth and certainty of the specific judgments that one ordinarily makes. They do so by bringing to one's attention the fact, ordinarily overlooked, that one's everyday attitude toward what constitutes certainty embodies a theoretical stance that cannot be justified by the methods that one normally employs, and the fact that there are alternative stances that those methods are powerless to rule out. Therefore, doubt about claims to certainty does creep in, not because one thinks one has failed to live up to one's normal standards, but because one finds that one can question the assumptions that underly those same standards.

As long as one cannot rule out talk about possible worlds in which one's beliefs and attitudes remain as they now are but in which there is nothing that corresponds to these beliefs, then one cannot rule out the possibility that *this* world is in fact one of those possible worlds. It turns out that one's ordinary attitude is every bit as "metaphysical" as the skeptical alternatives that clash with it. It is from this perspective that one realizes that there is room for an unusual kind of doubt about ordinary claims. One sees that it *is* relevant to point out that a given assertion is contingent, for this means that its opposite cannot be ruled out (not being self-contradictory), there being no certainty that the state of affairs is not very different from what one ordinarily assumes it to be. The fact that one does not normally consider this a possibility does not seem to me to carry any weight when one comes to wonder about the reality of the alernative conception.

Nor does Malcolm's point about degrees of possibility seem a strong one to me. He claims that empirical possibility admits of both *tense* and *degree*, while logical possibility admits of neither (*CES*, p. 29). Thus, it is incorrect to argue that because something is logically possible, there is *some* possibility that it is the case. But if any philosopher were to so state his conclusion (and this is Malcolm's reformulation of Russell, not Russell's own words), he would not be using 'some' to indicate that there was partial evidence in favor of the event happening but that the evidence was not conclusive. He would only be saying that the logical possibility makes one aware of a real possibility that one ordinarily overlooks. The 'some' in 'some possibility' would be expendable and would not indicate a confusion between the two sorts of possibility. Then the issue comes down to whether logical possibility can call into question the certainty of claims that one ordinarily considered to be certain, and this issue cannot be decided by pointing out that different words can qualify the different possibilities.

Moore's discussion of possibility also fails to diminish the force of philosophical skepticism. One can readily admit that *if* one *knows* that one is standing up, then the logical possibility that one is sitting down could only mean that one *could have been* sitting down, or that one *would have been* sitting down if certain conditions had prevailed: for example, if there were a chair in the room, if one had been more tired than one was, and so forth. My claim, however, is that to point out the logical possibility of a state of affairs that is different from the one normally thought to obtain indirectly calls into question the knowledge claim and, thereby, indicates what might be the case now, not merely what could have been the case. We shall examine Moore's claims for knowledge later; at the moment I merely wish to indicate that everything hinges on the epistemic certainty with which Moore begins his analysis of 'possible'.

As Moore presents the skeptic's argument, it indeed does seem to be invalid. Nothing follows about the (possible) falsity of a present perception from the observation that sometimes one's senses are deceived. However, Moore's formulation omits what seems to be an essential premise which is needed if this way of arguing for philosophical skepticism is to be valid. The "slippery-slope" approach to skepticism (as contrasted with the logical-possibility-of-error approach) requires the assumption that there is no definitive, internal difference between cases of perceptual error and perceptual success. This condition is what allows one to claim the possibility of error in *this* case because of error in other cases, or the possibility that one might now be dreaming since sometimes one cannot distinguish between dreams and waking experiences.

It follows that Moore's argument from some humans being female and oneself being a human to the conclusion that one might be a female does not fairly characterize the skeptic's position. Since there is normally no difficulty in distinguishing between the two sexes, Moore's version of the argument rests on the assumption that he *knows* that he is not a female. This makes the conclusion sound absurd, and it begs the question in the process. But what if one grants that one knows only that one is in a human state, that one has no internal evidence to decide that one is male or female? (I hasten to add that this begs the question against Moore unless an analysis of experience shows this beginning to be reasonable.) One then has put oneself in a position that the skeptic thinks is like one's normal perceptual situation, and from it, the conclusion that one might be female seems to be justified.[13] Moore himself admits that if it is logically possible that one could both have the sensory experiences that one has and "remember" what one seems to remember *and* be dreaming, then one cannot know for certain that one is not dreaming.[14] But although Moore says that the logical possibility of this has not been shown, it seems to me that unless one can show that there is or must be an internal difference between dreaming and waking states, then the fact that others have been deceived about cases that seem to be indistinguishable from the one in which Moore finds himself is enough to prove the logical possibility of the skeptic's alternative.

Austin has tried to provide the internal difference that skeptics have said could not be found. He argues that because we have the phrase "a dream-like quality," which artists try to depict, it cannot seriously be argued that dreams and waking experiences are qualitatively indistinguishable (*SS*, pp. 48–49). But all that the skeptic needs to argue is that there is no experiential element that is *uniquely* associated with either dreams or waking experiences. As long as there is not, an experience may be other than what we think it to be; its qualities will not serve to distinguish it from another type of experience in such a way that the logical possibility of error is ruled out. In this way I think that the skeptic can avoid Austin's stronger point that

> if the fact here alleged *were* a fact, the phrase would be perfectly meaningless, because applicable to everything.

> If dreams were not 'qualitatively' different from waking experiences, then *every* waking experience would be like a dream; the dream-like quality would be, not difficult to capture, but impossible to avoid. [*SS*, p. 49]

If one were to consider judgments about the past for a moment, one might put the skeptic's position as follows: Since there is no way to *directly confirm* which judgments are true and which false, it may be that despite one's usual way of distinguishing true from false, all such judgments are in fact false. Similarly, unless one can "directly" (and presumably internally) distinguish absolutely between dreaming and waking, it is possible that even one's so-called waking experiences are in fact dream experiences. It does not matter that some of one's experiences have a "dream-like quality" and others do not, as long as I admit that some experiences that are otherwise classified as dreams lack this quality and some that are otherwise classified as waking share it. And Austin does admit the latter. Then it will remain possible that those that lack it are in fact dreams as much as those that share it, and this seemingly is all that the skeptic needs in order to get his argument under way. There will be a use for the term "dreamlike," but it will not demarcate waking from dreaming in a way that will forestall skepticism.

The Argument from Meaningful Contrast

Austin does raise a point, however, which threatens a characteristic that is typical of philosophical skepticism, namely, generality. The philosophical skeptic would have us believe that *all* one's judgments about the external world, other minds, the past, and so forth, might be mistaken. Everything might be the result of deception or error or dreaming. In Malcolm's example, all of our empirical judgments are, or might be, merely probable (*CES*, p. 38).[15] But, so the argument goes, in the very act of spreading a term, which is normally limited in its scope by a contrasting term, over an entire area, one robs that term of any possible meaning. For to be meaningful requires, for many terms at least, that there be a significant contrast to the term in question. Thus it must at least make sense to say that this empirical proposition is certain or that this is a waking experience or that this is a veridical perception. But, argues the ordinary language philosopher, the heart of the skeptical position is that it is contradictory to imagine that any empirical proposition can be called knowledge or 'certain'. Thus the skeptic rules out a meaningful contrast even as a logical possibility, and in so doing, he robs his thesis of any meaning. The skeptic faces this dilemma: if he uses 'probable' meaningfully, then his thesis is false; if he uses it in a way that would allow his thesis to be true, then what he says is empty, having only the semblance of meaning, because one continues to treat the term as the ordinary one with its ordinary contrast.

A good example of this argumentative technique in action can be found in O. K. Bouwsma's article "Descartes' Evil Genius,"[16] in which Bouwsma imagines two stages in the deception arranged by the genius. In the first stage, he turns everything to paper, making everything so lifelike that one could easily mistake the paper objects for real objects. It is assumed, however, that one knows the difference between something made of paper and something made of flesh or rock and that one can detect this difference if one examines the newly created paper objects carefully. Thus, even if every human observer is deceived, at least the deceiving genius knows what the difference is between his creation and the real thing.

The second level of deception is quite different; it is analogous to that pictured by Descartes. In this case the Evil Genius destroys everything and allows only a "stream of seemings" to remain. He refers to his illusions as "thick illusions," because they have no detectable difference from real things, and he contrasts them with the "thin illusions" that are presented in mirror images (p. 34). Bouwsma's reply is that the Evil Genius means by "illusion" what one means by "flower," "rock," and so forth. The Genius uses the word "illusion," perhaps, because of his "sixth" sense, which does not detect what one calls flowers, as one's sense of smell does not detect the flowers seen in a mirror. Bouwsma comments that this added sense has "done wickedly with our language," for if your intention was to deceive you must learn the language of those you are to deceive" (p. 34). As he says:

> If we admit the special sense, then we can readily see
> how it is that the evil genius should have been so con-

> fident. He has certainly created his own illusions, though he has not himself been deceived. But neither has anyone else been deceived. For human beings do not use the word "illusion" by relation to a sense with which only the evil genius is blessed. [P. 35]

The Evil Genius is ignorant of the difference between our use of 'illusion' and his. And while there is an analogy between these two uses, "the difference is quite sufficient to explain his failure at grand deception."

First, a general comment: the Argument from Meaningful Contrast (sometimes called the Argument from Excluded Opposites) is a disguised version of the Veriability Argument. Verification requires the possibility of both validation and falsification, and talk about the need for contrasting terms is simply a way of making this point in the verbal mode. The Evil Genius fails at his "grand deception" because he uses his key terms in an empty way, with the result that his proposal is not really a proposal at all; and to say all of this is akin to saying that philosophical skepticism is not a genuine, meaningful alternative to ordinary speech. In fact, one can unearth the verification principle that is embedded in Bouwsma's presentation: a term is used nonemptily if the propositions in which it is used can in principle be verified (or falsified?) by humans.

Two questions arise here: (1) Is Bouwsma saying that Cartesian skepticism is meaningless or that it is false? (2) Why doesn't the conceivable verification of the skeptic's claim *by any being* allow one to say that the skeptic's proposal is at least meaningful? Bouwsma might be saying that the "grand illusion" fails because one can determine conclusively that, as one uses 'deception', not everything is deceptive. Or he could be saying that the different use of 'deception' means that for us the "grand illusion" does not really propose an alternative to our usual conceptions. It is, for us, empty or meaningless.

But either alternative has difficulties. The former implicitly admits that skepticism is meaningful, and once this is granted, the weight of the supposedly conclusive tests against it becomes highly dubious. The skeptic can brush them aside as distinctions within a context that cannot refute a claim that the entire context may not have the status that it is usually assumed to have.

The second alternative, which seems closer to Bouwsma's meaning, is difficult to maintain, because Bouwsma himself does a good job of making the alternative *from the Demon's point of view* perfectly meaningful and vivid. But it must then be meaningful *for us*, since we understand how this could be at least analogous to deception for him.

We understand what the Evil Genius has done and how it appears to him (the "thin illusions" of mirror reflections provide the bridge between our sense of deception and that of the Demon). We simply do not have a word for it, since our word 'deception' cannot be used, because of all its normal implications, to stand for the Demon's deception. But then, it seems to me, Bouwsma's point appears to be a rather uninteresting verbal point. One knows that there is a shared core of meaning between the two kinds or degrees of deception, and once one realizes this, there seems to be little reason to fret over the fact that our word 'deception' has implications that the other "deception" does not have.

In short, Bouwsma provides no justification for his apparent assumption that unless the skeptic's use of 'deception' is equivalent to one's normal use, there is no reason to think that one is deceived all the time. Since one understands clearly the sense in which it is deception for the Demon, Bouwsma seems to be left with nothing more than the claim that we do not ordinarily use 'deception' in this way. This point seems to be of no philosophical interest. One would not even have to invent a new word to cover the skeptic's proposal. All that one would have to do is to notice what state of affairs one's normal use of 'deception' is getting at, extract that intention from the normal contrasts that surround the term in everyday verification processes or situations, and one would have a perfectly good sense of what the Evil Genius is suggesting. Of course, what he is suggesting is highly unusual, but it is not something that is beyond one's ken when one understands the meanings of ordinary words. The success of the Evil Genius is perfectly complete and undetectable, but it is a success for all that, even if one does not and cannot recognize it.

One might add that Bouwsma seems to be allied with the form of Verifiability that is known as Strict Verifiability. The difference between his first and second deceptions is that one is detectable, whereas the other is not. But if this is enough to make the proposal in the second case empty, or irrelevant to our normal worries about deceptions, then Bouwsma must be rejecting that form of Verifiability which says that a proposition is meaningful if there is any evidence that is *relevant* to the truth (or falsity) of the proposal; for he makes no attempt to show that the fact of ordinary deceptions and the fact that one regards some cases as instances of nondeceptions are not facts that are relevant to assessing the validity of the skeptic's claim. If they are "relevant," then the proposal is meaningful even though one cannot determine its truth or falsity. Since there are well-known difficulties with Strict Verifiability, difficulties that are admitted even by champions of the general identification of meaning and verification, this would be another weakness in Bouwsma's case.

Ryle's well-known example of counterfeiting offers another case of this kind of antiskeptical argument. He says:

> The counterfeiting might be so efficient that an ordinary citizen, unable to tell which were false and which were genuine coins, might become suspicious of the genuineness of any particular coin that he received. But however general his suspicions might be, there remains one proposition which he cannot entertain, the proposition, namely, that it is possible that all coins are counterfeit. For there must be an answer to the question 'Counterfeits of what?' . . . Ice could not be thin if ice could not be thick.[17]

For the sake of discussion, let us agree that as one uses the term 'counterfeit', it must be contrasted with 'genuine', and that this in turn requires that there actually be or have been genuine coins. The following points still seem decisive against Ryle. (1) Is Ryle saying that there *now* must be genuine coins in order for there to be counterfeit ones? But this seems completely gratuitous. One can easily imagine counterfeiters slowly replacing genuine coins with counterfeit ones until there are now no genuine coins in circulation. In such a case, it would be shocking but perfectly intelligible for one to entertain the proposition that all coins are counterfeit and then even to discover the ring that has perpetrated this fraud.

(2) Then is he saying that there *must have been* genuine

coins at one time? This seems equally gratuitous. There might have been plans to produce genuine coins, but imagine that before that could take place a gang of thieves abducted those who knew of these plans and made their own coins, which were counterfeit coins. Once again, the concept that all the coins are now counterfeit is perfectly intelligible. (3) If Ryle objects that the false coins would not be "counterfeit" in that case, one can reply as above: there is a normal, central meaning to 'counterfeit' which one can extract from the ordinary contrast with 'genuine' (that is, from those ordinary *uses* in which we distinguish one from the other) and which suggests falseness. And one can then say that all coins might be false, and understand what one means, even if there be no answer to the question, "Counterfeits of what?" (4) As C. K. Grant has pointed out, a term can be used meaningfully without its normal contrasting term either if there remains a contrast of these terms in another related area or, for example, if one has a conception of another state of mind in contrast with which one's normal waking state is rather like what a dreaming state is in comparison to normal waking consciousness.[18] In either case the term that has enlarged its use is still meaningfully used if an analogy is preserved with its ordinary contrastive use. The fact of the analogy would preserve enough contrast so that one could identify the content of the enlarged term in a nonempty way. (5) Those who employ this mode of argument must show that they are not merely pointing out that terms used without an opposite are useless *for certain purposes* but also that they are not assuming that there could not be any legitimate philosophical purposes in terms of which they have both a meaning and a use.[19] One would have to show that distinguishing between items in a given situation is a legitimate use of terms, while the reordering of our conceptual scheme is not. In Ryle's comments, this point is assumed, not proved, and we shall have to look elsewhere for the argument to support this claim.

The Argument from Paradigm Cases

When Malcolm distinguishes between terms whose meaning is learned descriptively and those whose meaning is learned ostensively, and concludes that in the case of the latter, "it follows, from the fact that they are ordinary expressions in the language, that there have been *many* situations of the kind which they describe," he employs a mode of argument that is closely related to the one discussed immediately above and is called the Argument from Paradigm Cases (*MOL*, p. 18).

The principle of the argument is easily understood. One can undercut skeptical attempts to question the existence of empirical claims that are certain, of valid perceptual experiences, and so forth, simply by pointing to cases that serve as paradigms for one's use of that term and by which one was taught that term. One says: "This is what free-will *means*. What sense does it make to doubt its existence when one can point to undoubted cases of it?" Of course, the argument will not work, as Flew points out, in the case of a "compound descriptive expression," for a thing so described need not exist.[20] But in the case of a true paradigm, there is no sense in which one's use might be incorrect; one has the meaning, and no theory can convince one that there is "really" nothing that corresponds to the term in question.

The strength of this approach to skepticism comes out when one considers the following statement by Russell: "When I 'touch' the tree, certain electrons in my finger are sufficiently near to certain electrons in the tree for violent forces of repulsion to be generated."[21] But why does he put 'touch' within quotation marks? Because we never really touch anything? How absurd that is! Right now I am touching the keys of a typewriter. Russell is mixing two worlds to the detriment of common sense.

In her famous critique of Eddington, Susan Stebbing stresses the danger of mixing scientific talk with ordinary talk. As she states, "Nothing but confusion can result if, in one and the same sentence, we mix up language used for the furniture of the earth and our daily dealings with it with language used for the purpose of philosophical and scientific discourse."[22] And surely she is right that when Eddington says that the plank on which he stands isn't solid or that the paper on the writing desk is supported by electric particles hitting its underside, he is uncritically uniting two radically different views of the world. 'Solid' derives its meaning from solid planks, and *paper* isn't supported by atomic particles.

Still, Stebbing's account of the famous two-tables example is unsatisfactory, for she believes that it is nonsensical to speak of two *tables*, one being the "shadow" of the other. Perhaps it is silly to speak of the scientific *table*, since 'table' is a common-sense notion, but it is not absurd to wonder about the relation between the common-sense table and those entities that replace ordinary physical objects in the scientific account of what there is. Stebbing seems to think that *any* supposed clash between the two images is nonsense and not merely that Eddington's way of stating that clash is absurd. Appeals to our ordinary use of 'solid' and 'table' only serve to point out that these terms do have uses within ordinary discourse; they cannot do away with our underlying belief that the scientific account of the world represents a competing view of the world.

The Paradigm Argument seems to require a certain view of what the skeptic or the revisionary philosopher is trying to do; and if that view is incorrect, the Paradigm Argument seems to be irrelevant, strangely off the mark. The view that I refer to is the one that Malcolm adopts when he interprets the skeptic's claim about certainty to be a "disguised recommendation that the phrase 'it is certain that' be applied to a statement if and only if the statement has a self-contradictory negative" (*CES*, p. 34). Thus, such philosophers are said to want to "abolish" one ordinary use of the word and, strangely, to retain only a useless sense of 'certain'.

Elsewhere, Malcolm refers to such proposals as "disguised linguistic *statements*" (my emphasis) rather than as disguised linguistic *recommendations* (*MOL*, p. 13). If there is any difference here it might lie in the suggestion that a statement actually claims to tell us what the ordinary usage is, while a recommendation tells one only what it ought to be. In any case, the proper method of dealing with the skeptic's proposal on either interpretation is linguistic. One should produce (as Moore did on Malcolm's interpretation of him) paradigms of the ordinary use, which will reveal either (1) that there would be something queer about adopting the skeptic's terminology (in case he is making a recommendation) or (2) that the skeptic's language is "wrong" and "improper" and can be refuted by noting ordinary usage (in case the skeptic is ignorant of how one normally speaks and thinks he is telling one about actual speech patterns).[23]

63

Now, all of this seems to be clearly wrong for the simple reason that there is no reason to think that the skeptic (or the revisionary philosopher) is making a linguistic statement of any kind, disguised or not. His subject matter is not words but the things for which words stand, and he is not even *implying* that ordinary speech is wrong *for ordinary purposes* and that it should be replaced as one's means of communication by "stricter," philosophical speech. He is quite willing to leave one's ordinary speech distinctions alone and to grant that a more philosophically accurate language would make a mess of everyday intercourse; he only insists that such speech is too loose and inaccurate *for philosophical purposes*. But then, merely citing paradigm uses of ordinary terms, far from constituting a refutation of the skeptic, is simply irrelevant.

Presumably, in most cases the skeptic knows that the ordinary usage is different from his philosophic usage, and nothing that he says denies anything about the ordinary usage. He is not misusing words as someone learning the language might do. Nor is it relevant to point out that *by the ordinary use* the "strict" use is queer, unless one can show that any departure from ordinary speech is ipso facto a mistake. Merely saying that ordinary language is correct language grossly begs the question. Short of this, one must examine the arguments that philosophers present in order to justify their claims; and once this is done, reference to a paradigm starts but does not finish the discussion. One cannot, as Malcolm claims, reject "them as false statements without even examining them" (*MOL*, p. 10), for the paradigm method of refutation does not directly link up with the intention of the philosophic skeptic.

That reference to paradigms begins but does not end philosophical arguments can be shown in another way. The Paradigm Argument seems to rest on the view that some words can be learned descriptively, whereas some can be learned only ostensively. In the former case, one can use such terms without knowing that the items that they describe or refer to exist; but in the latter case, one cannot. Apparently, this is because the former use of words is "theoretical"; whether the things that it speaks of exist remains for verification to determine, and as long as that verification is indirect, it remains possible that there is another and better way of describing the given situation. (Malcolm's example of this is the word 'ghost'.) But in the latter case, one uses the words in a simple, nontheoretical manner, a manner that carries with it no suggestions or overtones that might be questioned. One has experienced the thing referred to; therefore, one *knows* that there are such things. One's words in this case refer to the thing experienced, and that is all. Shades of Locke and simple versus complex ideas!

Three questions immediately arise: (1) Is this sharp distinction defensible? (2) Even if it is defensible in some cases, does it help one to settle issues that particularly interest philosophers? (3) Is the claim being made that one *must l*earn words in a certain way or only that one *may* do so or *usually* does so?

About the first question, I will say only that even in the case of 'yellow' and 'left', it is not beyond question that such words refer to what we claim exists but about which some doubt is possible. If the circumstances in which one learned the reference of the word turn out to be other than one thought at the time, or if one later decides that the color patch was misclassified, or if one produces an argument to the effect that there *appear* to be such things but *really* there are not (as did Bradley and as some contemporary Scientific Materialists do), then one may be led to question the existence or reality that the "simple quality" was thought to have. If all of one's words make a claim on the future, then learning them in the immediate present does not guarantee that the things *so described* have the status one assumes them to have.

The second point is more interesting. If one does not begin by assuming that certain words can be understood by reference to paradigm cases (those, of course, that one wishes to justify and keep from the clutches of metaphysicians), how will one show that these interesting words are simple and not complex? Flew's example of 'free will' is a good case in point. One might well admit that willful, nonpressured acts are "paradigms" of free acts, but it is still plausible to see 'free will' as implying that there are no hidden causes, since simple external pressure is often easy to detect. Said another way, the discovery of hidden causes, which have an *analogy* with the causes that are normally thought to oppose free acts, may cause one to revise one's original application of 'free will' to the paradigmatic situation.

There are assumptions, which well may not be fulfilled, which surround the paradigm use of 'free will' and make that use theoretical. The facts that the use of such words is possible for those who show little capacity for abstract thought and that one can use them without reference to theoreticians do not rule out the possibility that they involve commitments of a theoretical kind.[24] When these commitments are brought out in the open, they may convince one that one's paradigm really only meets some of the criteria of a free act.

Similarly with 'certain': Does it have the required simplicity, or are there considerations that will convince one that cases of "empirical certainty" are only approximations to real certainty? We can learn from paradigms how we use words, but can we learn that that use is justified no matter how one's beliefs change or no matter what new things one finds out about the world? As Watkins points out, there does not seem to be any way to rule out the possibility that what one took to be paradigms may turn out on examination to be "bogus examples which did not fit the specification."[25] After all, as he also points out, one might learn the word 'miracle' by being confronted with clear examples of miracles. But one would not want to say, in this case, that a later reinterpretation of natural events might not make one say that one only *took* them to be miracles because of ignorance, superstition, or what have you. And outside of merely arbitrary, question-begging selection, where is the argument that shows that one should not regard key philosophical terms in this light rather than in Malcolm's and Flew's way? Meaning overflows the banks established by reference to such paradigms.

The third question reveals some hesitancy in the formulation of the Paradigm Case Argument. It would be an interesting fact if any words could *only* be taught ostensively. Then, one might be led, in those cases, to believe that the objects referred to are so basic that any attempt to doubt them would be absurd. But it is not clear how one might prove that 'certain' or 'free' could only be taught in this way. Despite what Malcolm says (*MOL*, p. 18), it seems perfectly possible that one might be taught the meaning of 'certain' (as applied to empirical statements) in terms of other words, and one might then proceed to check whether there are in fact any such cases of certainty.[26]

Realizing that "could only" is too strong, Flew suggests that all that the defender of the Paradigm Argument needs to support is the claim that the terms in question "*can be* elucidated by looking at simple paradigm cases . . . such as those by reference to which the expression *usually is* . . . explained" (my emphasis).[27] But this seems much too weak a case to make the Paradigm Argument of much philosophical interest. If one could elucidate certain words in terms of other words, but for some reason happens to do so in terms of paradigms, then it is hard to see how one's way of doing it can claim to have any metaphysical advantage over the other way. The certainty of existence that comes (supposedly) through reference to paradigms will be undercut when one realizes that others do (or even might do) it another way. A visitor to one's culture or group will think that one is ignorant of conceptual possibilities because of a cultural feature that one has taken to have ontological implications.

As a result, the strong version of the learning theory that bolsters the Paradigm Case Argument seems to be impossible to defend, while the weaker version, even if true, provides no reason for thinking that reference to paradigms decisively refutes certain skeptical and revisionary theses. Presumably, the skeptic could well agree that such reference makes it incumbent on him to provide good reasons for not taking these paradigms at face value, but this modest claim leaves completely open the possibility that good reasons are forthcoming.[28]

CRITICISMS OF MALCOLM

I append the following criticisms of points that Malcolm makes in his discussion of knowledge and certainty: (1) Malcolm points out that when one is using 'know' in the "strong" sense, one would refuse to count anything as *evidence* against one's claim (*KB*, p. 72); and he makes a similar point with regard to verification, when he states that it is a mistake to think that more looking counts as more verification no matter what the circumstances (*VA*, p. 54). If one has looked carefully a moment before, continued looking would not be called further verification.

The question is what follows from these speech habits. Malcolm himself says that it does *not* follow from one's using, and from one's knowledge that one is using, 'know' in the strong sense that one in fact knows what one claims to know.[29] But then, I think it is fair to say that his original article was misleading, for he spoke of statements in which one would use 'know' in the strong sense as "beyond the reach of doubt" because they form the foundation of one's reasoning (*KB*, p. 79). Either these remarks are further statements about one's attitudes toward some statements, in which case one still knows nothing of their truth; or they imply something about truth, in which case one *does* know them in knowing that one is using 'know' in the strong sense. The former alternative, while not "autobiographical," is "psychological" and says nothing with which the skeptic need quarrel. The latter is rejected by Malcolm, and in any case it carries the unwelcome implication that by being stubborn enough, one can know anything that one pleases. Malcolm's two senses of 'know' represent, then, an effort in what might be called "cultural linguistics"; they carry no implications for the existence of knowledge.

I think that the same could be said for his remarks about 'verify'. One may normally think that more and more observation is a sign of neurosis, not of investigative care, and may refrain, therefore, from dignifying those efforts with the term 'verification'. But is this attitude not born of practical necessity, and is it not without theoretical justification? The fact that one does not pursue verification beyond a certain point in specific circumstances says nothing about whether what one sees might surprise one and might suddenly need to be counted as evidence; nor does the fact that a surprising conclusion might leave one momentarily dumfounded rather than leave one thinking that what one said before was false (*VA*, p. 13). The skeptic need not be bothered if in ordinary speech one arbitrarily limits the extent to which one is willing to apply certain epistemic terms.

(2) Malcolm's remarks about "conclusive evidence" and "complete verification" in regard to empirical propositions can, I think, be dismissed by the skeptic as mere reports of how one uses those phrases in everyday discourse. Malcolm himself says in several places (*VA*, pp. 38, 52) that certain grounds or evidence

would *ordinarily* be regarded as conclusive, but since the skeptic is not interested in what one ordinarily says, he can ignore this bit of evidence. The problem, as I see it, is that one wants to *understand* how evidence can be conclusive when one cannot rule out the possibility that future events may make what now seems certain seem misleading. And if the grounds for an empirical assertion do not entail the truth of that claim, as Malcolm acknowledges (*VA*, p. 49), then it seems that such an understanding is ruled out in this case. As long as the gap between evidence and conclusion is not bridged by a logical bond, all that one is left with is the admitted fact that in everyday life, one accepts certain evidence as conclusive.

Malcolm, it seems to me, has at least two possible responses to this criticism: (a) Since the notion of verification applies to empirical statements, the notion of complete verification must also be applicable, at least in theory (*CES*, p. 31). (b) Probability and certainty can differ in kind, even though they differ principally in the "number of favourable tests" that favor one over the other (*CES*, p. 40).

I simply do not see why it follows that because evidence weighs in favor of an empirical proposition, there must be a conceivable state of highest evidence. One might as well say that because quantity applies to numbers, therefore "highest quantity" must also apply. There is nothing in applying a process to something that compels one to say that this process must have an end in regard to this same something. Second, I cannot understand how if two propositions differ only in that there is more evidence for one than for the other, one can be certain and the other merely probable. What is it about the extra quantity of evidence that makes this qualitative change occur? At what point does it occur; that is, how many observations are needed for certainty? These questions seem absurd just because it is obvious that they have no answer.

Malcolm's own analogy shows that his case is bankrupt. He claims that the skeptic's position is exactly analogous to saying that "because the difference between 'being bald' and 'having a full head of hair' is only one of degree, therefore all men are really bald" (*CES*, p. 42). But the skeptic need not be saddled with the thesis that in no case need a process that proceeds by degrees have an end that represents a qualitative change. His claim is that because the process of verification is theoretically *without limit,* the addition of more verifications cannot make the qualitative difference that certainty brings. Baldness can be reached by degrees, but how can certainty? Malcolm makes it clear that his claim for absolute certainty for some empirical assertions must not be interpreted as mere practical certainty (*VA*, p. 55). But the fact that we normally distinguish the two kinds of certainty is not sufficient to show that Malcolm's certainty amounts to, or could amount to, anything more than practical certainty. That some empirical statements are certain does not show that one is not settling for far less than theoretical certainty. Malcolm's claim that sometimes one can be certain and sometimes one cannot (*CES*, p. 43) amounts to no more than the observation that one ordinarily thinks that in favorable circumstances one can know things with certainty. But then, skepticism is not a doctrine that is identical with common sense.

(3) Malcolm says that to suggest by the words 'merely probable' that empirical statements fall short of some goal is "totally misleading," since they cannot possibly attain certainty (*CES*, p. 22). Two remarks seem to be in order. First, there is a well-known argument in the rationalist tradition which claims that empirical assertions probably understood (by God, perhaps) would attain to rational, logical certainty. Thus, one cannot *assume* that under no conditions could the empirical attain this ideal. Second, even if one grants that they cannot, I do not see that the use of 'probable' is misleading. There is an ideal of certainty that cannot be realized in the empirical realm, but why cannot the ideal (realizable in its proper realm) and the empirical be related by referring to the latter as probable? Under such conditions, it would be a waste of time to try to make the empirical over into the certain, but as long as the notion of certainty makes sense—or has a conceivable application *somewhere*—it seems informative to bring out the contrast with the empirical by use of the term 'probable'.[30]

KNOWLEDGE AND CERTAINTY: PART 2

ARTHUR DANTO: A LINGUISTIC REPLY
TO SKEPTICISM

In his *Analytical Philosophy of Knowledge*, Arthur Danto formulates an answer to philosophical skepticism that finds a linguistic mistake at the heart of it but that rejects the ordinary-language version of this mistake. According to Danto, an Austin or a later Wittgenstein talks at cross purposes with the skeptic, the former two insisting that words *do* have a descriptive use, whereas the latter says nothing that denies this claim. As Danto says, "In the sense of 'real' which is *skeptically* relevant, *descriptively* real Rembrandts are no better off than their non-genuine counterparts."[1] Not only is there a failure to make contact with skepticism here, but on the view that Danto calls "Internalism," there is a self-defeating attempt to avoid the very possibility of skepticism.

For Danto, "internalists see language primarily as a set of instruments for the facilitation of social existence and, in the extreme version, questions of truth-and-falsity collapse completely into empirical questions of use" (p. 233). On such a view, skepticism cannot arise, because language and the world do not have the requisite distance from one another; the only questions that can arise are those empirical ones that a study of word use can in principle settle. Yet, Danto urges, this position is suicidal, for the attempt to state it presupposes the same distance between language and the world that the position is trying to deny. Language must "withdraw" from the world in order to present Internalism, and one then assumes that language is outside of and related to the world of which it speaks. Thus, Internalism tries to overcome skepticism by a version of the "quest for certainty"; it tries to ignore the gap between language and the world. And this way of opposing skepticism must fail, for it ignores the gap that makes knowledge possible (p. 237).

What, then, is characteristic of philosophical skepticism, and how should one deal with it? In Danto's view, the skeptic is concerned with the semantical uses of words, not with their descriptive uses. That is, he is concerned with the true and false semantical values that assertions acquire in their relation to the world. "The skeptic so phrases his questions that they cannot be answered *within* experience, and then flaunts us with our incapacity to go outside experience and to see whether, on the other side, there is a relationship satisfied or not" (p. 195). The skeptic is not concerned with errors that are discoverable within experience; he is concerned with questioning "the *whole* of experience, including that to which we would ordinarily appeal in the removal of error" (p. 196).

Danto is willing to accept the fact that there is no internal determination of semantical values and that, therefore, there is a gap between language and the world. This gap is necessary for the possibility of truth and, hence, of knowledge, and in one interpretation of skepticism, all the skeptic is doing is pointing out the conditions of knowledge (p. 181). But insofar as he insists that he is calling knowledge into question, his view rests on the following mistake: he treats the elements or objects of experience as semantical vehicles that are capable of truth or falsity. In effect, this is to treat experience as a language (p. 200) and to insist that there is the same gap between experience and the world as there is between language and the world. Danto speaks of this as "*neutralizing* the content of experience" (p. 191) and as "*externalizing* the world . . . from experience" (p. 194), a process that he sees as a response to the Argument from Illusion.

Once one is convinced that there is no internal mark that reveals whether an experience is veridical or not, one accepts the view that this mark can only be external and is conferred on experience by the world that one experiences. As Danto says, "What we have done has been to open up a semantical gap between experiences, taken now as semantical vehicles, and the world" (p. 191). In so doing, one transforms the problem of illusion from a descriptive problem to a semantic one, one that philosophers, not psychologists, are qualified to handle (p. 200).

This semantic transformation of experience is the key mistake on which skepticism rests, according to Danto. Now, granted that the skeptic does treat experience and the world as semantically separable, and granted that the skeptic, in so doing, is concerned to call all of experience into question (and I think that Danto's presentation of skepticism and its immunity from the type of ordinary-language criticism that we have considered so far is well taken), one must still show that this process amounts to a mistake. Danto's way is to argue that the very gap created by the skeptic, which is essential to his case, is also fatal, providing the basis for a conclusive self-refutation of skepticism.

His strategy is to show that by the skeptic's own standards, one cannot understand the sentences that he utters. Of course, the skeptic assumes that he and others have no trouble understanding his claim that "meaning must remain invariant under changes in semantical value" (p. 186). But if we cannot tell for certain that any utterance is true, "we can in principle never apply the rules of meaning for these sentences, which means we do not understand these rules, which means we do not understand those sentences" (p. 187).[2]

Put in more simple terms, Danto is saying that if one cannot in principle know that any sentence is true, then one must not know in what circumstances the truth of a sentence could be determined. But if one does not know this, one, by definition, fails to know the descriptive meaning of the sentence and does not, therefore, understand what is meant by the sentence in question. Where knowledge is impossible, understanding and meaningful utterance are also impossible. So, although the skeptic requires that the descriptive meaning of semantic vehicles remain the same despite changes in semantical value and although he does not deny that words have descriptive uses and criteria for those uses, in fact, his position requires that no sentence have a clear meaning and, therefore, that he understand no sentence, his own included. I suppose that Danto could grant that the skeptic might be under the impression that he understands what he says, but the logic of meaning indicates that this impression is without foundation. The skeptic must face the dilemma that "either he is incoherent or wrong" (p. 186).

This is an interesting approach to skepticism, one that first grants what the skeptic thinks will prove his case (the gap between semantical vehicles and the world) and then argues (1) that identifying this gap is harmless and (2) that the claim that one cannot cross the gap turns out to be self-defeating. However, neither of Danto's claims seems to me to be satisfactorily proved. One important observation to make at the outset is that Danto's case that the skeptic is mistaken in treating experience semantically (that his neutralized experience is a "mythical replica" of the neutrality of genuine semantical vehicles, p. 195) rests entirely on his argument that this move leads to incoherence. If it does not, then Danto's pejorative remarks about skepticism can be ignored, while one can retain his description of the origin and nature of skepticism. A second observation is that Danto's theory is a version of the Verifiability Theory of Meaning: there is no meaning where there is no possibility of verification.

Danto's first point is clearly the less important of the two, but it is unconvincing to say that skepticism is a "disguise for the description of the conditions of knowledge" (p. 181). Rather, the skeptic insists that once one knows what these conditions are, one sees that they cannot be fulfilled. Thus, the skeptic's claim *is* that the "very character we are obliged to ascribe to the structure of knowledge itself" *is* a "fatal impediment to the possibility of knowledge" (p. 182). There is nothing necessarily self-defeating or harmfully paradoxical in the view that the certainty that "knowing" seeks could be attained only by the transcendence (and destruction) of the conditions under which ordinary "knowing" takes place. Those who quest for certainty might be right: one can reach "knowledge" only by crossing (or denying) the gap between experience and the world; but as a thinking being, one may well find that one is always on the near side of that gap and

74

that one is, therefore, always prevented from realizing the goal that one seeks as a thinking being. In any case, skepticism is not harmless, as Danto suggests one might take it to be.

The difficulty that I have with Danto's main contention is that I see no connection between philosophical skepticism and the loss of descriptive meaning. That is, I do not see that the *philosophical* questioning of knowledge leads to an inability to specify the descriptive meaning of a sentence or a term and, hence, to an inability to understand what the skeptic is saying.[3] Just as Hume went right on with his ordinary beliefs and anticipations despite his skepticism, I see no reason for the philosophical skeptic not continuing to determine the truth or falsity of claims in the ordinary way that one does such things. I am almost willing to grant that if there are no conceivable conditions in which one is willing to say that the statement "This tulip tree is dead" is true or false or in which one is willing to say that the animal before one does or does not meet the specifications of "dog," then one cannot claim to understand what those terms mean.[4] But just as Hume's view of physical objects does not make it wrong to speak of things remaining the same, when one is speaking *within* one's ordinary framework, so the skeptic continues to "know" when it is correct to say that he is having a veridical experience, "knowing" something, and so forth. And this knowledge of one's ordinary criteria provides the basis from which one can well understand the skeptic's claims, even though those claims say that in an ultimate sense the ordinary distinction between true and false is not as justified as one ordinarily thinks.

Because there are circumstances in which one would be willing to say that something is an x or that a sentence y is true, one demonstrates that one understands those words or sentences. But then, one also understands what the skeptic is denying when he criticizes our claims to knowledge: he claims that although our normal tests for truth have been fulfilled, there still are good reasons for thinking that this fulfillment does not guarantee truth. Even Danto makes what seems to be a crucial admission in this regard. He states that normal errors and illusions are "irrelevant" to the skeptic's position, that they "give no evidence" for it, because the skeptic is concerned with the illusoriness of experience as a whole (p. 195). However, he immediately grants that there may be a "proportion" (p. 196) between mistakes and "correct takings" within experience, on the one hand, and "correct takings" within and without experience, on the other. But this seems to say that experiential errors are at least *relevant* to the skeptic's claim, even if there is no direct road from the one to the other. As we argued above regarding meaningful contrasts, this proportion helps us to understand the generalized error or illusion that the skeptic wishes us to acknowledge as possible.

Nor will it do to say, against the skeptic, merely that he creates a gap that one *cannot* cross, when, in fact, "through discovering our mistakes we demonstrate ourselves as capable of crossing the gap between semantical vehicles and whatever confers semantical values on these" (p. 196). For this assumes that what one ordinarily calls "discovering one's mistakes" involves crossing the gap between one's semantical vehicles (words and sentences) and reality. But the skeptic claims that one cannot know that what one compares one's assertions with is in fact reality; he relies on the arguments from illusion and from dreaming in order to convince one of the "neutrality" of experience. For him, what we take for reality is, for all one knows, simply another semantical vehicle. Danto, of course, stresses these latter points, but then he cannot begin against the skeptic by asserting that one does know that certain of our assertions are false and that the skeptic has to invent another gap, because the one between language and the world has already been crossed.

Such remarks would have explanatory force only if one were convinced by Danto's argument that the second gap leads to impossible difficulties about descriptive meaning. And since I have argued that skepticism does not impair one's understanding of the normal application of words and sentences and, hence, leaves descriptive meaning where it was before skepticism, I do not think that we can assume that this underlying claim against skepticism has been proved.[5] Thus, I find that Danto's main thesis—that "we are *defined* through the fact that we exactly occupy the space between representations of the world and the world" (p. 63)—remains ultimately undefended. If his thesis is true, skepticism is overcome; but since skepticism has not been shown to be self-defeating, one has no conclusive reason to think that his thesis is true.

G. E. MOORE: THE COMMON-SENSE REPLY TO SKEPTICISM

G. E. Moore's defense of knowledge, although closely related to the ordinary-language approach to skepticism, represents a distinctive and powerful means of overcoming radical skepticism.[6] In his "Reply to My Critics," he says that in his lecture called "Proof of an External World" he thought that he offered only *a* good reason, not a proof, against the claim that nobody knows for certain that there are any material things, while he thinks that he has disproved the claim that there are no material things.[7] This remark suggests that Moore's criticism of philosophical skepticism may not be meant to be as final as it has been thought to be. And some remarks in "Certainty" suggest that Moore's claims for certainty are not as powerful as one might think. For example, he states that there is at least *one sense* of 'known' and 'certain' from which it does not follow that because a proposition is contingent it cannot be known or be certain. Since this sense is contrasted with 'know' and 'certain' as used in relation to mathematical propositions, one might read this qualification as meaning that it is all right, as one normally speaks, to say that one knows that the sky is blue today.[8] Or when Moore claims in the same article that the statement "It is certain that *p*" is "relative" to the person who says it (p. 236), one might think that, for Moore, 'certain' only describes a personal, psychological attitude, one that one often has and one that makes the use of 'certain' appropriate. Again, this would make the contrast between the skeptic and Moore less marked.

However, I do not think that this interpretation would be correct. Moore makes it quite clear that he is claiming absolute certainty for his common-sense assertions. And while certainty does not commit others to being certain (this is the subjective element in 'certain'), it is used by Moore in the strict sense favored by the skeptic. In "A Defense of Common Sense," one learns those propositions that, when taken in their ordinary sense, he and other human beings know with certainty to be true.

Therefore, his attack *is* directed at skeptical claims about knowledge as well as against claims that certain things do not exist.

Second, I want to insist that, despite important areas of agreement, Moore's approach to skepticism differs significantly from that of ordinary-language analysis. Malcolm has claimed that Moore's approach to the skeptic "consists in pointing out that these statements *go against ordinary language*."[9] Like the skeptic, Moore is said to offer "disguised linguistic statements" and to "appeal to our language-sense" (p. 13).[10] Moore's reply works because we do speak as Moore says, and it would not be correct to speak as the skeptic suggests that one should. But it is hard to see why Moore should be taken in this manner. He speaks rather, in an old-fashioned way, about knowledge, material things, and the like, not about their verbal counterparts; his claims just are not couched in the linguistic idiom. In addition, Moore's approach to skepticism is radically different from what Malcolm suggests that it is. Moore begins by granting to the skeptic that the issue is over whether one has knowledge in the "strict" sense about the existence of physical objects, the past, and so forth; and he then claims to show that one does have such knowledge. The skeptic's claims are wrong, although they might have been right.

Playing the skeptic's game makes Moore's task at once extremely difficult and worthy of a try. One does not have here a case of two ships passing in the night. The ordinary-language philosopher does not proceed in this way, at least some of the time. He may suggest that skepticism is incoherent or that it uses its terms in an empty, noncontrastive manner or that it wins an arbitrary, empty victory by so defining his terms that only knowledge in the strict sense is denied; and whoever thought that one had or needed that anyway? Moore does not try to undermine the force of skepticism in any of these ways, and he does not (explicitly) rest his case on the way that we ordinarily speak. His approach is more bold: let us take skepticism on its own terms and show that it is wrong about the reality of knowledge, not merely wrong about how one uses words.

Moore's answer to the skeptic is disarmingly straightforward. He merely states that he knows certain things that skeptics have said one cannot be sure that one knows: "But do I really *know* all the propositions in (1) to be true? Isn't it possible that I merely believe them? Or know them to be highly probable? In answer to this question, I think I have nothing better to say than that it seems to me that I *do* know them, with certainty."[11] Sometimes he offers a proof (e.g., that external objects exist), but even here he merely states that he knows the premise of the proof to be true: "But I *do* know that I held up two hands above this desk not very long ago. As a matter of fact, in this case you all know it too. There's no doubt whatever that I did" (*PP*, p. 146; see also pp. 41 and 145).

Second, he explains why people might tend to doubt that he has the knowledge that he claims to have. But here again, much of his explanation consists in bare assertions. (1) Knowing the analysis of a proposition is an "entirely different thing" (*PP*, p. 37) from not understanding the meaning of the proposition. Therefore, one should not fail to claim knowledge of common-sense statements on the ground that one does not fully understand them. (2) Since one can know things without knowing the evidence for them, one should not doubt statements because they are based on evidence, known or unknown (*PP*, p. 44). (3) "I can know things, which I cannot prove" (*PP*, p. 148). Therefore, one should not doubt Moore's proofs merely because he cannot justify them.

Third, and here Moore joins with the ordinary-language approach to skepticism, Moore tries to show that skeptics run into logical difficulties of one sort or another. Some skeptics, those who hold that Moore's common-sense propositions are not wholly true, presuppose in their denial that *some* of these statements are in fact true (*PP*, p. 40). As Moore says,

> The strange thing is that philosophers should have been able to hold sincerely, as part of their philosophical creed, propositions inconsistent with what they themselves *knew* to be true; and yet, so far as I can make out, this has really frequently happened. [*PP*, p. 41]

Other skeptics actually contradict themselves, for they deny that one knows for certain any of Moore's common-sense propositions, and in so doing, they actually assert the existence of other human beings. But if one can know that other human beings exist, one knows an instance of one of Moore's general common-sense assertions (*PP*, p. 43). And the skeptic who appeals to the fact that he may be dreaming in every case of a supposed veridical observation seems to be involved in a contradiction in implying that he knows dreams that have occurred while he says that he does not now know that he is not dreaming (*PP*, p. 244). (We will discuss the Argument from Dreaming in the next section of this chapter.) And as we have seen, Moore thinks that some skeptical arguments arise from a confusion between different senses of 'possible' or 'may' (*PP*, p. 216).

One question that arises immediately is whether Moore is not simply begging the question against the skeptic. If he merely asserts that common sense is a reservoir of knowledge in opposition to the reasoned case of the skeptic, then his case seems to be a good example of old-fashioned dogmatism. But Moore need not be read in this way. First, if his arguments against the logical consistency of skepticism are valid, then they can provide a basis for his bare assertions concerning knowledge claims. Second, Moore's bare assertions actually rest on a principle that makes these assertions seem more rationally justified, to wit:

> But it seems to me a sufficient refutation of such views as these, simply to point to cases in which we do know such things. This, after all, you know, really is a finger: there is no doubt about it: I know it, and you all know it. And I think we may safely challenge any philosopher to bring forward any argument in favour either of the proposition that we do not know it, or of the proposition that it is not true, which does not at some point, rest upon some premiss which is, beyond comparison, less certain than is the proposition which it is designed to attack.[12]

There seems to be a great deal of sense in this. If one does know what Moore claims one knows, then there seems to be nothing more certain that one can point to in order to justify one's knowledge claims. All that one can do is to make this claim seem reasonable and to challenge the skeptic to make his case seem as reasonable. Confronting the skeptic with an exception to his denial of knowledge need not be a harmful begging of the question if the contrary position can be approached in no other way. After all, the skeptic can be equally said to beg the question; Moore at least gains a stand-off with the skeptic on this point. The dilemma, as Moore puts it is, "How on earth is it to be decided which of the two things it is *rational* to be most certain of?" (*PP*, p. 222).[13]

One of the main problems that arise in trying to decide what weight to give to Moore's principle, stated above, is that the issue with skepticism revolves around a distinction that tends to undermine the obvious appeal of his principle. The distinction between the practical and the theoretical, if legitimate, suggests that what seems most rational in one's daily life and concerning one's common convictions may not be what is most rational to believe when the special doubts of philosophical skepticism are raised. From this point of view, Moore's principle correctly captures one's everyday response to skepticism, but if it *merely* does that, it will have no effect on the skeptic who thinks of this attitude as limited and impure when measured by the highest standards of theoretical certainty. The skeptic would seem to gain a stand-off with Moore here unless Moore can show that what is most rational to believe ordinarily is most rational to believe under any conditions; and presumably that is the issue between himself and the skeptic.

And there is another reason for distrusting Moore's principle. As he acknowledges in his *Common Place Book*, in Ann Arbor he said that there was a window in the roof and later asserted that "if I didn't know this, when I said it, I never know anything of the kind" (p. 193). Later, Moore was told that "what looked like a window merely covered an opaque portion of the dome." On reflection, Moore wants to claim that at the time he only *thought* there was a window and did not *feel sure* that there was. But he says that he cannot prove this, and in fact, there seems to be no essential difference in one's attitude toward this case and one's attitude toward the claim that this is a pen on the desk before one.[14] If one can be wrong in such a case, how can one claim certainty in cases that exhibit no decisive differences from this one? To be sure, in other cases, objects may be closer to one, situated in better light, and subjected to the scrutiny of more than one sense. But as we have shown, the relevance of further testing cannot be ruled out, and one's attitudes do not differ markedly from one case to the other. There seems to be no barrier that we have come across so far to extending Moore's mistake at Ann Arbor to reveal the possibility of mistake in cases that are essential to his attack on skepticism.[15] If so, rationality would seem to fall with the skeptic, and Moore's principle would appear to be a reflection of the hastiness with which one claims certainty in ordinary life.

Yet another shaky underpinning to Moore's position lies in his sharp distinction between understanding the meaning of a term or expression and being able to give a correct analysis of its meaning (*PP*, p. 37). This is a crucial step in Moore's attack on skepticism, for it enables him to keep common-sense propositions free from the doubts and intricacies of philosophy. Such difficulties will lie with analysis, while, there being no question about meaning, ordinary folk may remain certain of the truth of common-sense propositions. It seems to me, however, that the distinction blurs as soon as one examines it. If an analysis gives one the meaning of a term, then how can one understand the meaning of that term before one has the analysis? To be sure, there is something that Moore calls "*the* ordinary or popular meaning" (*PP*, p. 36), but how can one *know* that a statement taken in this way is *true* before one is convinced that the ordinary meaning of terms is acceptable. And presumably one learns this from one's analysis. For example, how can one know that "the earth has existed for many years past" until one is convinced that there are such things as "earth," taken in its common-sense way? If our analysis finds this concept inadequate and replaces it with, say, a Humean one, then (if we follow the analysis) one's judgment of the truth of the assertion will be modified. One will be led to say that the statement contained hidden ambiguities which make one's knowledge claim premature or hasty. The ordinary meaning will come to be treated like a theory; and the analysis, like a test of the adequacy of the theory.

At this point the Moorean may well point to his principle and insist that when faced with the choice between knowledge that the earth exists and has existed and an analysis that seems to question this, the rational thing to do is to hold on to the former, rejecting, thereby, the implication that the analysis holds sway over the truth of the assertion taken commonsensically. As

I understand Moore, one need not take the apparent conflict as a sign that the analysis is wrong; what is wrong is the belief that there is a conflict. But then, it is hard to understand why one thinks that there is such a thing as "*the* correct analysis" of the meaning or what it gives to one, if, when one has it, one keeps it at a safe distance from common sense. Interestingly, on Moore's own analysis of "I see a hand," it seems to me that one cannot say that this statement, taken in its ordinary sense, is wholly true. Rather, it is true in what it suggests, but misleading in the form that it gives to this suggestion. The metaphor that one needs is not one of direct conflict but of dimmer and sharper focus. At the very least, I think Moore's division here is questionable, thus making his knowledge claim also questionable.[16]

It is worth noting that at the end of "Certainty," Moore seems to take a slightly different approach toward skepticism than he did in "Four Forms of Scepticism" (*PP*, p. 216). There he is willing to grant both that it is logically possible that one might be having the sensory experiences that one is now having and still be dreaming *and* that this fact (assuming no additional information) makes it impossible for one to know that one is not dreaming (*PP*, p. 245). However, he adds that if one considers memories of the immediate past along with present sensory experiences, then this combination *may* rule out one's dreaming as a logical possibility. At least, Moore claims, no one has shown that this *is* logically possible, so that one gains at least a stand-off with skepticism.

This is not convincing (as Moore himself seems to have granted), for there seems to be nothing in the addition of memory experiences to one's present experiences that could guarantee one's knowledge claim. Perhaps such an addition makes it more unlikely that one is dreaming, but if a guarantee is needed and if it is not found in one's present experiences, then how will one's memory experiences make that much difference? As Ayer points out, Moore seems to be seeking for some combination of experiences from which it *logically follows* that one is not dreaming. But (as Malcolm agrees) there are no such experiences from which it follows either that one is not dreaming or that certain propositions are true.[17] Here Moore seems to grant too much to the skeptic.

Let us now return to Moore's attempt to show that skepticism is logically incoherent and, hence, that it is not a genuine alternative to one's common-sense knowledge claims. The weakness here is that Moore makes no attempt to show that the skeptical assertion either that certain common-sense beliefs are not true or that at least one does not know them to be true *must* be formulated in such a way that it presupposes the truth or knowledge that it wishes to question. For, as Passmore points out, "if we can say whatever we wish to assert about the 'common-sense view of the world' without actually using that descriptive phrase then it appears that nothing of any consequence can be deduced from the presence of that phrase in our ordinary way of talking."[18] One might add that a reformulation of the skeptic's position without the unwanted implication is rather easily made.[19] It does not seem, then, that Moore can rely on his attempt to eliminate skepticism as a possibility; therefore, he must rely on the plausibility and rationality of his principle and of the truth claims that implement that principle.

I wish now to consider another kind of criticism of Moore, one that finds his claims for knowledge not merely unjustified as definitive answers to the skeptic, but finds these claims to be mistaken. This view constitutes an "answer" to the skeptic in that it treats both Moore and the skeptic as victims of the same mistake, namely, that doubts and knowledge claims make sense in almost any context.

Malcolm claims that Moore was not, in fact, defending common sense, for "Moore's assertions do not belong to 'common sense,' i.e., to ordinary language, at all."[20] They involve a use of 'know' in cases in which there was no doubt to be removed, no reason to be given for a claim, and nothing that could count as a proof of that claim—no mode of investigation that would be relevant. In breaking these normal connections with 'know', Moore misused that word and departed thereby from the common-sense viewpoint.

Obviously, this account of Malcolm's is saddled with explaining away the fact that philosophers have in fact considered Moore's arguments to constitute a defense of common sense. Presumably, they must have been overlooking Moore's alleged "misuse" of 'know', for they otherwise would not have so regarded his arguments.[21] When Malcolm replies that amusement, puzzlement, or annoyance is really more typical of reactions to Moore's proofs, he misses the point.[22] For many would find it hard to see how this method could succeed against the skeptic. Hence, the amusement. These reactions do not stem from a sense that Moore misused words or that he was mistaken in thinking that he was defending common sense but from doubts about the possibility of success or shock over the simplicity and directness of Moore's approach to skepticism. Otherwise, Malcolm is faced with explaining why philosophers cannot spot a misuse of their native language when they hear one. Further, I think we can see where Malcolm went wrong and why the ordinary opinion is correct.

I would like to suggest that we think of Moore as a philosopher who is making a philosophical defense of common sense. To respond to the skeptic, he must defend claims that ordinarily need no defense, and to do this is to treat common sense *as* a philosophy or theory. To do so, Moore must extend the normal range or use of words such as 'know' into situations in which one would normally never think of having to claim knowledge because everything is obvious. But I do not see that this means either that Moore is misusing 'know' or that he is not defending common sense. Since doubts have been raised about areas that are normally thought to be free from doubt, Moore finds it necessary to put into words convictions that are so obvious that they normally go unspoken.

Malcolm's reply to this description of Moore's technique seems to be that it is a mistake to think that there is any doubt involved at all (thus, a mistake to think that his first condition of the normal use of 'know' is fulfilled). He states that "to call a philosophical doubt a *doubt* is as misleading as to call a rhetorical question a *question*" (*DCS*, pp. 207–8). And he adds that situations that are candidates for philosophical doubt are precisely those in which no *doubt* is *possible* (p. 216). Now Moore is clear that the skeptic is not in doubt, in the sense that he feels no doubt about that which, as a philosopher, he questions (*PP*, p. 195). He recognizes something as doubtful without being in doubt about it. But then, Moore, in replying to the skeptic, is using 'know' to respond to something, now thought to be doubtful, that is normally not so considered, and this makes his use of 'know' perfectly intelligible by providing a reason that explains why he should be speaking in this unusual way. And there seems to be no reason not to consider this a defense of common sense.

Malcolm's criticism seems to amount to nothing more than pointing out that Moore's use of 'know' is unusual. Thus, Malcolm says that "by calling it a 'misuse' I think I meant only that it was not an ordinary use," and he retracts the claim that Moore's use was "senseless."[23] But this point seems to me to carry no philosophical weight; certainly it does not at all show that Moore was not defending common sense. And unless Malcolm can show that philosophical doubts are not *genuine* (this is the suggestion of his comparison with rhetorical questions), as contrasted with not being *ordinary* or *practical*, he will not have shown that they cannot provide a rationale for Moore's claims and one that gives these claims a perfectly clear sense. (Malcolm claims that this sense is unclear in "Moore's Use of 'Know'," p. 243). If Malcolm tries the stronger assertion, that Moore is radically misusing language, then he has not shown why the kind of extended use of 'know' described above is not a perfectly acceptable, if somewhat unusual, use and one that makes Moore's undertaking what he and most others thought it to be.[24]

However, I think it would be a mistake to reject so quickly the view that Malcolm expresses. We need to understand its foundation and development more fully before passing final judgment, and the place to find these features is in Wittgenstein's *On Certainty*. There Wittgenstein asserts that "Moore's mistake lies in this—countering the assertion that one cannot know that, by saying 'I do know it'."[25] In order to understand why this is a mistake one must understand the nature of a language game.

Language games are said to be possible only "if one trusts something (I did not say 'can trust something')" (§ 509). One cannot say that "in any *individual* case that such-and-such must be beyond doubt," but there must be *some* empirical judgment that is beyond doubt. Otherwise, orders could not be carried out, and doubt itself would not have the proper foundation on which to operate (§ 519). Wittgenstein speaks of Moore's truths as the "unmoving foundation of his language games" (§ 403), which form "the basis of action, and therefore, naturally, of thought"

(§ 411). Assertions of, or doubts about, these foundations lead to confusion. Thus, "if someone were to look at an English pillar-box and say 'I am sure that it's red,' we should have to suppose that he was colour-blind, or believe he had no mastery of English and knew the correct name for the colour in some other language" (§ 526).

A crucial part of Wittgenstein's account is his explanation of the trust, or lack of doubt, that is necessary for any language game. It is helpful, he says, to consider man "as an animal; as a primitive being to which one grants instinct but not ratiocination. . . . Language did not emerge from some kind of ratiocination" (§ 475). Given this perspective, one can see that a lack of doubt does not imply knowledge (§ 480). It may be enough simply that experience does not show otherwise (§ 477). That is, the success of the language game is not the ground or reason for our adopting it, although it may cause one to do so (§ 474).

One does not satisfy oneself of the correctness of one's "world view" either when one learns it or later. Rather, "it is the inherited background against which I distinguish between true and false" (§ 94). The language game can be learned purely practically (§ 95), with the result that mastering a language game presupposes that one can do certain things but not that one knows certain things (§ 534). Wittgenstein adds that one's world view, which he compares to a mythology, may change so that the foundations—empirical propositions that are "hardened" and serve as "channels" for "fluid" empirical propositions (§ 96)—shift; and he says that this division need not be a clear one (§ 97). Nevertheless, he says, "Something must be taught us as a foundation" (§ 449). Wittgenstein is "trying to say something that sounds like pragmatism" (§ 422).

This account reveals the ultimate nature of a language game: "It is not based on grounds. It is not reasonable (or unreasonable). It is there—like our life" (§ 559). We find "the groundlessness of our believing" difficult to accept (§ 166), but the claims and doubts that one has have value only within a world view (§ 110). For example, "a doubt about existence only works within a language-game" (§ 24). To give up the foundations of one's language game would be to give up judging altogether (§ 494), and would be properly dealt with by the admonishing "Oh, rubbish" rather than with a reasoned reply (§ 495). Similarly, if two persons are in disagreement over fundamentals, then one has reached the end of reasoning and must rely on persuasion or conversion (§§ 92, 262, 612).

The results of this analysis for Moore's truths is reasonably obvious. Mathematical and empirical statements need not differ as far as certainty goes (§§ 447, 651–57); both are capable of a "direct taking-hold," a "sureness" that is not to be confused with a knowing (§ 511). Wittgenstein refers to Moorean assertions as "immediate utterance (s)" (§ 510). But there are two main points that relate to Moore. Concerning statements that oppose those that are fundamental to our language game, Wittgenstein says, "I should not call this a *mistake*, but rather a mental disturbance, perhaps a transient one" (§ 71; see also §§ 281, 659); but the inability to be mistaken does not guarantee infallibility (§ 425). Second, Moore's claim that he knows that this is a hand *could* make sense *if* he meant something "quite particular by it" (§ 387). If one can imagine particular circumstances that make such a statement appropriate, then one can understand what is being said; the strangeness of Moore is that he supplies no such context and suggests than none is necessary (see § 423). Interestingly, when one explains what move in the language game one's assertion is by filling in the relevant particular circumstances, the assertion loses "everything that is philosophically astonishing" (§ 622).

Wittgenstein suggests that we might interpret Moore's knowledge claim to mean that certain things "stand-fast" for him and others (§ 116). As Wittgenstein says, "Regarding it as absolutely solid is part of our *method* of doubt and enquiry" (§ 151; see also §§ 86, 112, 136, 371). In any case, merely saying that one knows or enumerating what one knows proves nothing (§§ 487–88).

Although Wittgenstein's portrayal of Moore is fascinating, it does not convince me that one should regard him in the way that Wittgenstein suggests. I say this because I think that Wittgenstein can be interpreted largely as spelling out the characteristics of one's ordinary language game, a procedure that cannot show one that either skeptical doubts or knowledge defenses of that language game are out of the question. And I shall urge that his remarks that do try to argue this point are not nearly sufficient for the purpose.

For example, it is harmless to the skeptic to point out that certain "doubts" are normally thought to be signs of disturbances, not genuine doubts at all.[26] And pointing to the particular circumstances in which 'I know' might normally be uttered does not show that one cannot understand the extended range of use that this phrase has when used in reply to the skeptic. And of course, that doubt presupposes certainty is compatible with Cartesianism and even with doubting at a later time what I now take as certain in order to doubt something else.[27] Further, to suggest that philosophical doubt can be safely ignored ("But if anyone were to doubt it, how would his doubt come out in practice? And couldn't we peacefully leave him to doubt it, since it makes no difference at all?"; § 120) is an effective retort only if one can show that theoretical doubts make "no difference at all" in other than a question-begging sense.

Wittgenstein's pragmatism, as present in his remark that giving grounds ends in an ungrounded way of acting and not in an ungrounded presupposition, is unconvincing as it stands (§ 110). If on reflection, one wants to say that one knows that such-and-such, then the fact that one usually does not consider these matters and (seemingly) simply acts in certain ways is reason to think that the practice is supported by unquestioned beliefs. It also seems silly to me to deny that one does not "know" that physical objects exist merely because one never worries about the matter. The way in which one acts cannot be said to be a final, reasonless fact if one can see that its finality is only the result of an attitude that one normally passes by (§ 148). And unlike Wittgenstein (§ 204), I feel that basic claims, not acting, do rest at the bottom of our language game. The problem then becomes one of justifying those claims, but Moore seems to me to have demonstrated that they are claims.

Is doubt about a language game possible? Clearly, some kinds of doubts would so unsettle one that one would not know what judgments could be made. In fact, newcomers to philosophy are often subject to this disorientation within philosophy. But this does not show that such doubts cannot make sense within a framework that replaces the ordinary one. On the Idealist's view, the law of contradiction is a case of "this or nothing"; one might say that Wittgenstein's remarks force one to see that the skeptic asks one to choose between "this or something else." Thus, one might agree with Wittgenstein that doubts occur within a particular language game, but he does not show that the debate between Moore and the skeptic does not constitute such a language game. Thus, he does not show that questions that threaten one's normal language game are necessarily unjustified even if one grants that doubts must have a system within which they exist (§ 247).

There is one point, however, on which I think Wittgenstein was correct. I have argued that Moore succeeded only in detailing those convictions that are fundamental to our language game, and so I accept Wittgenstein's interpretation of Moore's achievement. I do not agree, however, that this is because his knowledge claims can only be understood in this way, nothing more being possible in this area. Moore failed to do more, but he intended to break out of his own framework; and in the area of logical laws I think a proof is possible that shows that there is a basis for *any* language game. It is simply that on the skeptic's terms there is no way of showing that one's normal, empirical convictions constitute knowledge. All that one achieves here is a pointing to those knowledge claims on which one's ordinary world view rests.

I might add that the evidence does not seem to me to favor Wittgenstein's claim that a clash between language games brings an end to reasons and calls for "conversion" or "persuasion." Certainly, it is difficult for either side to accept the primacy of the points urged by the other side, but the skeptic does produce reasons that the ordinary language game will not do for strict philosophical purposes, and Moore tries to defend the rationality of remaining with the usual language game. In its better moments, neither side merely wants to win the assent of the other; rather, each wants to persuade the other by the truth of its position. If this is thought to be a façade for rhetorical, nonrational techniques, then it must be shown that philosophical debates of this type cannot be argued with an eye toward the truth. One can conceive of alternative language games; one's problem is then to assess the validity of the skeptic's case in favor of one such alternative. This is difficult, but unless one can show that the skeptic's case *cannot* succeed rationally, I see no reason to doubt that rational argument is the means by which he tries to present his case. (More about this when we discuss the private-language argument.)

THE ARGUMENT FROM DREAMS

To make his case for possible error more striking and to give it greater plausibility, the philosophical skeptic reminds one that one dreams and that one mistakes dream experiences for veridical experiences; then he tries to convince one that one cannot be certain that any candidate for a real experience is not in fact a dream experience.[28] The ordinary-language philosopher has basically several ways of rejecting the skeptic's conclusion. He may simply say that one must be able to distinguish between waking and dreaming states.[29] He may then proceed to find other logical difficulties in the use that the skeptic makes of his premises. And finally, he may develop a view of dreaming that helps to explain why nothing of philosophical interest follows from the fact that we dream. This last step calls into question the seemingly true premise that while dreaming, one often thinks that something is occurring to one.

The discussion focuses on the notion of being deceived in dreams. Bouwsma finds the source of this conviction to lie in one's mistaken, overly strong allegiance to the "grammatical" analogy between telling what happened and telling one's dream. Ignoring the fact that one can get the former wrong but not the latter, for "his dream is what he remembers, what he tells,"[30] one imagines that what one tells is false (p. 166), since it never happened. Thinking of oneself as a witness to a happening when one dreams, one thinks of dreaming as a kind of perception. Then it is natural to think that one has an "attitude of acceptance" in one's dreams, as one might have such an attitude in perceiving. Bouwsma suggests that one can cure oneself of this confusion (a confusion that makes skepticism seem to be a problem) if one emphasizes a favorable analogy, that between dreaming and "seeing stars." As there is no inclination to think that one is deceived

91

in the latter case, so there will be no such temptation in the former case.

Even more strongly, it has been argued that there is

> no incompatibility between dreaming that I believed your house is small, and the fact that it is quite large. . . . While I was asleep I did not think your house was small. Sleepers are not thinking about things at all. When I was asleep I was dreaming. I did not think it; I dreamt I thought it. . . . People who do not know they are dreaming when they are dreaming, are not making any mistakes. . . . Even when I dream about whether I dream or not, I am dreaming the question and the answer; I am not asking the question or giving an answer.[31]

Ebersole adds that the Cartesian view of dreaming seems to imply that I am "a late listener to my own dream story, one who does not know that what is described is a dream" (p. 339). One cannot use as a premise to skepticism the claim that one is sometimes deceived in one's dreams because acts of judging, whether failures or successes, make sense only if one is awake. The skeptical argument cannot get off the ground.

Malcolm develops the above position by asserting that claiming one is sound asleep, questioning whether one is sound asleep, and even thinking or being under the impression that one is asleep are all self-contradictory in the sense that each "is an assertion that would necessarily be false each time it was made."[32] In fact, this holds for thinking, doubting, and so forth—"anything whatever." The reason for this is that whatever serves as a criterion for saying that one is thinking, doubting, and so forth, also serves as a criterion for saying that one is not sound asleep (p. 62). Therefore, there would be a contradiction in affirming the former and denying the latter. This train of thought leads Malcolm to the conclusion that it is "senseless" to think that it is impossible to distinguish between waking and deep sleep, because the latter can have no "content of experience" at all and, therefore, not one the same content as waking (p. 66). One cannot express fear when sound asleep (p. 75) or determine whether one is awake or asleep (p. 67). In fact, it is wrong to think of a dream as an occurrence of any kind, for one has no criterion for answering the questions that one might ask about occurrences, such as: How long did it take? When did it happen?[33]

Since Malcolm is merely trying to restore one's normal conception of dreaming, he does not expound on the nature of dreams. But one can say that, for him, there is no contrast between correctly remembering and seeming to remember a dream,[34] and he claims that dreaming and telling about dreams are numerically different things.[35] Their connection, however, is said not to be one of logical independence, presumably for the above reason that what one says about one's dreams is the criterion for what was in fact dreamt.[36] Certainly there is a question of what correspondence with the facts about one's dreams would amount to in such a situation, and Malcolm admits that one's talk of remembering a dream may seem strange in this context (*DS*, p. 74).

I think that it is important to point out at the beginning that Malcolm's depiction of dreaming suggests a view of it that is not ordinary. The "Cartesian" ideas that he attacks are largely part of our ordinary thinking about dreams (minus the skeptical conclusions that the Cartesian draws from them). By contrast, Malcolm seems bound to philosophical doctrines about criteria which he is determined to push at any cost. This is worth noting only because he *claims* to be spelling out our ordinary talk about dreams in an attempt to save one from problem-making philosophical doctrines about them. However, I take this to be a good example of a case in which much revision takes place under the name of description.

The result is that one can use common sense as a weapon against Malcolm's claims. For example, it seems clear to me that, on reflection, one does want to say that, when dreaming, one takes something to be happening that wasn't, or thought that one was dreaming, or whatever. Afterward one feels the same commitment that one felt then; this is the testimony of the experience of dreaming and not the result of some complex argument from analogy. One need never have been seduced by philosophy to think this. One wants to say that one can judge while dreaming or in dreams, but that this does not make these judgments any the less genuine assertions.

Malcolm's argument from self-contradiction does nothing to

show that one is wrong. For if one is speaking of the difficulty of *saying* "I am asleep" or "I am doubting" while one is dead asleep, then one can grant this difficulty with no harm to the skeptic. And if one is saying that to think or judge while one is dead asleep is a kind of contradiction, then his case is without sufficient support.[37] Malcolm can still claim that it *follows* from the fact that I am thinking (not the assertion that "I am think-ing") that "I am awake" is true, but he offers no defense of this supposed inference, and it seems clearly to be question-begging to assume that it holds. On my reading of common sense, it does not hold.

A further defense of the argument from self-contradiction appears in Malcolm's introduction of the notion of a criterion. But it seems irrelevant to point out that when one is concerned with *others*, one's standards for determining that they are think-ing and not asleep are the same; for the ordinary view is based on one's experience of one's own dreams, and there is no such imposition of third-person criteria in this case. Malcolm has simply picked the case that is favorable to him and has treated it as if it were the only relevant case. More charitably put, Mal-colm's argument here demands that we accept Wittgenstein's saying that inner processes stand in need of outward criteria. We shall examine this saying later, but for the present let me say only that it smacks of Verificationism.

Nor do I see any reason to accept Malcolm's judgment that whatever one says about one's dreams is correct. A psychoanalyst, knowing one's personality, may well discern in one's dream re-port an overlay of commentary which has distorted or enlarged one's dream, and he may gain one's agreement that this is the case when he calls it to one's attention. Of course, this distinction is hard to draw clearly in any case, but this is not a good reason for thinking that there is no such distinction. Indeed, one may correct one's own statement about one's dream, in the process implying that one's first report was not the whole truth when one uttered it. In addition, if Malcolm's remarks concerning the "logical" connection between the dream and its report are inter-preted correctly as implying that the latter is a necessary condi-tion for the former, then this seems clearly false. There is no contradiction whatever in the notion of an unreported dream or of one so forgotten that it is at least practically impossible for one to remember it. To think otherwise is, one suspects, to make *existence* depend on *verification by others,* a view that is extreme to say the least.

Malcolm betrays the radical nature of his view when he suggests that remembering dreams may seem to be a surprising notion. There is nothing surprising about it for common sense, since the latter holds that there is both something to remember and a right-wrong possibility in our attempts to remember. In fact, when Malcolm acknowledges that dreams and dream reports are numerically different, he at once puzzles his readers (for what can dreams be for him?), and despite himself, he seems to create a situation in which distinctions of right and wrong do have a place.

To deny that dreams are occurrences seems equally dubious to me. Let us agree that one has no everyday way of deciding how long a dream takes or precisely when it occurred. To argue that one's lack of decisiveness here means that there is no sense to the speculation seems backward to me. One *knows* that the question *does* make sense, for one experiences dreams as taking time. The lack of certainty about the specific time that a dream takes does not suggest to one that the entire category of time does not apply to dreams; it suggests only that there are questions that one cannot yet answer about dreams. A stronger association of criteria and meaning strikes one as yet another philosophical correction of common sense.[38] This is perhaps most striking in Malcolm's claim that it is "logically impossible" that one expresses fear while sound asleep. Anyone who has suffered from nightmares can testify to the contrary. I conclude that there is nothing about deep sleep that precludes judgment, although one's beliefs-while-asleep may escape the knowledge of others.

POSTSCRIPT

Danto offers an argument against the Argument from Dreaming which purports to show that it is involved in a self-defeating dilemma. If the Argument from Dreams is to be taken seriously, "it must be presupposed that he who offers it is awake. Or else he is not arguing but only talking in his sleep. . . . So either there is no Dream Argument, or else the Dream Argument is refuted through its very presuppositions" (*Analytical Philosophy of Knowledge,* p. 170). One might grant that the proposer of this theory assumes that he is awake when proposing it, and the hearer makes the same assumption, "being awake" and "being asleep" being taken in their usual, contrasting sense. But one makes no assumption about whether one is awake or dreaming when "dreaming" is used to cover both normal waking and normal dreaming. Thus, one's argument can work only if one isn't dreaming or asleep in the normal sense of these words, for one might be asleep$_2$ but awake$_1$ and one need not cancel out the other. There is no reason, then, to think that the Dream Argument is either no argument at all or false simply because one does not (and need not) presuppose that one is not dreaming in the sense of dreaming which the argument insists is a pervasive possibility.

I might add that there seems to be no necessity to limit intelligent discourse to one's waking moments. One can imagine that under certain unusual circumstances one might well consider a person who shows some signs of sleep, but is also "arguing" a point, to be both asleep and asserting something. If this is possible, then all Danto's argument could possibly prove is that one *now* divides sleep and waking in such a way that one cannot argue in one's sleep. This leaves the Dreaming Argument as a perfectly reasonable possibility; at the very most there would be a difficulty in stating it *now,* but that is hardly an important point against philosophical skepticism.

5

THE EXISTENCE OF THE PAST

Now that we have dealt with philosophical skepticism (and the ordinary-language reply to it) in general outline, we should consider what such skepticism entails when it is applied to specific areas of philosophic concern. The topic of this chapter grows out of a famous statement of Russell's in *The Analysis of Mind*. There Russell says that because

> everything constituting a memory-belief is happening *now*. . . . It is not logically necessary to the existence of a memory-belief that the event remembered should have occurred, or even that the past should have existed at all. There is no logical impossibility in the hypothesis that the world sprang into being five minutes ago, exactly as it then was, with a population that "remembered" a wholly unreal past. There is no logically necessary connection between events at different times; therefore nothing that is happening now or will happen in the future can disprove the hypothesis that the world began five minutes ago.[1]

Russell adds that this skeptical hypothesis is "logically tenable, but uninteresting." Since if one genuinely remembers p, p must have happened, Russell's suggestion amounts to saying that one can never know whether there have been or will be cases of genuine memory. No doubt there have been and will be many cases of what one believes to be memory (one might say what "feels" as if it were memory), but there is a possibility that one is cruelly deceived in these beliefs. I presume that when Russell says that such a possibility is "uninteresting," he is referring to the impossibility of testing the truth (or even of estimating the likelihood) of the skeptic's possibility. Nonetheless, there is one way in which this possibility is highly interesting. As long as one cannot show that it is somehow incoherent or irrelevant, its existence means that none of one's knowledge claims about the past can be valid.[2]

Of course, the skeptic might argue that the evidence for any historical claim is never strong enough to rule out the possibility that the claim is false. Some reevaluations of so-called historical facts would, no doubt, shatter one's ordinary conception of the past and destroy one's confidence in the method that historians use to uncover past events; but difficult as such reevaluations might be, new evidence might require them. If one treats claims about the past as the components of a theory, then one cannot rule out violent upheavals in one's theories.

But I think that Russell's hypothesis has a distinct advantage over the above approach. It makes crystal clear that the skeptic is challenging the entire framework within which historical investigation takes place by questioning the assumption that even radically conflicting views of the past share. That one is wrong about key events in the past might well be accepted without one's doubting that there is a past for authorities to disagree about. The latter doubt leaves one's ordinary framework for historical investigation without its most basic support. By the same token, I suppose that the logical possibility of total error is harder to believe than the logical possibility of error about well-established particulars, but this psychological difficulty is irrelevant to the strength of the argument if one is convinced that the logical possibility of error is a relevant consideration in the evaluation of knowledge claims.

Ayer points out that the skeptic seems to require for historical knowledge the logical impossibility that "someone, being at the point of time at which he is, should also be at a point of time at which he is not."[3] But Ayer adds that one need not follow the skeptic here, for "historians do have canons of evidence; and it is no criticism of these canons that they do not require for their satisfaction a logical impossibility." Of course, this is obviously true when one is thinking of these canons as rules for weighing evidence within the *framework* of historical investigation. But then the skeptic has nothing to say about how distinctions within a framework should be made. But now if one thinks of these canons as indicating when an assertion is true or well founded, no matter what criticism is brought to bear against it, the very fact that these judgments are based on evidence introduces a weakness in the judgments, which the canons overlook, since they assume this notion and then make distinctions within it. Perhaps this means that historical claims *cannot* support claims to knowledge, but unless one can show that criticism of frameworks is inadmissible, I do not see that this is a reason for ignoring what the skeptic says. The historian does not need to consider logical possibilities of error, and the skeptic is not suggesting that the historian should develop new canons of evidence in order to meet these possibilities. The skeptic is saying, however, that one should not confuse meeting those standards within historical investigation with justifying the assumptions on which those standards rest. Once one keeps this distinction in mind, it is not hard to see how a claim could pass the former test, and thus be a bit of knowledge, without finding the full justification that the latter vindication would bring.

THE ORDINARY-LANGUAGE ATTACK
ON RUSSELL'S HYPOTHESIS

For our purposes, I will divide the ordinary-language response to Russell into seven claims against the skeptic:

1. Russell's hypothesis is senseless since it cannot be answered.
2. Skepticism *cannot be believed* because, if believed, it would destroy all understanding.
3. Skepticism is unacceptable because it is *unimaginable.*

4. Russell's hypothesis can be refuted by noting that *incorrect memory presupposes correct memory.*

5. Skepticism cannot be stated because *the skeptic is not entitled to his use of the past tense.*

6. Assuming that Russell's hypothesis is correct, one can show that it entails the notion of an *instantaneous world* and/or of *instantaneous belief.* But since these notions are unintelligible, so must Russell's hypothesis be unintelligible.

7. That sincere memory reports are generally true is a *conceptual truth,* for if this seems not to be the case, one reasonably assumes that the person in question does not understand the use of the past tense and not that he simply misremembers most things. Therefore, Russell's hypothesis does not project an intelligible situation (although it seems to).

1. According to Marcus Singer, Russell's hypothesis is "literally senseless, not in the sense that it is pointless, but in the sense that it is logically impossible to answer it."[4] Russell's hypothesis is so framed that any use of evidence in regard to it is question-begging, since that "evidence" is itself subject to Russell's doubts (p. 190). Yet, the question that Russell asks "is a demand for evidence or a way of knowing" (p. 190). Since one does not know what an answer would look like, since no amount of knowledge would help and since the difficulty is logical and not factual, the question is without sense.

Singer calls such questions "non-terminating," and he admits that they may be understood, if only to the extent that one sees that they are absurd. He also says, however, that "there is absolutely no reason for it and every reason against it" (p. 195). Singer adds that what Russell says cannot be considered as a "hypothesis," for the test of a genuine hypothesis is that it has "empirically testable consequences (which) are different from the consequences of its denial" (p. 194). Yet, he refrains from saying that it is "meaningless" or "self-contradictory" (p. 197), describing the distinction between the former and senselessness as follows:

A statement *S* can be meaningful, whereas the claim to know that *S* is true or that one has evidence for *S* may

100

be senseless, since the statement may be such that, although it is logically possible for it to be true, it is logically impossible to have evidence or a good reason for it or against it; in such a case S can be said to be "senseless." [P. 200]

I think that it is helpful to think of Singer as trying to carve out a response to skepticism that will fall between two extremes: rejection as meaningless through adherence to the Verifiability Theory of Meaning and straight-out acceptance as a relevant possibility. My problem is that I do not see where the "logical space" is that can accommodate such a compromise.

Consider Singer's remarks about 'hypothesis' and 'senseless'. Singer so characterizes 'hypothesis' that Russell's assertion clearly does not qualify as a hypothesis, but that is because Singer uses 'hypothesis' synonymously with 'empirical hypothesis'. And this use of terms obviously constitutes a begging of the question against Russell. Singer offers no argument to show that there cannot be nonempirical hypotheses, one of whose characteristics is that they cannot be tested by empirical means, which remain hypotheses because they are estimates of what is the case. Perhaps one does not ordinarily *call* them hypotheses, but then that is a rather uninteresting fact about ordinary speech which does not prevent philosophers from seeing a generic connection between scientific hypothesis and those employed by philosophical skeptics.

Singer's remarks about 'senseless' are equally harmless. If all that Singer *means* by 'senseless' is that a certain kind of answer is logically precluded, then Russell's hypothesis is senseless. But then 'senseless' in this sense does not preclude the possibility that the hypothesis is perfectly sensible, even if one accepts the general belief that an assertion is senseless if it is logically incapable of being answered in any manner whatever. Russell's hypothesis might be "empirically senseless" and yet have all the sense that Russell could want. I might say that Singer's discussion of evidence, and his examples thereof, suggest that he might be limiting an answer to what can be empirically confirmed.

Since this use of 'senseless' would be true but harmless to Russell, let us assume that Singer means to claim that Russell's hypothesis "has been so worded as absolutely to preclude the possibility of answering it" (p. 189). His language often does suggest this unqualified version of the Argument from Senselessness, but how does he defend it? To begin with, he wishes to admit the meaningful, non-self-contradictory nature of what Russell says; it is logically possible that Russell is right. Yet, he wants to deny that what Russell says is "significant." Once again, I am puzzled by what appears either to be a harmless remark (in case 'significant' is no different from 'empirically significant') or to be indistinguishable from meaninglessness, despite what Singer says. If the "tough" sense of 'significant' is to have a real impact on Russell's hypothesis, surely it must imply that although what Russell says appears to say something, it does not in fact do so. Since Singer does not accept this interpretation of 'significant' (or of 'senseless'), I do not know how to understand his charge against Russell.

Singer's "hard" line against Russell remains, finally, undefended. He tells one that "naturally there is no logically necessary inference from logically necessary premises to the conclusion that the world did not begin five minutes ago. If there were, this conclusion would be analytic" (p. 193). In so saying, he rules out one possible kind of answer to Russell on the slender thread of a dogma about necessary truth. Of course, it then appears to him that no kind of answer whatever is possible to Russell because of the way his hypothesis is worded. We *can* imagine what an answer would look like (*pace* Singer, on p. 190), as any Rationalist will tell you, if only one is not blinded by the dogmas of Hume and Logical Positivism. Perhaps Russell's question cannot be answered, in which case one would think that the appropriate response would be to marvel at the necessary truth that he has uncovered rather than to berate him for senselessness. Apparently, for Singer complete success turns into its Hegelian opposite, complete failure. I conclude that he has not shown that what Russell said is senseless in any sense that detracts from the philosophical significance of his remarks.[5]

2. Malcolm claims that Russell's hypothesis is "incompatible with our concept of evidence" and that to "accept this 'hypothesis' as true would mean the destruction of *all* our thinking" (*MP*, p. 264). Thus, if Martian scientists were to claim that *they*

had created our planet five minutes ago, we would think that they had confused our planet with some other one.

Three comments seem relevant here. First, skeptical hypotheses do not require one's "real" belief, anymore than they require "real" doubt. To be effective, they only need be regarded as logical possibilities. Thus, it is no criticism of them to point out that belief in them would be disorienting. Second, while such belief would require that one give up one's usual notions about how one acquired one's knowledge, language, and so forth, it does not require that one abandon all knowledge of how things are and how they work. One now simply must accept that such knowledge was given to one by one's recent creator. To be sure, this would be extremely disorienting, but it would not mean that one would have to renounce one's "entire store of common knowledge" (*MP*, p. 264).

Third, even though one normally means by 'England' and 'Bertrand Russell' entities that have existed for a long while, I do not see that one would have to stick with these convictions and thereby reject the claims of Martian scientists. If Martians displayed enough amazing powers, I see no reason that one might not abandon one's normal commitments in favor of the recent-creation theory. If one's current meanings are regarded as theoretical commitments, then one might well come to accept another theory, although one would not do so lightly. The psychology of belief does not seem to be a good reason for denying the relevance of Russell's hypothesis.

3. Consider the following quotation:

> When I sincerely say that I remember, and then say things which there is no reason in the world to doubt, these are not things which I just say that I remember. They are my memories. I cannot imagine that they are all to be questioned for some completely unknown reason or for no reason at all. I cannot then go on to imagine that they are all somehow not memories or are all wrong.[6]

I can agree with Ebersole that just because the nonexistence of the past cannot be tested by conventional methods will not make a difference in what one ordinarily does and says, and I can also agree that if one is thinking within the framework of our ordinary validation of memories, one may well find the skeptical hypothesis unimaginable. I do not see, however, that this leads to the conclusion that the hypothesis has no "sting" at all or that it is unimaginable in the sense of inconceivable without qualification. The "sting" is felt, not in our normal practice, but in our reflections on the validity of that practice and in our subsequent evaluations of the knowledge claims that our normal practice encourages. And the fact that doubting memories and relieving those doubts occur normally in specific contexts, with approved ways of dealing with such doubts, does not show that we cannot understand the possibility of another kind of doubt, which is not so restricted and which cannot be so resolved.

Russell does give reasons that explain why he considers his hypothesis to be a logical possibility, but of course they are not the kind of reasons that one might give for doubting a specific memory claim. The result is that Ebersole's distinction between what one *calls* memory and what *is* memory cannot sustain the weight that he needs from it. Certain claims *are* memories *for us*; in certain situations it would be misleading to speak of such claims as merely what we *call* memories. But then one's normal conception of memory does not include an awareness of Russell's hypothesis, so that one would not expect one's normal standards to reflect this as a possibility. In no way does this constitute a criticism of either the possibility or the relevance of what Russell says, however.

4. The claim that incorrect memory is possible only within a context of correct memory can be thought of as a version of the Argument from Meaningful Contrasts, with the additional assumption that the negative notion is less basic than the positive one.[7] Peirce's conception of belief and doubt is formally similar to the present one. Obviously, such a conception rules out the possibility of there being only error or doubt with no corresponding truth or belief.

Malcolm asserts that one's memory of a dinner party might be partially incorrect as long as there was in fact a dinner party, attended by certain persons, and so forth. But if nothing one "remembers" is correct, if in fact there was no dinner party even approximately similar to the one recalled, then one would have to speak, not of incorrect memory, but of "delusive memory."

And he adds:

> But a memory which is totally delusive, . . . is not a
> memory. It stand to an erroneous memory as a counter-
> feit diamond stands to an imperfect diamond. The lat-
> ter is a diamond, the other not. A totally delusive
> memory is no more a memory than a fictitious occur-
> rence is something that happened, or no more than a
> painted fire is a fire. This is not quibbling. A painted
> fire does not have the important properties of fire and a
> totally delusive memory does not have the important
> properties of memory. Nothing could be more unsound,
> therefore, than to base one's philosophical treatment of
> memory on the notion of a total delusion of memory, as
> Russell does. [*MP*, p. 251]

One might well grant that one tends to take memories as
true unless there is some reason to think otherwise and that,
therefore, the notion of memory mistakes is parasitic on the
notion of memory truths. One might well grant, further, that no
study of fake or pseudo objects is likely to reveal the properties
or nature of the real thing. But neither admission leads to the
conclusion either that Russell was not studying memory at all or
that he was studying it in a misleading way. More importantly,
nothing that Malcolm says shows that there is something logically
defective about the notion of a totally erroneous memory.

Studying copies of diamonds, even clever copies, would result in some misunderstanding of what diamonds are like. However, Russell is not suggesting that one learns about memory by
studying cases of nonmemories, that is, of delusions. Unlike the
diamonds case, there is no ordinary empirical way of determining
that what one is studying are delusions, not memories. Russell is
studying what one normally considers to be memories, and truth-
ful ones at that! And he reveals the possibility that all memories
may be false in order to highlight the validity of the knowledge
claims of one's most highly substantiated memories. Nothing that
he says implies that if one wants to know about the details of
memory, one should not study the distinctions that one normally
makes concerning memory.

Perhaps one might think of Russell's memory as perfectly
ordinary memory that has been reconceived or viewed from an

unfamiliar angle. It is not correct, then, to say that he is speaking of "totally delusive memory" as that notion is usually contrasted with genuine memory, for one cannot detect the delusiveness of Russell's memory. Yet, one wants to say that Russell's memory *is* delusive in the same generic sense that some ordinary memories are delusive. Russell extends the range of 'delusive' but retains its basic meaning.

I think that this point effectively undercuts Malcolm's claim that incorrect memory is possible only within a context of correct memory. Ordinarily, one does view error as the exception, assuming the basic trustworthiness of memories. But Malcolm says nothing that shows that this *must* be so, that one could not come to think of memory as generally delusive or perhaps as completely delusive in the way that Russell suggests is possible. Even if it were necessary that one learn the concept of faulty memory in such a context, this does not prevent one from deepening one's sense of error far beyond one's original confines. The debate between determinists and free-willists is a good example of this process.

In addition, neither Russell nor the determinist is going to deny that as one normally uses 'incorrect memory' or 'unfree act', these concepts must arise and operate in a context of trusted memory or free acts. All that is claimed is that one can call into question the standards that allow one to establish certain memories as correct and, in the process, to question the correctness of any memory. One leaves the ordinary distinction and its requirements, if any, standing unharmed, as marking off differences between memory claims within a given context. In effect, one is objecting to the interpretation of that difference which it is usual to make and offering an interpretation that makes it seem possible that delusive memories may form a wider class than one normally thinks, or needs to think, that they do.

In short, I am suggesting that Malcolm's claim can be seen as a statement that reports correctly at least the ordinary way in which one does arrive at a notion of incorrect memory and the role that notion ordinarily plays in normal discourse. As so interpreted, however, it is harmless against the skeptic who is willing to work with this distinction and, in the process, to reverse its normal weighting. All that the skeptic need claim is that once the distinction is made, there is no necessity in forever being limited in one's use of 'incorrect memory' by the ground rules that first established the normal use of that term.

5. Edward J. Bond has proposed linking questions concerning how one understands statements in the past tense, how such statements have meaning, and how one has a concept of the past, with questions concerning the reality of the past. The former could not be the way they are unless one knew that the latter was also the case. He argues for this claim by saying that

> we would not be able to understand or use the past tense if there were not circumstances concerning which there was general agreement that in those circumstances the use of the past tense expressed a true judgment. For if this were not so, we could never learn the use of the past tense, since there would be nothing which could determine that its use in any particular case was correct or incorrect or, to use Wittgenstein's expression, there could be no past-tense language game.[8]

Bond concludes that in these learning circumstances "it will therefore necessarily be true that something was the case or that something happened or occurred" (p. 543).

Once again one has an argument from within the language game that employs the past tense. In effect, Bond is pointing out that a precondition of one's use of the past tense is that one considers certain statements about the past to be true. This may well be the case, but it does nothing to show that these preconditions are justified. After all, what one takes to be true may not in fact be true, and only the former can be invoked by the above argument. Thus, when Bond speaks of its being "necessarily true that something was the case," all he can be referring to is the necessity that one *consider* something to have been the case. Since the skeptic is not worried about such necessities, nothing that he says can deny their force within their own proper sphere. There is no difficulty in the skeptic's using the past tense and holding the philosophical view that he does.

6. The next criticism of skepticism argues that it can be forced to a position that is unintelligible. By reducing skepticism to its most extreme form, one can show that it cannot avoid employing two notions—instantaneous world and instantaneous

belief—that are unintelligible. The less extreme form of skepticism seems to state a real possibility, but its purified version in fact presents no possibility at all.

Danto quite correctly points out that the time specification in Russell's hypothesis is arbitrary; the same point is made even though the time dimension be adjusted in an infinite number of ways. And since one of these is not more justified than another, there is no "evidential friction" that can keep them all from sliding into instantaneous skepticism.[9]

This skepticism is incoherent, for instants are not units of duration, and "just to be a world at all requires that it have *some* duration, and the only remaining question is how much" (p. 85). Danto claims that the skeptic is faced with a dilemma. If he allows nothing to count as evidence for the existence of the past, then he must adopt an incoherent instantaneous skepticism; if he allows something to count as evidence for the existence of the past (whatever suggests an event occurring within the arbitrarily set time limit), then he cannot justify any preset limit as to how far back in time the evidence will apply. The issue over the duration of the world will be seen as an empirical issue that has nothing about it to interest philosophers.

Danto's charge that the arbitrary time set of historical skepticisms begins the ride to instantaneous skepticism I find to be unconvincing. One would have thought that these time sets were arbitrary at any point *beyond the present*. Since the issue is whether one can be certain of the existence of the past on the basis of what one *now* observes, the limits of the "now" seem to set the common starting point for a version of Russell's hypothesis. Yet, what reason is there for thinking that skepticism must take this "now" to be a durationless instant? A "specious present," in which everything is present for some small slice of time, provides a sufficient common basis for the skeptic. And as Danto himself points out, when one says that something exists now, "we are not saying . . . that its existence is confined within the present instant" (p. 84). The limitation of one's starting point to the noninstantaneous present would not be arbitrary, and it would retain the thrust of the skeptic's argument. Just because *some* time limitations are arbitrary for the skeptic, it does not follow that all such limitations are arbitrary. Existence within the noninstantaneous present is not known by evidence, but rather is known directly; therefore, the skeptic can avoid Danto's charge that he is allowing evidence to apply over a limited span but cannot justify this limitation.

I conclude that the arbitrariness with which Danto begins does not constitute the "fatal difficulty" that he envisioned. One might add that the notion of consciousness or knowledge at an instant is a puzzling one. But if one grants it for the moment, it becomes only a verbal point to say that one could not know a "world" in an instant. The skeptic could well reply that one must infer a world from this "data" but that such an inference is unjustifiable. He need not speak of what has instantaneous existence as a world if this is troublesome.

An argument that Sydney Shoemaker uses could be understood as a criticism of Russell's type of skepticism. Let us assume that beliefs that are well grounded constitute knowledge. Shoemaker asks: Can there then be a problem about the retention of the knowledge that one has acquired in sense perception or otherwise? His answer is: Only if it is conceivable that the beliefs of one moment might be completely different from the beliefs of another moment, for then what one believes now about the past may not accord at all with one's beliefs of a moment ago. It is possible that none of one's previous knowledge will be retained in one's current beliefs, and so there will be no accumulation of knowledge. Russell's hypothesis might be thought of as an extreme case of this exchange of beliefs, one in which beliefs appear for the first time.

If the above is to be a genuine possibility, then the notion of an instantaneous belief must be a sensible one. One's beliefs must be able to come and go, much as Hume imagines that one's impressions whirl in and out of existence. Of this assumption Shoemaker says:

> What ought to seem puzzling is not the idea that beliefs can be simply retained once acquired, but the idea that they cannot be. . . . No sense can be given to the notion of a belief lasting no time at all, and if someone is said to have believed something for only a few seconds or minutes, then what requires an explanation (if what is said is to be even intelligible) is not his retaining the

> belief for that length of time, but rather his losing it
> after so short a time. . . . But if beliefs can, indeed
> must, be retained for some period of time, the same must
> be true of knowledge.[10]

I agree that for Russell's hypothesis to make sense, it must also make sense to be able to have current beliefs that are totally different from one's beliefs (or lack of beliefs) of a moment ago. One must also grant that one does not ordinarily *say* that someone believes something unless his behavior (including what one says) is of a certain kind, and this ties what one says to an extended period of time. Also one could never *know* that a person believed something if there were no time in which the belief could be displayed.[11] And indeed, one would not know about *oneself* whether what seemed to be a belief really was one unless the belief was retained for a period of time. (At least this is true of beliefs that are of a practical nature. I am not certain that the same restriction holds for beliefs that are theoretical and that have no necessary forms of expression.)

Nevertheless, the notion of a momentary belief does not seem a senseless one to me. It seems perfectly possible that one's current beliefs are brand new, only seeming to be about a nonexistent past, or that they are simply completely different from one's earlier beliefs, thus preventing earlier bits of knowledge from being retained. One cannot determine if this is the case by evidence, and in many cases, one could not be certain that these were beliefs (let alone whether they were true), but they could be beliefs for all that. Shoemaker says that beliefs must be retained for a certain period, or they would not be beliefs, but this does not seem to me to be so. There is no contradiction in the idea of a person attaining a belief that X, then dying immediately after.

Normally one takes the retention of belief for granted and therefore focuses one's attention on failures to retain beliefs. But this does not show that the wholesale failure to retain beliefs does not constitute a skeptical possibility, one that simply does not attract one's attention as one goes about acquiring knowledge. There is no short way home to establishing what must be true (or at least a candidate for knowledge) simply by meeting the conditions that one normally sets ups for something to be a belief. Meeting these conditions may require one to *say* that some of one's beliefs must be the same as a while ago (and thus that knowledge achieved earlier is retained), but it cannot rule out the possibility that one is simply mistaken about the length of time that any of one's beliefs has been in force.

7. We now come to the most important and powerful argument against philosophical skepticism about memory that ordinary-language philosophers have devised. The claim is that in order to say what one remembers, one must presuppose an understanding of past-tense speech, and such understanding presupposes that the statements that one makes in the past tense are usually true (*MP*, p. 255). Malcolm reaches the conclusion that it is a conceptual or necessary truth that one's statements about the past are usually true. As he says: "If this were not so then his sentences, even though they had past tense grammatical form, would not express statements *about the past*. It would not be *that* 'language-game,' but some other one, or none at all" (p. 255).

Malcolm argues for this claim both by means of illustrative analogies or examples and by general theses about language mastery. For the former, he asks one to consider a child who is first using the past tense but is saying things that are usually false. In such a case, one would have no right to say that the child means to say that he remembers something or that he means anything at all. Second, he employs Wittgenstein's chess analogy. A person who usually made illegal moves while appearing to play chess would not correctly be said to be playing chess, or any game at all for that matter.

For more general support, Malcolm refers to Wittgenstein's principle that "our concepts, our language-games, presuppose *agreement in judgments*" (p. 256). If such agreement is lacking, then one says that the person who is speaking in this way is not using our words. In turn, the concept of truth is involved with the notion of agreement in judgments. He says, "This agreement in language makes it *true* that this is red and that is blue" (p. 257). Expanding on this latter, crucial point, Malcolm claims that where memories agree with each other and with "records of the past," then these memories are verified as true, for "this is what the *verification* of apparent memories *means*. . . . And if the apparent memories were verified it would not be intelligible to hold that, nevertheless, the past they describe may not have existed" (p. 261–62).

One might think that although persons could not express "remembrances" that were generally false either in language or in behavior, they still might *have* such memories. And such having would be enough to make Russell's hypothesis present a genuine possibility (p. 260). Malcolm's rebuttal to this suggestion is that in order to even have the experience of *seeming* to remember, there must be at least the possibility of expression. Behavior and/or language are said to be necessary to having beliefs about the past.

Malcolm sums up his position by saying that the reference to the past, which Russell takes for granted, is possible only if one's assertions about the past are largely true. Even an omniscient observer would have to conclude that where this is not the case, people just do not have a past tense in their language.

Sydney Shoemaker agrees with Malcolm that it is a necessary or conceptual truth that "when perceptual and memory statements are sincerely and confidently asserted, i.e., express confident beliefs, they are generally true,"[12] but he includes two arguments which are well worth mentioning. First, in translating a newly discovered language, one would have every reason to think that the translation was incorrect if the utterances of persons tended to be false. One would think that one had not understood what the sentences meant, rather than thinking that one had understood them but that the people in question misremember most of the time (see pp. 232–33).

Second, if one applies to oneself the notion that it is only a contingent fact that one's sincere memory and perceptual reports are generally true, two important consequences follow. One seems to be involved in a "kind of inconsistency," for it would mean admitting that confident reports must be thought of as being irrational. Yet, Shoemaker asserts, it is "not a psychological fact, but rather a logical fact, that one cannot help regarding one's confident perpetual [perceptual?] and memory beliefs as constituting knowledge" (p. 234). The other consequence is that in the imagined circumstance, one could never know this to be true, since such "knowledge" would have to rely on the suspect memory and perceptual claims, and, in fact, that one could "never be justified in asserting anything on the basis of observation and memory" (p. 235). Shoemaker regards this consequence as "absurd."[13]

The account given by Malcolm and Shoemaker presents a plausible rendering of one's reaction to constantly mistaken assertions or uses of words. One naturally would turn to an explanation of mistranslation or failure to understand the language if there were more errors than one could tolerate. However, the question at issue is not what one *would say* in certain circumstances, but whether it would make any sense to offer an explanation that was consistent with the skeptic's hypothesis in the same circumstances. I do not think that the latter has been shown to be incoherent.

After all, it is easily understood *why* one normally looks to the kind of explanation of constant error that is mentioned above. It represents a fruitful way of treating this unusual circumstance, one that improves communication (as far as we can tell) and that is in accord with one's normal assumptions about error and truth (namely, that faculties are trustworthy unless there is a special reason to think otherwise; that error, not truth, needs explanation; etc.). Since one does not ordinarily entertain the possibility envisioned by Russell's hypothesis, one does not consider any explanation that would be in accord with it; and just as Russell's hypothesis is not productive of further investigation into the truth about history, so an explanation that implemented this hypothesis would also provide a dead end for further investigation. However, none of these considerations rules out the possibility of such an explanation, one that would be appropriate only for special philosophical purposes.

In other words, I see no reason that Russell could not accept the Malcolm-Shoemaker thesis about the relation between truth and language mastery, insisting only that it be understood as applying *within* the normal framework of language use. When one is speaking of detectable error, then it is reasonable to link truth and language mastery; but no such restriction need apply when one has already fulfilled the normal criteria for language mastery and wants, in addition, to raise questions about even those cases that one normally considers as truths. In essence, Malcolm and Shoemaker treat skepticism as if it were a thesis that occurs within our normal framework and one, therefore, that directly threatens our normal distinctions. They then see its application as wreaking havoc with the language mastery that is assumed in normal assertions. But if skepticism has no such application, it need not run into the kind of difficulty that a mere enlargement of the number of ordinary errors might encounter.

Putting these general considerations aside, let us look further at some of the details of the ordinary-language position. First, there seems to be nothing that is obviously absurd about the following scenario. It gradually comes to the attention of historians and others that more and more material is accumulating that contradicts supposedly verified claims about the past. After a certain point, this evidence becomes so overwhelming that one begins to correct one's historical judgments, finding to one's horror that now the majority of one's old judgments are regarded as false.[14] Yet, one need not then say that one had no mastery of the past tense at the earlier time. Malcolm's conceptual truth seems to rule out by fiat a genuine possibility, and this discredits it.[15]

One might add that the skeptic need not worry over Malcolm's claim that if beliefs are verified, then the denial that the past existed is unintelligible (*MP*, p. 262), for this verification takes place within the normal context of investigation, whereas the skeptic wants to ask about the justification of the entire context. Normal verification cannot settle *this* question and so says nothing about its possibility.[16]

Second, consider Malcolm's chess analogy for a moment. It is self-serving in that a move that breaks a rule of chess is not a move in chess, whereas a false assertion *is* a move in the game of assertion and denial. One is not playing chess *every time* one violates the rules, but even Malcolm does not say that one ceases to be playing the language game every time that one says something false. But this is just the relevant disanalogy from the skeptic's point of view. It is easy to see why one would say that someone who made a large number of illegal chess moves was not playing chess, since each such move was in itself a failure to play chess in miniature. But it is hard to see why a single false statement can refer to the past but that when one has a large number

114

of such errors, one no longer has a reference to the past. This transition from quantity to quality is a baffling Hegelian change.[17]

As a result of these reflections, I cannot accept Malcolm's tight connection between having a memory (or even a seeming memory) and being able to express it in behavior or language. One might become disoriented and confused if most of one's memory claims were false, but this is no reason to say that one could not be remembering in such a situation. Others might even doubt that one was remembering or be unable to detect that one was remembering, but that is a problem of communicating what one does, not a problem of doing it. Unless Malcolm can show that the possibility of expression is constitutive of memory, and I do not think he has done this, he cannot justify making the possibility of expression a necessary condition for the existence of even a seeming memory.

Neither can I find much force in Shoemaker's attempt to reduce the skeptic's position to absurdity by tracing its consequences to their bitter end. Of course, a "kind of inconsistency" is introduced if one applies skepticism to one's own confident reports and still retains one's allegiance to those reports. In so doing, one has mixed skepticism and common sense in a way that the skeptic need not intend or require. One need not actually doubt one's confident reports in order to embrace skepticism. And while it *is* absurd, by one's normal standards, to hold a position that calls into question the justification of all observational and memory reports, the question is whether this absurdity makes Russell's hypothesis a logical absurdity. Rather, it seems to me, the former claim of absurdity reflects the assumptions of common sense that conflict with philosophical skepticism. Any reference to them, then, merely begs the question.

I conclude that Malcolm and Shoemaker have failed to show that there is a conceptual connection between the meaningful use of the past tense and the frequency of true assertions about the past. And even if there were such a connection, it would only hold within the sphere of normal assertion and counterassertion. As such, it would not show that a skepticism was impossible that tried to undermine the entire framework, one of whose necessary elements was the above connection. Such internal necessities need not bother the skeptic until it can be shown that they cannot be transcended.[18]

Two other ways of trying to answer Russell's hypothesis are relevant for our purposes here. The first finds skepticism about memory to rest on two mistakes: (a) "treating memory in an isolated first-person context instead of an interpersonal or social context" and (b) "treating every reference to the past that meets the 'nonrelative' or 'absolute' criteria for being a memory as an instance of memory."[19] The latter criteria are defined as those that "must be satisfied *in any circumstance* by a claim to remember"—for example, they must refer to the past, not be based on hearsay, and so forth.

The error of philosophers is to assume that such criteria are sufficient criteria for something being a memory claim. To show that this is a mistake, Nelson introduces the notion of a ground statement. These are statements that we use in order to settle questions; they are not themselves subject to question, and it is not proper, therefore, to say that one 'remembers' or 'knows' such things to be true, since such words suggest a certain amount of risk-taking. Absolute ground statements "remain fixed and permanent through changes of circumstances" (p. 39), whereas relative ground statements change with the nature of the conditions surrounding the question asked. The former usually do not come into play in the normal course of justification, and they are said to stand behind relative ground statements as the girders of a building stand behind its façade.

Thus, although memory statements are logically open to question, not all past-tense statements are memory statements. Ground statements provide the independent confirmation of memory statements that one needs if one is to overcome skepticism. They give certainty, and they allow one to go beyond one's own ground statements in order to confirm one's memories by relying on the ground statements of others.

Two criticisms that immediately come to mind render Nelson's claims harmless against the skeptic. First, even absolute ground statements are known only because they are remembered.[20] But if memory is logically open to question, one cannot rely on any "knowledge" that rests on our faith in memory.[21] Second, Nelson at most has succeeded in pointing out that one normally takes certain claims to be unquestionable. This explains why one finds it strange to speak of remembering what just happened. But this is a mere fact about our ordinary attitudes and does not by itself show these attitudes to be beyond question. Perhaps their overthrow would suggest madness (p. 38), but this does not show that the skeptic is wrong in claiming that they are in principle questionable. Nelson's description of our ordinary views does not, and could not, constitute a defense of those views.

One last way with skepticism is provided by Locke in his book, *Memory*. There he admits that no one has shown Russell's hypothesis to be incoherent, inconceivable, or logically impossible; and he says that he cannot prove it false. But he claims that one has reasons for rejecting it, since "rationality itself requires that we accept our evidence for the past as evidence for the past . . . it is not just a matter of what proves convenient; it is a matter of what presuppositions or assumptions we have to make if knowledge is to become possible at all."[22] Somewhat surprisingly, given these remarks, Locke proceeds to offer a "transcendental" argument for the reliability of memory. One admits that the reliability of memory is a contingent fact that might be otherwise. One then claims that it is a first principle, without which knowledge is impossible. (Locke says that it is logically necessary that one cannot prove that memory is reliable; p. 134). Finally, one asserts that since such a proof is logically impossible, it is a mistake to think that we somehow cannot do something that we ought to do.[23]

While Locke may have shown what one must assume if there is to be knowledge, he has not answered the skeptic at all. He may have shown what one must assume to overcome skepticism, but that does not show skepticism to be false. If this road is to be followed in combating skepticism, then one needs a transcendental argument that will show its very possibility to be incoherent, much as Kant tried to show that Hume's views on causation lead to a radical incoherence when their implications are thought through. Otherwise, the skeptic can regard Locke's argument as merely the construction of a fools' paradise. Skepticism *is* hard to digest, but one needs more than that to rid philosophy of its presence. As long as the "has" in "one has to accept the assumption of the reliability of memory" is conditional, one will have failed to answer the skeptic.

6

THE CLASSICAL PROBLEM OF INDUCTION

In this chapter I shall not be concerned with either the New Riddle of Induction or with a survey of all the responses that have been formulated to meet the Old Riddle of Induction. Instead, I shall concentrate on the problem of induction as argued by Hume and Russell (since ordinary-language philosophers have concentrated on this formulation of the problem) and on the response of ordinary-language philosophers to the arguments that Hume and Russell present. My goal, as throughout this book, is to show that these responses do not succeed in dissolving Hume's and Russell's difficulties, in explaining the origin of these difficulties, or in showing that there is some rather obvious way in which the problem of induction can be overcome.

The bare bones of the Hume-Russell view are well known. Hume points out that "all reasonings concerning matter of fact seem to be founded on the relation of *Cause and Effect*,"[1] and he adds three observations: (1) one learns of causes and effects by experience, not reason (p. 28); (2) the contrary of any proposition about a matter of fact is possible because it never implies a contradiction (p. 25); and (3) past experience can give one "*direct* and *certain* information" only about past (and present) objects (p. 33).

The question is how one is to justify transferring what one has learned about causes and effects from the past to the future. Or as Hume puts it, What is the "medium" that enables one to pass reasonably from the observation that an object in the past has had a certain effect to the claim that similar objects in similar circumstances will have similar effects in the future? Can one show in this way that it is reasonable to believe that nature is uniform? The second of Hume's observations rules out the possibility of a demonstrative proof that nature will maintain the same uniformity in the future that it has in the past. One can always accept the antecedent but deny the consequent without contradiction. As Hume puts it, "The connexion between these propositions is not intuitive" (p. 34).

But if one cannot be certain that the future will resemble the past, perhaps one can establish that this is *probable* by utilizing Hume's second type of reasoning, that "concerning matter of fact and existence." That is, perhaps one can adduce arguments drawn from experience that will weigh in favor of the uniformity of nature. But such arguments will have to rely on past observations in order to support claims about the future, and to do this is to assume the very principle that one is seeking to justify.

To sum up: if one understands the nature of empirical propositions, one will quickly see that none follows necessarily from any other and that there is a necessary circularity in any attempt to support experiential claims about the future (or past) with other experiential claims. Hume is clear that the skepticism that results from this conclusion will not undermine ordinary reasoning, but he insists that it shows that the basis of this reasoning is habit or custom, not reason.

Before going on, there is another interpretation of what Hume is trying to show that differs from the above in one important respect. Brian Skyrms points out that the only reasonable request that one can make of the defender of scientific induction is that he show that "inductively strong arguments give us true conclusions from true premises *most* of the time."[2] To ask for more—namely, that such premises *always* yield true conclusions —is to ask that inductive arguments match the standards appropriate to deductive validity. According to Skyrms, Hume's argument should be understood as claiming only that no rational justification can be found for the belief that one's properly formed inductions yield true conclusions most of the time. This cannot be shown by deduction, since the premises of any such attempted proof must refer only to the past and since the conclusion cannot extend beyond the premises; nor can it be shown inductively, on pain of circularity. On the other interpretation of Hume, he denies that one's belief that the past causal uniformity of nature will continue in the future is certain. That this will be so is not a logical truth and cannot be deduced from logically true premises; thus, there can be no demonstrative arguments in this case. What cannot be demonstrated is that nature will *always* be uniform. Failing certainty about absolute uniformity, Hume then concerns himself with trying to establish that it is *probable* that nature will be uniform, and he finds that an appeal to past experience cannot establish even this much.[3]

There seems to be evidence on both sides. Hume does speak of the impossibility of demonstrating that "similar sensible qualities *will always* be conjoined with similar secret powers,"[4] and he says in the *Treatise* that if one were determined by reason, one would follow the rule that "the course of nature continues *always* uniformly the same."[5] These remarks suggest that Hume was interested in showing that one cannot prove an exceptionless constancy about nature. And while this is undoubtedly more than the minimum that induction needs as a justification, Hume's apparent consideration of it in turn suggests that, for him, it might be a desirable kind of justification.

On the other hand, if this is Hume's intention, one wonders why he did not consider the attempt to prove demonstratively that one can usually rely on one's inductions; that is, show that what is necessary is the probability that true premises will yield true conclusions. This is particularly strange because his reason for denying the possibility of demonstrative proofs relies on the observation that there is no contradiction in the assertion that nature may change.[6] Yet, this reason does not seem to rule out a demonstration that inductions guarantee the probability of their conclusions. Nature could change to some extent, and still our faith in induction could be rational if we expect only probability from it.

In addition, if one looks to Russell's formulation of the problem of induction, one finds him insisting that "it is to be observed that all such expectations are only *probable*; thus we have not to seek for a proof that they *must* be fulfilled, but only for some reason in favour of the view that they are *likely* to be fulfilled."[7] He adds that since the observed connection of things can at most yield a probability that is close to certainty, "probability is all we ought to seek" (p. 66).

This suggests that, for Russell, if experience could establish that the "inductive principle" could be relied on in most cases, that would constitute a rational justification of induction. However, even in Russell's case the evidence is confusing. For Russell also says that the belief in the uniformity of nature is a belief that there are *no* exceptions to the most general laws and that "science habitually assumes, at least as a working hypothesis, that general rules which have exceptions can be replaced by general rules which have no exceptions" (p. 64). *This* suggests that we have a deep commitment to absolute uniformity and presumably would wish to justify *that* commitment in justifying the inductive rule. That is, presumably the inductive rule itself would reflect that commitment, not the lesser one of probability.

Nonetheless, there are two considerations that make it clear that at least part of the criticism of induction is that its conclusions fall short of deductive certainty. First, there are philosophers who have taken this view quite explicitly. For example, Donald Williams holds that a justification of induction consists in showing that induction is a perfectly logical process; for him, this means that the conclusion of an induction follows from its premise by a probability relation that "is a logical credibility relation justly to be described as analogous to strict entailment."[8] As he says, "The most, but also the least, which we can ask is to vindicate for induction a validity which is like that of deduction in an essential respect but of less degree" (p. 31), and he seems to hold out the possibility that a truly deductive justification of induction is possible when he says that he has decided to opt for a more modest aim than that.

A. C. Ewing has elaborated even further on this type of criticism of induction. He states that "some *a priori* principle about the world is required if induction is to be justified,"[9] and he makes it plain that this principle is the principle of induction referred to by Hume and Russell. Second, he makes it clear that the a priori character of this principle derives from a view about causality according to which the relation between cause and effect is "closely analogous to that of logical entailment."[10] On the regularity view of causation, no justification of induction is possible. Ewing admits that "we cannot say that the conclusion of an inductive inference follows from its premises with the same necessity as does the conclusion of a deductive one,"[11] but he ascribes this fact to one's lack of insight into the nature of causes in the physical world, a lack that he thinks does not apply when the cause is mental.[12]

Ewing's fundamental argument is that inductions require that one be able to argue from cause to effect, "but no inference can possibly be legitimate unless the premises really entail the conclusion" (*Idealism*, p. 167). And Ewing asks: What can 'entailment' mean in such a case if not that the conclusion is logically tied to the premise such that it could not be otherwise, the premise being what it is? Ewing admits that causes and premises are radically distinct, but he claims that his view does not involve confusing the two. The claim is, rather, that unless what propositions refer to in the world are related by an entailment relation, one is not justified in reasoning from one to the other as if they were so related. Thus, if one holds to a regularity view of causality and if one's thoughts are intended to capture the nature of the world so pictured, then one should never allow oneself to reason that because something is the case, something else must be (or probably is) the case. In short, the claim is that the justification of induction lies in a certain metaphysical view about the nature of relations between items in the world.

Of course, this solution amounts to conceiving of induction as a species of deduction; but Ewing argues that this is consistent with there being differences between the two, is not objectionable in principle, and would not *directly* conflict with the fact that inductions are at best probable.[13] I say "directly" because Ewing's explanation relies on the fact that his philosophical view would have no effect on normal inductive practices, since he admits that we do not possess insight into the necessary connection between cause and effect that is required if induction is to be capable of justification. This means that his view *is* incompatible with the probabilistic character of induction if one thinks of this as an ultimate fact about the world and of our reasonings about it. Ideally, from God's point of view, so to speak, one would see that probability is tied to one's lack of insight into necessity and does not reflect accurately the relation that actually holds between real things or events. Hume was right about what insight one has into the physical world (that is, none), but he was wrong about the relations that one is led to think really do hold in nature.

It is important to notice that this view takes quite a different view of what "rational justification" of induction involves than does the one advocated by Skyrms. For Skyrms, one would have justification if one could be guaranteed that inductions from true premises are *likely* to be true. But for Ewing, this could at most be a step on the way to a final justification, for it does not make the transition from premise to conclusion reasonable. Only an understanding of *why* this connection will continue to hold in the future can do that, and such an understanding presupposes the insight that the items mentioned in the premise are bound together in such a way that one entails the other. A guarantee of probability leaves one without an understanding of the "why," and while this would provide a support for scientific induction, it would fall short of being fully reasonable. How could one be fully satisfied with a justification of induction that shows one that probability is necessitated but that does not go further to show *why* this is so? And it is hard to see what this "why" might be if it did not involve some type of logical connection, a connection that would make one's acceptance of probability a half-way house on the way to a fully reasonable view of the way things are.

The second part promised above is more comprehensible in light of Ewing's criticism of induction. I think that one might well interpret Hume's disclaimer that no demonstration about the uniformity of nature is possible as a deduction from his view of causality (which is how he discusses induction) and that, in turn, as a deduction from his metaphysical view that all events or impressions are "loose" and separate. According to this view, no fact can ever require another or have power over another. Thus, one would never be able to deduce the strict uniformity of nature from the observed uniformity of the past. Since Hume's metaphysics rules out any "tight" relation among impressions, it is reasonable to think that he is rejecting any knowledge of such assumed tightness in his discussion of causality/induction. Having rejected a necessary bond between past and future, Hume then shows that even a probabilistic bond cannot be proved, and since these represent the two ways that justification can be obtained, that no justification is possible.

My hypothesis is that *one* reason—and the more important, underlying reason—that induction remains unjustified is that it cannot meet deductive standards of justification. Russell's discussion of induction revolves around the lack of an inductive justification, but Hume's discussion betrays that he is hankering after the Rationalism that he is determined to reject, much as any rebel longs for the comfort that the old order provides.

I shall divide the ordinary-language response to the classical problem of induction into four overlapping categories. (1) Specific criticisms of inductive skepticism: (a) the error of trying to reduce induction to deduction and (b) the claim that inductive inference need make no appeal to nonempirical principles. (2) The attempt to show that a general criticism of induction is incoherent. (3) Explanations of how skeptics seem to generate philosophical skepticism about induction. (4) Presentation of alternative ways of justifying induction once the errors of skepticism have been exposed: (a) the claim that induction can be defended inductively and (b) the claim that inductive inferences *are* logically conclusive. As is to be expected, the emphasis in the first three groups is on dissolving the specter of skepticism, and even in the fourth group there is an attempt to clear the land of needless debris and to show that this clearing process reveals the natural mode of justification that was obscured by unnecessary philosophical perplexity.

SPECIFIC CRITICISMS OF INDUCTIVE SKEPTICISM

(A) In this case, the charge against the skeptic is that he points out the differences between induction and deduction, but that he claims that these differences show that the former is cognitively inferior to the latter. Stated otherwise, the skeptic hits hard at nonparallelisms between induction and deduction, and in the process makes one feel uneasy about the cases in which there is a distinct parallelism. Finally, the skeptic's use of such key terms as 'evidence' and 'justification' betray his unspoken allegiance to deduction as *the* proper mode of inference. But once his allegiances are out in the open, along with the shifts in meaning of terms caused by such allegiances, one can see that the differences pressed on one by the skeptic provide no justification for his skepticism. One is left with two legitimate modes of inference, whose differences form a natural area of study.

Let us first consider the charge that the Rationalist or Deductivist critique of induction would make normal regularities into accidents or miracles if necessary connection is denied,[14] or would imply that there is no real distinction between well-founded and poorly founded inductions.[15] This would result either in emptying the term 'accident' of all meaning, or it would lead to practical frustration and chaos. But this criticism, besides resting on the exploded Doctrine of Meaningful Contrasts, assumes that the critic of induction wishes his criticisms to directly affect ordinary practices, and he hopes that his conception of justification will become operative in science and common sense. This is incorrect. The philosophical justification of induction must not be confused with the ordinary justification of inductions; if the former suggests that an ultimate irrationality underlies induction, it is not an irrationality that need make one pause before drawing an inductive conclusion. In criticizing the framework of ordinary induction, the Deductivist *is indirectly* criticizing the confidence that we place in well-founded inductive conclusions. But as Ewing points out, his position does not permit its being adopted as a practical measure. One lacks the insight that the Deductivist finds at the heart of the problem of induction.

To explain, and at the same time to explain away, the appeal that the Deductivist's program has for philosophers, Ambrose cites both disanalogies and analogies between deduction and induction which, she thinks, first cause us philosophical (but not practical) doubt about well-formed inductions and then make a justification of induction seem both necessary and possible. Ambrose notes that some inductive arguments are extremely uncertain, and one's tendency is to allow this uncertainty to spread to all inductions.[16] On the other hand, some inductions are such that it would be a "misuse of language" to say that certain results were only "probable." These cases bring out the analogy between deduction and induction and make one feel that a justification of the latter is something that can be accomplished. Ambrose adds that the analogy between the legitimate doubts of scientists and their requests to justify inductions, on the one hand, and the doubts of philosophers and their desire to justify induction, on the other, make the latter seem genuine; in truth they are equally disanalogous, for no testing procedure is even relevant to the philosopher's doubts about induction (pp. 197–98).

The problem with Ambrose's psychology of the inductive skeptic is that one can note carefully these possible causes for skepticism and nevertheless find persuasive *reasons* for skepticism. The riskiness of some inductions need not be the reason that one finds even well-formed inductions to be without a rational justification, as Hume and Russell have shown; and the fact that the philosopher's doubts do not affect one's behavior and are not testable shows nothing about their legitimacy, unless one can show in general that only ordinary doubts are legitimate. I see no reason that the Deductivist should accept this account of why he finds the foundations of induction to be suspect.

Now consider the following arguments: 1. "What reasonable ground can be given for arguing from the mere difference of two things to the lesser cognitive value of either term of the inequation?"[17] The two have different strengths, and since one needs both kinds of strength, to rank one lower than the other "is as absurd as to assert that the walls of a house are more important than its rafters" (p. 63).

2. The Deductivist's critique of induction can be understood as relying on either (a) an equivocation between the ordinary sense of such key terms as 'justification', 'knowledge', 'possibility', and so forth,[18] and a strict or deductive sense, or (b) on a sense of 'evidence' that simply does not allow examined cases to count as evidence for unexamined cases. The mere numerical difference between the two prevents the former from weighing in favor of the latter.[19] The point in both cases is that the Deductivist's case seems to be made out only because he adjusts the meaning of

his terms to suit his arbitrarily adopted standard of legitimate inference.

3. A deductive justification of induction *cannot* work because *"induction, by definition, is not a species of deduction."*[20] Or somewhat more mildly, to suggest that one ought to try to acquire knowledge by deductive procedures "is to propose a worthless ideal," for "there is no way in which an inductive argument can approach the ideal of deductive argument" (p. 77).

4. The formal beauty of deductive procedures is no reason for ascribing cognitive superiority to deduction over induction. Their relative values can be intelligently measured only if one compares their instrumental value (p. 83).

I think objections one, three, and four are rather transparently weak. No Deductivist need ever appeal to the *mere* difference between induction and deduction in questioning the justification of the former. One simply wants to understand the inference from premise to conclusion, and such understanding is clear in the case of deduction but not in the case of induction. And merely pointing to the *amount* of evidence in the case of some inductions does not help one to *understand* the transition in question. This difference is what the Deductivist emphasizes and tries to show to be relevant.

Similarly, the definition of induction that Black cites represents the ordinary division between these two procedures. Since no one doubts that, *as practiced*, the two differ, and since the Deductivist wants to question this division, it is an uninteresting verbal point to remind him of the ordinary view. This poses no barrier for the Deductivist. Nor is he suggesting that one ought to learn about the world deductively or that induction is less important than deduction. The writings of philosophers on this subject simply do not make these claims. Thus, no one doubts the instrumental value of induction; the Deductivist would gladly agree that one needs both in order to help one know one's way about in science and common life.

The Deductivist can also distinguish truth and beauty as well as the Inductivist. What interests the former about induction is its questionable intelligibility. As a thinker, one wishes to understand why things happen; that is, one seeks reasons. But unless one's conjunctions are more than mere conjunctions, or unless they rest on events bound together by entailment, it is hard to see how induction can provide this insight. If one says that this ideal is arbitrary and has been invented by Rationalists, then one can only request a reexamination of one's own experience as a thinker and of what seems to be the end of disinterested speculation generally.

I have saved the second criticism for last, because it seems at first blush to offer a genuine challenge to the Deductivist. However, it really is no more than a type of criticism that we have earlier found mistaken. The skeptic is not claiming that it is wrong, within one's ordinary framework, to say that one knows or is certain of a given inductively reached conclusion, as Black notes (pp. 77–78). The ordinary senses of 'conjecture' or 'guess', as contrasted with 'know', remain in force. But this does not mean that the skeptic's use of 'know' is not pertinent to the ordinary use, for the ordinary use carries with it the conviction of absolute certainty or justification; and it is this implicit claim that the skeptic questions. There is then no equivocation; the skeptic merely suggests that the ordinary distinction cannot hold up in the final way that one's ordinary use of it suggests. Will, on the other hand, is mistaken to think that mere numerical difference is what the Deductivist condemns. Rather, the Deductivist is bothered by the lack of necessary connection between what is numerically distinct, and *this* lack explains why he does not accept inductive evidence as justification of conclusions so reached. To simply rule against induction would indeed be arbitrary, but this ruling is a conclusion and not a premise of the Deductivist's case.

(B) This point takes us to our second specific criticism against critics of induction. Paul Edwards notes that ordinarily when one is asked if one has a reason for believing that a man will fall if he leaps from a building, one replies unhesitatingly that past experience and science provide such a reason. One then tries to show that this is the correct answer, needing no reference to a nonempirical principle of induction, by arguing that skeptics are guilty of an "*ignoratio elenchi* by redefinition."[21] Skeptics are said to be guilty of "high redefinition" of a term such as 'reason', by which locution Edwards means that they pack additional meaning into 'reason' until almost nothing could count as a reason. Such claims, then, do not in fact contradict ordinary claims, although they appear to do so since the same word is used by both the philosopher and the ordinary man (p. 153).

Edwards issues a familiar challenge to the skeptic: either you are using words in their ordinary senses, in which case what you say is false; or you are using words in a special way (at least a way that is special for this context), in which case you are guilty of an *ignoratio* by high redefinition (p. 149). Let me note at the outset that even if Edwards were right about skepticism, it is hard to see how he could be defending or justifying induction in any interesting sense. For if no criticism of ordinary notions is possible (I take it that any criticism could be dealt with as Edwards deals with Russell) and if other people might well use terms differently from the way we do, then one seems bound to conventionalism. One can note what we mean by 'reason' or 'justification', but there will be no sense in which one sense of those terms is "truer" than another. The kind of assurance that Edwards gives of induction, namely, reasonableness, only points to the use that we make of that term, and unless saying it is so makes it so, one must wonder what assurance this information brings.

Of course, I do not think that skepticism about induction must select one of the horns of Edwards's dilemma. If the skeptic can show that the various senses of 'reasonable' share a commitment to understanding one thing in terms of another, then these senses can be rated by their effectiveness in helping this understanding. Evidence that there is this common core to 'reasonable' would come if the common man would admit on reflection that his unquestioned assumption of the reasonableness of induction was not thought out fully and that it is not finally justified. That is, if the common man recognizes the claim of Russell's rationality, then he treats it, not as a foreign imposition on his own meaning, but as a development of the meaning that he only partially realizes. An examination of the goal of thought would, I believe, lend further weight to the view that common sense represents a practical compromise with ultimate standards. Certainly, Edwards's case is weakened by not considering the possibility of criticism from within, even when different senses of the same word are involved.

Thus, I think that one can counter Black's attempt to meet the Argument from Greater Intelligibility of Deduction (p. 82). Black claims that we *can* explain why physical events occur; and if this is denied, then one is equating intelligibility with logical intelligibility and is saying nothing that is relevant to inductive reasoning. But isn't it clear that the intelligibility of which Black speaks ends with the uniformities whose intelligibility we assume in order to see why the events that they explain occur? We have simply pushed the problem back one step. To say this is not to impose a foreign standard on empirical explanation but to point out that the desire to see why has not been fulfilled, and cannot be fulfilled, in the manner suggested.

IS SKEPTICISM ABOUT INDUCTION INCOHERENT?

The most important attempt to cut off skepticism at its roots is the one by P. F. Strawson. He begins by drawing a parallel between asking about the general validity of deduction (a question that does not make sense) and whether induction in general is rational. In both cases, it seems, the key terms, 'validity' and 'rationality', have meaning only when applied to deductive or inductive standards. One thinks immediately of Kant's analysis of 'cause'. Just as causal terminology works for Kant within a context and cannot be applied sensibly to that context as a whole, so 'valid' and 'rational' work for Strawson within deductive and inductive contexts, respectively, and cannot apply to either process as a whole.

Strawson claims that doubting the rationality of induction stems from a desire to make inductive arguments deductively valid. And he adds: "Of course, inductive arguments are not deductively valid; if they were, they would be deductive arguments. Inductive reasoning must be assessed, for soundness, by inductive standards."[22] It is, Strawson claims, *analytic* that one is reasonable if the strengths of his beliefs are proportional to the strength of the evidence in favor of the propositions in question (p. 256); this is what being reasonable means in this context. And to ask for a justification of induction is to invite the response that until one states the standards by which this question is to be answered, the question has no sense. Strawson here compares such an inquiry to the question, "Is the law legal?" (p. 257).

However, Strawson is well aware that his answer is more liable "to produce irritation than relief," and so he promises something more. (1) Since it is an analytic proposition that any successful method of finding out about the unknown is justified inductively, it is strange to speak about induction as if it were one method among others. (2) Attempts to show that induction is rational seem justified only because they represent the conflation of two separate matters. One can legitimately wonder whether inductions will continue to inform one about the unknown, for that they continue to do so will depend on the constitution of the universe; and it is a contingent claim, not a necessary one, that the universe will continue to exhibit certain regularities. On the other hand, it is a necessary statement, one about the meaning of 'rational', that induction is a rational policy. Induction would continue to be rational no matter what characteristics the universe might display. The distinction is between the ability to form rational opinions, on the one hand, and what a rational opinion is, or what one means by 'rational opinion', on the other.

As I read Strawson, the confusion of these two matters is partly or largely responsible for one's doubts about the certainty of the principle underlying the rationality of induction. Being confused, one feels both that it must be necessary (since one senses that the rationality of induction is not a contingent matter) and, yet, that it must be a contingent matter (since one cannot claim that the universe must exhibit any order). This ambivalence makes both the principle behind induction and, by extension, induction itself seem questionable or even contradictory.[23]

Let us begin by granting the Strawsonian point that if any method of finding out about the unknown works, it will have to be an inductive method. Whatever it is, one will adopt it because it has been successful—that is, because there is strong inductive evidence in its favor. The method itself may not be what one would call scientific induction; for example, it might involve falling into a trance and then saying something about the future on waking, but it will be *justified* because one thinks its working in the past is a good reason for thinking it will work in the future.

But I do not see that this necessary truth prevents one from asking whether full justification by the ordinary standards of induction is enough to make an argument rational. Thus, I do not think that the two matters that Strawson separates so sharply are in fact that separate. It seems perfectly possible to ask why one calls inductive arguments "rational" when they meet inductive standards. Why must one rest content with the answer that this is the way in which we use 'rational'? The obvious answer to this question is that one has tied 'rational' to 'inductive' so closely because inductive arguments, when well formed in fact, lead us to truth more often than not. And this fact is obviously dependent on the universe being a certain way. Once this question is asked, it becomes apparent that the success of induction cannot, on pain of circularity, be used to justify the rationality of induction. More directly, one has a clear standard of rationality, and induction simply does not meet that standard.

For this reason, I see no absurdity in measuring induction by deductive standards when questions of rationality arise. One can see why the conclusion of a deductive argument follows from its premises, and one cannot see the same with an inductive argument. That seems reason enough to say that the latter is not fully rational.

Consider Strawson's example of asking whether the law is legal. If this questions whether the law is the law, then it is obviously without sense. One can ask whether *this* is legal—that is, whether it is within the bounds of the law—but not whether the law is within its own bounds. But there is another sense to the question which makes it far from senseless. One might be asking whether the law, including its principles and particular statutes, is in accord with moral principles which, many think, it is supposed to reflect and by which it can be criticized. Here one asks whether an entire framework meets a certain standard in a way that is analogous to asking whether a given law meets the standards within that framework.

I see a precise parallel with the skeptic's questions about the justification of induction. One asks whether the framework of induction adequately reflects the standard of rationality that is embodied in deductive inference. One does not impose this standard on induction from without; rather, one recognizes this standard as what one means by 'rationality' and finds induction lacking in the one kind of rationality that one knows. To say that induction has its own kind of rationality, one that is self-justified by its own standards, makes no more sense to me than saying that the Chinese have their own logic or their own mathematics. In the case of induction, there is no mystery about what one's standard for rationality is or why induction falls short of this standard; therefore, there is no reason to think that the questioning of induction is without sense, a question that is asked in a vacuum, with no means of answering it.

There is both a strangeness and a troublesome result in the view that one cannot criticize the rationality of induction. Since Strawson supposes that the connection between rationality and induction is analytic, one may assume that this connection is conventional and tells one nothing about anything in the world. It would be strange if one could not wonder about the justification of such a linkage when other linkages are possible. What barrier prevents one from wondering about the reason for so defining rationality and from finding reasons for disputing this definition? The point that any successful method of finding out about the unknown must be justified inductively will not help one here, for the success of induction is not in question when one asks about its justification. The only method that one can, in fact, use to justify reasonings about matters of fact may not be rationally justified. As long as this remains even a possibility, the critic of induction will have opened the door to inductive skepticism.

The unwelcome result follows from the above and has been pointed out by Salmon.[24] Strawson's view makes empirical knowledge conventional, for it forces one to accept induction as it is, not allowing one to find "cognitive considerations" that would serve to justify it. But then, others might have other rules; they would not be rational by our standards, but then our standards would hold no sway over alternatives. Seemingly, both sides would be faced with a stand-off; but one would find this result disturbing, I believe, because one wants one's methods to have more than conventional force.

I believe that Strawson's reply to Salmon actually plays into the latter's hands. Strawson, citing Hume, makes a distinction between conventional and natural.[25] He asserts that merely because induction does not have a general justification, it does not follow that induction is conventional. For Hume, one has no choice at all about what basic inductive rules to follow; these are mandated by nature, reason merely spinning out the details of this basic commitment. There is no opportunity for arbitrary choice to make its presence felt, and in this way, Hume can be said to have "solved" the problem of induction.

The problem with this reply is that it does not cut deeply enough. Normally, one does contrast 'conventional' and 'natural'; the former is changeable and variable in a way that the latter is not. But what is natural is itself variable, and in this sense is conventional, since it is not necessary or in any way determinable by reason. Perhaps these alternatives are not chosen alternatives, but as long as they are conceptually possible, the person who finds induction natural will have no leverage against the person who finds a counterinductive policy natural. If Martians do it differently from humans, there is nothing that humans can say except that as a matter of fact they do it another way and that *they* so connect the concepts of rationality and induction that the Martians' procedure is irrational by those standards. Salmon's point that the "basic cannons of induction . . . are arbitrary in the sense that cognitive considerations do not force their acceptance" (p. 39) would still hold even if his remarks about choice do not. No matter how natural induction may be, in lacking a rational justification and in being merely factually compulsive, it leaves itself no avenue by which it might be judged superior to other, perfectly possible, modes of inquiry. And this is surely a result that grates against our sense that induction is *the* proper way of learning about the unknown.

ORIGINS OF THE APPARENT FORCE
BEHIND INDUCTIVE SKEPTICISM

I wish now to consider briefly two accounts of what "really" sparks the skeptic's dissatisfaction with induction, accounts that, when exposed to the light of day, are meant to dispose of this dissatisfaction by showing it to be unjustified or unreasonable.

According to Ambrose, "The dissatisfaction with inductive

inference which prompts the quest for a hidden principle which justifies it arises from the following commonplace: that instead of certainty that 'p is probable' follows from the empirical facts, in case after case there is indecision."[26] That is, the skeptic is actually dissatisfied with the linguistic fact that we use 'probable' in such a way that there is no rule that specifies some exact number of cases from which it follows that 'p is probable' is true. Just as there is no precise point distinguishing 'rich' from 'poor', so "we have no fixed criteria in our language for saying whether an inductive argument is correct" (p. 202). Ambrose concludes that our language contains no hidden principle that might sharply demarcate probable from nonprobable, and if one then interprets the skeptic as claiming that there *should be* such a dividing line, one can observe that 'probable' is as sharply defined as one needs it to be. Ordinary language is satisfactory.

In my view, the above misconstrues the dissatisfaction of the skeptic, and it also contains an extremely weak defense of ordinary language. The skeptic is not concerned with that middle range of cases in which one does not know whether to say 'rich' or 'poor', 'probable' or 'not probable'. His claim is that probability is not entailed by *any* number of favorable past instances. Second, he does not suggest, therefore, that ordinary language should contain such a dividing line. He does not even suggest that ordinary language should meet his standards of logical adequacy, though one might add that it does not follow that ordinary language has all the characteristics that philosophers find necessary for philosophical purposes. The uses to which ordinary language is put may simply preclude the inclusion of such philosophically warranted elements.

A second source of skepticism about induction is suggested by Morris Lazerowitz. According to him, philosophical theories about inference, as is the case with philosophical theories generally, despite their "ontological mask," represent "alterations in the use of terminology."[27] They introduce "stretched" uses of terms that are "academically superimposed on ordinary language."[28] The Deductivist adds a "sham" use to the actual use of 'deductive', although he hides this "artificial redrawing" of inference language behind a vocabulary that suggests that he has discovered some new fact about the world. Once one recognizes the true nature of the skeptic's suggestions, Lazerowitz claims, one will recognize that what the skeptic says warrants a dissolution rather than a solution and calls for an explanation rather than an assessment of its truth value (p. 247).

The type of explanation that Lazerowitz thinks appropriate is taken from depth psychology. The philosopher is said to give expression to emotional problems in his rearranging of language, problems that are characterized as a "tendency to obsessional doubt" (p. 256). The philosopher who questions induction is said to be finding reassurance that his affliction is universal, not merely personal (p. 257).[29]

To this charge I append the following comments. (1) Lazerowitz does not show in any way that such philosophical proposals *must* be viewed as *only* verbal alterations, even if one agrees that they do involve a departure from ordinary use. (2) These proposals are not "superimposed" on ordinary language, if this means that they are combined with it or that they are meant to replace it for ordinary purposes. (3) Since Lazerowitz does not take seriously the reasons that philosophers give for inductive skepticism, he can make such proposals seem strange. But what is strange to the ordinary man may be perfectly normal in another context, *unless* one has antecedently decided that the other context is without justification. Take away the negative implications of Lazerowitz's descriptions of the philosopher's activities, and one has a description that does not suggest anything strange. (4) Even if Lazerowitz is right about the *cause* of philosophical perplexity, there is still the issue of the truth of what is said. No one, including Freud himself, is immune from the charge that there are unconscious forces behind his activity. But if Freud's ideas are not to be dismissed because they have such a background, why are the ideas of philosophers to be so dismissed— unless, again, one has previously decided that they are bogus? Psychoanalysis is irrelevant to the evaluation of philosophical proposals that concern reasons and truth; if this is not the case, then I see no alternative to throwing out Lazerowitz's own philosophical theories along with those of philosophers of whom he disapproves. In short, unless one is already convinced by other arguments that philosophy or philosophical skepticism is an illegitimate enterprise, one can find nothing in what Lazerowitz says that would support his claim that one should take philosophy in the way that he suggests.

JUSTIFICATIONS OF INDUCTION

(A) There is some sentiment among linguistic philosophers for arguing that once the confusions surrounding the skeptic's criticism of induction are exposed, it will be clearly seen that there is evidence in favor of induction, even if this evidence does not constitute proof of the validity of induction.

Frederick Will believes that the skeptic thinks of the future as in principle beyond investigation, as if the future were behind some impenetrable barrier. He treats the ever-receding border between past and future as if it were stationary, for he claims that when the future events referred to in one's induction occur, they are considered past rather than future. Therefore, one is always trapped in the past for one's observation, making guesses about a future that one will never experience. Given this situation, nothing can count as evidence in favor of an inductive generalization.

But, says Will, one's predictions are not about a future never to be revealed, but about an ever-revealing future, whereas the skeptic makes his claims about the former type of future, albeit seeming to speak of the latter type of future. He so manipulates terms such as 'evidence' and 'future' that his skepticism must be justified, but then "the argument has no bearing whatever . . . upon the soundness or success of any inductive inquiry."[30] One need not worry about the skeptic's future; the skeptic has no case against induction when he is taken to refer to the future that is constantly being revealed. The conclusion is that one is constantly learning how the future will be like the past, and in the process, one presumes that one is justifying the inductive method.

It is hard to see the force that the above argument would have against the skeptic. He may readily accept all that Will claims, short of admitting that this constitutes a proof of induction. Thus, he can willingly admit that the future event to which he was referring in an inductive leap has become present and observable. He can also admit that this occurrence either proves one's prediction to be true, if it referred only to a limited time

138

span, or allows one to know that more A's are B, or have been B, than one knew previously. However, the skeptic insists, at this point, that this increase in one's knowledge of "A's that are B" can be used as evidence in favor of induction only if one has reason to believe that a claim that has once come true will come true in the future. And this claim assumes the validity of the very principle of induction for which one thought that one was presenting evidence. As long as events are separate, the skeptic insists that successes, no matter how numerous, do not justify a belief that there will be similar successes in the future. This point involves no arbitrary use of terms and no confusion over different senses of 'future'. It simply does not allow that the normal build-up of evidence is justified.

In fact, one can see that Will's case against skepticism is built upon assuming the validity of the normal way that one uses 'evidence'. And of course the skeptic *does* think that this use has no ultimate philosophical justification in cases of induction, but this does not make him like the prophet who claims that "next year" is always the year beyond; and so, nothing that happens can falsify what he says.[31] He admits that the future will come, but he denies that its coming will provide the proof of induction or natural regularity that one normally assumes that it will. I conclude that Will has not correctly diagnosed a conceptual confusion which supposedly generates inductive skepticism and that his attempt to make experience cumulative is circular.[32]

(B) Another, more direct, means of justifying inductive inference has been proposed by Casimir Lewy. Lewy claims that the true premises "Whenever I have heard barking in the past there was always a dog somewhere near" and "I am hearing barking now" *entail by themselves* the conclusion "I have good reason to believe that there is a dog somewhere near now."[33] One need invoke no Russellian principle of induction, which one must assume but cannot prove, to make the above argument a sound one.[34]

Lewy supports his claim by further asserting that it is *self-contradictory* to accept the above premises and then to deny the conclusion. Reflection on the normal use of 'probable' or 'good reason' will, Lewy adds, substantiate this further claim, although he does not claim to be able to prove that this is so. The result is that inductive arguments are on a logical par with deductive arguments; in both cases the premises logically entail the conclusions. Therefore, there is no problem of justifying induction; one might say that it is self-justifying in the way that deduction is.

One might agree with Lewy that if events in the past were as the first premise states and one heard a dog barking, one would feel oneself justified in drawing the conclusion mentioned above. That is, one would normally *say* that past regularities provide good reasons for thinking that such regularities will probably continue in the future. It might well be that in such circumstances there would be a verbal contradiction in denying that one had a "good reason" for believing the conclusion or in denying that the conclusion was probable. However, these linguistic facts will not help to justify inductive inference.

After all, the skeptic can acknowledge one's use of 'good reason' and merely add that he wishes to question whether what one calls 'good reasons' are in fact the same as 'logically compelling reasons'. Lewy seems to think that this is the case and that it can be shown to be so by an examination of the ordinary use of 'probable' and of 'good reason'. However, it seems clear to me that there is no contradiction whatever in denying that the conclusion of Lewy's argument is probable while accepting the truth of the premises. One can well imagine a run of coincidences that would cause one to think that this connection of events probably will continue in the future, only to find out that one's conclusion had been hasty and had been based on too narrow a base. Or the regularities in nature may simply turn out to be variable if one sees things in the perspective of the long run.

Lewy's mistake, I think, is that, finding that ordinary language sanctions the use of 'good reason' in this case, he assumes that 'probable' and 'logically entails' are equally sanctioned. The problem is that the skeptic need not be bound by the dictates of ordinary usage; at most, Lewy can be calling one's attention to the logical structure of ordinary speech and thought, but such observations do not touch the skeptic. Second, while one would normally sanction the use of 'good reason' in the above case, and even that of 'probable', I do not think that one would be prepared to extend this sanction to 'logically entails' or (in the case of denying the conclusion) to 'self-contradictory'. Even rather ordinary reflection would make one question the latter, while it would take the extraordinary reflection of philosophy to make one question (for special purposes) the use of 'probable' or 'good reason'. Treating them all on a par seems to me to be a mistake.

I conclude that the resources of ordinary-language analysis have failed to show that the skeptic's call for a justification of induction is based on a confusion, and therefore, it can be safely ignored.

7

CRITERIA AND OTHER MINDS

The philosophical problems of whether one can know on specific occasions the state of another's mind, of whether there is only a more generalized certainty available to us, and of whether one can know even so little as that there are other minds at all rest on the same generic base that supported other forms of philosophical skepticism. The skeptic wants to claim that there is a gap between the evidence that one has about the state or existence of another's mind and the mind whose state one is attempting to know. Since, the skeptic claims, one cannot cross this gap in order to "see" for oneself whether one's claims are correct, one has no way of conclusively verifying in even a single case that other minds are as one says they are. The result is that one cannot eliminate the possibility that one is generally and even universally wrong about other minds. Of course, we do not ordinarily countenance such a possibility, but if the skeptic is right, our ordinary attitude is epistemologically overconfident. Short of direct verification, one has only probability to fall back on, and likelihood is not strong enough a notion to counter the skeptic's abstract possibility. The skeptic demands that a case be made which will justify one's ordinary convictions; it seems that such a case would have to invoke certainty if it is to capture the strength of those convictions. Otherwise, one's "evidence" for other minds may not be evidence at all.

However, this sketch of the generic similarity between skepticism about other minds and skepticism about induction or about the past omits important details which are necessary to flesh out other-minds-skepticism and to reveal assumptions that go to the heart of Cartesian Skepticism. These assumptions concern notions about privacy and private language and are those against which ordinary-language philosophers have argued most originally and effectively.

If one looks at the skeptical argument, one will notice that it does not seem doubtful about *what* one is claiming when one claims, on the basis of another's words or gestures, that the other is in pain, afraid, or whatever. The doubt is only about whether this basis adequately supports the claim to know this to be the case. But then one must, in speaking of another's pain, be claiming that the same thing is being experienced as one experiences when oneself is in pain. In turn, this seems to mean that one knows what pain is, or what 'pain' means, on the basis of one's own experiences. According to this view, the man who can feel no pain is as handicapped in his attempt to understand what 'pain' means as is the blind man who tries to grasp the meaning of color words.

In clarifying this assumption, one might stress that in knowing what pain is solely on the basis of one's own case (where knowing involves no more than 'having' or 'experiencing'), one knows all there is to know about the intrinsic character of pain in the experiencing of it. (Of course, one knows nothing in this way about the causal background of pain.) Therefore, one omits *all* of one's knowledge, not merely a part of that knowledge, of the intrinsic character of pain if one lacks this type of experience. Thus, the behavior that tells one that another is in pain is not even a part of the meaning of pain. If it were, presumably one could know that another was in pain simply by noting his behavior, and still grant to the skeptic the claim that one cannot experience the "inner" part of that complex thing which is the pain of another. Or if one insisted that it would not be pain unless *all* the parts of the complex were present, so that I still could not claim to know that this was a case of pain, then one could at least say that one could know that a "part" of pain was occurring.[1]

However, the skeptic cannot rest with the assumption that nothing bodily is part of the meaning of pain. In addition, he must assume that the connection between the mental state and its behaviorial expression must be a contingent one; for if this were not the case, even if behavior were not an integral part of pain, it would still provide a basis from which one could claim knowledge of the presence of the mental state. If the two are related by an entailment relation or by something akin to one, then on the assumption that one perceives bodies and not signs of bodies, one could know of the quality and existence of other minds.

The remainder of this chapter is divided into three main sections. In the first I shall try to further clarify the skeptic's position by considering several objections to different pieces of his position. Second, I shall consider briefly whether either the Argument from Analogy or the Argument from Science will do as answers to the skeptic. Third, and most central, I shall consider in detail the Argument from Criteria, this being the major way in which ordinary-language philosophers have tried to undercut the skeptical argument by demonstrating that it is radically incoherent. In all of this, I put off a discussion of the possibility of a private language until the next chapter.

SOME OBJECTIONS TO OTHER-MINDS SKEPTICISM

In this section, I shall consider four notions related to the other-minds question: (1) self-observation, (2) logical and empirical possibility, (3) justification of knowledge claims, and (4) our attitude toward other minds.

1. As noted above, one premise of the skeptic about other minds is that he can know by experiencing his own mental states what these states are.[2] Presumably this is how he knows that in the behavior of another he is being given only the husk of the mental state. If there were no such self-knowledge through experience, then it is hard to see how the problem of other minds could ever be generated, for it is the contrast between the way that one comes to know of one's own mental states (and the way that one comes to know is intimately tied up with the character of

what one knows) and the way one "knows" of another's mental state that makes the latter seem less than knowledge to the skeptic.

As obvious as this assumption has seemed to philosophers steeped in the Cartesian tradition, it has been challenged by post-Wittgensteinian philosophers. For example, Bruce Aune tells us that a

> person's sensations are non-observable—even to himself. This is not because they are, as a matter of fact, invisible, intangible, etc.; it is because they are not the sort of thing it makes sense to say one observes: one can feel or suffer a pain, and one can observe its effects or manifestations; but the pain *per se* is such that nothing could count as an observation of it.[3]

Don Locke takes a somewhat more modulated position on this issue. He distinguishes between "bodily sensations" and "conscious processes." The former can be perceived (including after-images and hallucinations) only by the person who has them, while the latter cannot be perceived by anyone.[4] This is not because such processes elude even one's own detection, but because it is a "logical fact that in so far as perceiving, thinking, feeling are conscious processes they cannot occur without my knowing that they do" (p. 19). Belief in an infallible power of introspection, which reports the occurrence and nature of conscious processes, arises only because philosophers confuse the above conceptual, analytic truth with a psychological truth (p. 25). Finally, Locke claims that one does not even know what it would be like to perceive one's conscious processes (p. 34).

The quotation from Aune's article at first suggests that his point is a rather harmless one. When he distinguishes between feeling a pain and observing one, Aune suggests that although one does know experientially and directly one's own pains, he does not want to call this type of awareness "observation." And one can readily admit that the former awareness does not imply the distinction between subject and object that the latter does. But this would be an important misunderstanding of Aune, for his purpose is to show that it is reasonable to assimilate sensations to theoretical states of a person, and such an assimilation carries with it the claim that sensations do not have observable properties (p. 200). As Aune says, "They are specifiable *solely* in terms of the circumstances that occasion them and the behaviour, etc., that they themselves occasion" (pp. 200–201; my emphasis).

This suggestion is part of a larger project of justifying a conception of reality that is derived from physical science, and the status of such a grand project cannot be estimated here.[5] However, one can point out its rather obvious initial implausibility. To accept Aune, one must believe that one does not know the qualitative nature of pain through inner experience, in whatever way one might choose to characterize that experience. Yet, nothing seems more directly open to one than just the qualitative nature of sensations. That is why the insensitive man does not know what the pain-sensitive man knows; in feeling pain, he directly confronts pain in its various grades and distinctions. Therefore, it is highly implausible to suggest that one is aware *that something* is occurring in feeling but that one does not learn *what* it is at the same time. No matter what the theoretical advantages of Aune's view, it cannot succeed by ignoring obvious facts.

Locke's view of conscious processes is more plausible than Aune's view of sensations simply because it is harder to be certain that one knows by inner experience the qualitative features of thoughts than it is to be sure about sensations. However, I think that one does know "directly" that thoughts are intentional; one experiences this feature of thoughts in the very act of thinking. One does, then, "observe" one's thoughts. Second, Locke is forced to admit that what is conceptually necessary is that one be in a position to know that one thinks, not that one necessarily knows this. It is possible, then, to separate being conscious from being conscious that one is conscious enough so that the relation between then is not analytic (p. 22). And even if one grants that in normal adults (perhaps not in children, animals, and defective adults), consciousness by its very nature implies self-consciousness, this does not prove that this is a conceptual relation unless one can show that all necessary connections are analytic ones. If the relation be one of synthetic-but-necessary entailment, all one is saying is that it is necessary for one to know that one is conscious, and this in no way rules out the possibility that this knowledge is acquired by immediate inner experience.

I conclude that nothing that Aune or Locke has said shows

that there is something unacceptable or incoherent in the notion that one knows of one's own inner states via a direct inner experience which contrasts with the indirect experience that I have of other's inner states. This situation remains a viable starting point, then, for skepticism about other minds.

2. Locke asks the skeptic whether the fact that one cannot know of other minds perceptually or directly represents a factual difficulty or a logical one. If it be the former, then, Locke says, there will be something to the skeptic's case, for he will be lamenting the fact that one is not provided with a means of knowing (that our nervous systems might tell us of sensations in another's body) which one might have. If it is the latter, however, the skeptic's lament will be empty, for it will consist in asking for the impossible. On the latter interpretation, all that the skeptic can be doing is pointing out that one does not know other minds as one knows one's own, for he will accept nothing short of this as enough to guarantee knowledge. But, Locke insists, it is silly to worry about a complaint that one could satisfy only by being the other person in question (see pp. 33 and 40).

Of course, if Locke is right, the skeptic faces a dilemma. If the lack that the skeptic refers to is merely factual, then he cannot rule out the possibility that someone will come to verify statements about another's mind. Perhaps someone has already done so! And then he cannot have claimed to show that there is any *philosophical* problem about one's knowledge of other minds. Yet, if he claims to have shown that there is such a problem, that there is a necessary barrier to one's knowledge of other minds, then he seems to be faced with trying to raise a worry that, if realized, results in a logical absurdity. In either case, the skeptic seems to lose the distinctive point that he wishes to make.

The skeptic's doubts about other minds seem to rely on having one's inability to know another's pain "directly" remain a constant, no matter what unusual ways of knowing—telepathy, connecting nerve systems, and the like—one can devise. His doubts are not based on the empirical claim that in fact one cannot have this knowledge directly either now or under normal circumstances. Even supposed cases of split personality would fall victim to Locke's remark about telepathy: "What we would be aware of would not be the contents of other people's minds but rather various thoughts and ideas in our own minds which would inform us about what was going on in those other minds" (pp. 38–39).

But I do not think that calling attention to the fact that being a self entails having privileged access to the contents of one's own mind is an empty undertaking. The skeptic makes this disclosure simply to underscore the direct-indirect difference and to draw from this the necessary consequence that the latter is questionable in ways that the former is not. He does not *merely* point to the difference, but points out that the difference means that our ordinary knowledge claims about other's minds cannot have the total security that strict knowledge implies. Locke's formulation—namely, that the skeptic merely shows that one *knows* others differently from the way in which one knows oneself —begs the question against the skeptic who claims that the difference in access implies a lack of knowledge in the case of others (p. 40). Perhaps this lack cannot be helped, but this does not prevent the situation from containing the seeds of philosophical doubt. A doubt that cannot be removed is not one that one should ordinarily worry about, but it can still point to a logical feature of the knowing of others that is philosophically troublesome.

3. It might be argued that the skeptic's doubts about other minds seem to have merit only because they are so very abstract. Thus, Locke asserts that whether one is justified in one's knowledge claims "depends on whether or not it is a situation of the sort ordinarily accepted as providing knowledge" (p. 48). Since one does say that this is the case of other minds having seen certain kinds of behavior, one is justified in one's belief, "whether it is possible to prove the point or not." In another place, Locke puts the point thus:

> So if we, people generally, have the right to be sure of *p* it follows, logically, that we have good reason for believing *p* to be true, and no outweighing reason for believing *p* false. To show that we have good reason for believing *p* true and no outweighing reason for believing *p* false is, surely, an acceptable proof that *p* is true.[6]

One might add that for Locke, "having the right to be sure" is determined by whatever conditions are mandated by one's ordinary conception of knowledge.[7]

Here is a version of the familiar argument that the skeptic is a "revisionary epistemologist" who ignores our ordinary conceptions and simply imposes his own standards on them, thus creating the illusion of discovering a weakness in those common conceptions. But I would claim, in granting one the "right to be sure," one does more than acknowledge that one has met the common standards; one implicitly acknowledges the validity of those standards themselves. Thus, the skeptic in questioning those standards is questioning a dimension of the "right to be sure" which common sense acknowledges in the suggestion of certainty that 'sure' connotes. The challenge to common sense is indirect, but it is a challenge all the same.

One might add that Locke's conception of proof is a strange one even if one has doubts about philosophical skepticism. Having evidence for a proposition and knowing of no evidence to the contrary hardly constitute *proof* that the proposition is true. Let us grant that they constitute a good reason for asserting or believing the proposition, but the skeptic need not object to this. And in denying that this constitutes "proof," the skeptic need not be appealing to a special sort of proof, as Locke claims (p. 155). The ordinary notion of proof (though not perhaps the ordinary *use* of 'proof') connotes that what is proved true cannot be false. Yet, one's failure to know of counterveiling evidence leaves open just this possibility. And in any case, with reference to the other-minds problem, Locke admits that there is no proof that one's belief that we can judge of inner states from behavior is correct (*Myself and Others*, p. 49).

4. There is another kind of objection that one could make to skepticism about other minds, even though it is usually directed against the Argument from Analogy, since the latter can be said to accept the epistemological situation as described by the skeptic and then to work out a justification of one's ordinary convictions within that framework. This objection is to be found in Wittgenstein's famous aphorism, "My attitude towards him is an attitude towards a soul. I am not of the *opinion* that he has a soul."[8] As glossed by Malcolm, this means that "when he groans we do not *assume*, even tacitly, that the groaning expresses pain.

We fetch a sedative and try to put him at ease."[9] We *react* to suffering; we do not *believe* in it. Thus, "the thought that behind someone's pain-behavior is the pain itself does not enter into our use of 'He's in pain'" (p. 91). Malcolm claims that one's reaction to another's pain behavior constitutes a "form of life" and that it is a mistake to try to justify such forms. One must accept them.[10]

There is no doubt that when confronted by a person groaning and writhing, one does not adopt a theoretical stance and wonder about abstruse philosophical points about knowledge. One is engaged, and doubts would be out of place. Nevertheless, there is nothing in one's sympathetic reaction that rules out the presence of a judgmental factor in the background. After all, *why* is one sympathetic? On reflection, there is surely the reason that one believes another to be feeling the sensation that one calls pain. Otherwise, one's sympathy would be misplaced; and in fact, the Cartesians who watched animals writhing in ovens obviously had changed their reactions on the basis of their view that animals are complex machines. Malcolm's claim that one must accept one's reaction as ultimate, something for which no reason can be given, seems to me obviously false. It seems strange to me to suggest that in evaluating the elements that are present when one notices a person groaning, one should take the unreflective immediate situation as one's touchstone, rather than the reflective theoretical stance that one might assume after the fact. This is to assume that thinking distorts and that one knows best when one is thinking least. It seems more reasonable to me to read into the practical situation the theoretical commitments that reflection discloses, for I think that the practical man does recognize these commitments as in fact his own. The severing of the theoretical and the practical that is suggested by Malcolm makes the former useless and the latter unintelligible.

One might ask: Just what does one react to in the above case? Malcolm says that it is to the other's "suffering" or to his "groans" or even to "him." But if in one's reactions one does not distinguish between one's suffering and one's groaning, one does distinguish between the *statements* "He is suffering" and "He is groaning." The former mentions the sensation that the latter omits. Then it seems perfectly clear that one's reaction is to the other's pain and yet that one does not observe or see this pain.

The only alternative is that one unreflectively assumes that the behavior is a reliable sign of the sensation and so, in one's reaction, gives no thought to the distinction.[11] The fact that one does not overtly make a distinction in the heat of action shows in no way that this distinction is not present in one's action, all the while providing a rationale for that action.[12]

TWO ANSWERS TO SKEPTICISM ABOUT OTHER MINDS

Both the Argument from Analogy and the Argument from Science represent attempts to answer skepticism about other minds. They do not merely trace genetically the way in which one comes to *believe* in other minds; rather, they *justify* one's claims to *know* about other minds. These ways of answering skepticism differ from the Criteriologist's answer, to be discussed shortly, in that they accept both the skeptic's notion of evidence and the general situation as described by the skeptic, and then try to justify one's convictions about other minds.

It might seem as if one's inability to test the analogy with one's own pain-behavior relation in the case of another's behavior would mean that no argument relying on analogy could answer the skeptic. Such arguments, seemingly, could at most justify *belief* in the *probability* that there are other minds in certain states, and the skeptic can then point out that this account does not capture one's normal sense of certainty about such matters and that anything short of certainty leaves skepticism a real possibility.

Without challenging this point about logical possibility, Stuart Hampshire has argued that, properly understood, doubts about other minds are "testable and empirical." Hampshire says:

> All that is required for testing the validity of any method of factual inference is that each one of us should sometimes be in a position to confront the conclusions of the doubtful method of inference with what is known by him to be true independently of the method of inference in question.[13]

Hampshire then explains that one is in such a position many times, for one can know when others have been wrong about one's feelings or sensations and in the process can check possible error in one's inferences about others. This is described as a "circle of mutual correction."

Presumably, this account of analogy is meant to counter one of its central criticisms, namely, that arguing from only one's own case is too slender a base for an inductive conclusion. And while the testing that Hampshire mentions may not amount to strict verification (let alone logical certainty), still it does mean that one is able to check the reliability of one's statements about others by checking the truth of their statements about oneself. Hampshire grants the solipsist that at most one person can know directly that a given claim about one's feelings is true, but this does not lead to solipsism or to the solipsist's sharp distinction between those problematical statements about other minds and the certain ones about one's own mind. As Hampshire puts it, the relevant analogy is "between different uses of the same methods of argument by different people on different occasions. . . . Each of us is in a position to learn from his own experience that certain methods of inference to conclusions of the kind 'X feels giddy' are generally successful" (pp. 119–20).

The problem with this attempt to make the argument from analogy seem testable and cumulatively more probable has been put definitively by Malcolm.[14] As stated, Hampshire's model presupposes a community of intelligent beings and shows how, once within this community, one might learn more about its details. But since the very existence of other minds is in question and is to be justified by the argument from analogy, this assumption makes Hampshire's case circular. Confirmation or testing of the inferences of others presupposes the very point at issue.

If, on the other hand, one does not take the noises issuing from other bodies to reflect thoughts, one has no reason to think that one's use of those same noises, when one observes the same behavior, is justified. One might conclude that because one's noises represent thoughts, that a similar being's noises also represent thoughts, but that is merely the Argument from Analogy in its classical guise. Similarly, if one argues that taking the noises of others as assertions is the best explanation of their being uttered in the presence of one's behavior, one is basing one's estimate on the behavior that one sees and on its circumstances. In either case, one is limited to knowing one's own case and to judging about others on the basis of behavior that is like one's own behavior when one has a given feeling.

Alternatively, one might try to justify one's assertions about other minds by comparing them to theoretical claims in physical science. One would then stress that psychological attributions have explanatory power and that no alernative explanation is "in the field" as a developed, fruitful theory.[15] These factors do not prove one's theory to be true, but they do establish that nothing else is at the moment capable of "rational belief." It is worth pointing out, and this is not denied by Putnam, that the skeptic does not suggest that his possibilities are capable of rational belief or that it is rational to feel doubt as a result of them. He only insists that they are not to be dismissed and that they cannot be disproved; they may be "silly" (as Putnam says about Plantinga's demon hypothesis), but they are not meaningless or known to be false on that account. Putnam's account is unacceptable to the ordinary-language philosopher precisely because it does not eliminate skepticism as a genuine alternative. Rather, it ignores skepticism as not being "in the field," and while this attitude allows ordinary empirical inquiry to progress, it will not satisfy one who wishes to set limits to the range of meaningful utterances. Therefore, we pass directly to the attempt to cut off skepticism from any claim to being an intelligible alternative to common sense or common language.

THE ARGUMENT FROM CRITERIA

Two kinds of replies to the skeptic about other minds remain as possibilities. One might adopt a form of behaviorism, thus negating the risk in the inference to inner states, which generates skepticism. But while this approach seems to help with justifying one's references to another's mental states, it does so at an unacceptable cost. That cost is the implausibility of analyzing one's own inner states in a behavioristic way. To say that "I am in pain" means that I am behaving or am disposed to behave in certain ways does not accord with one's own experience of pain itself, and in addition, it fails to specify the behavior and dispositions to behave that are to be the pain. This is a failure of principle, for no matter what bill of particulars is conjured up in whatever detail one can imagine, one might still be in pain and yet fail to display the behavior in question. Behaviorism strikes me as a theory that one would adopt only if one saw it as the only way out of a philosophical predicament, a predicament that one was determined to rid oneself of at all costs.

The strength of ordinary-language philosophy is that it has tried to formulate a position that stands between the extremes of behaviorism and empiricism or skepticism. Unlike the former, it accepts the reality of inner states and does not try to reduce them to something else. Unlike the latter, it denies the logical gap between behavior and inner states that makes the inference from the one to the other seem so risky. If behavior can be shown to be a criterion and not merely evidence for inner states, then the presence of certain behavior can guarantee or justify one's assertions about other minds as it cannot if it bears a merely contingent relation to those states. Because the notion of a "criterion" has been used in several different ways, it is difficult to state briefly anything revealing about *the* Argument from Criteria, but one can say that a common goal is to provide one's claims about other minds with a stronger foundation than one finds in the Argument from Analogy, a foundation that will in some sense provide a justification for those claims.

The strongest conception of a criterion would be its identification as both a necessary and sufficient condition of the relevant mental state. This would guarantee both that no mental state could in principle be unknown (either because it was associated with no behavior or because it was associated with a limitless variety of behavior) and that the behavior in question was a guarantee of the presence of the mental state that it signifies. Such a position would provide the clearest and strongest answer to other-mind's skepticism. The correlative problem of this strength is to show that one has, in fact, such criteria for inner states. For example, if one thinks of a complete definition as providing sufficient criteria for the definiendum and if one assumes that no other thing could have the features mentioned without being that thing, then one normally thinks that one has given the *meaning* of the term in question. A "perfect" criterion for X gives the meaning for X.

154

But this option does not seem open to one in the case of pain or other sensations. Even the criteriologist does not claim that the behavioral criteria for sensations constitute the meaning of sensation words. Such a position amounts to behaviorism and is subject to the criticisms mentioned above. To borrow Wittgenstein's terminology (to be explained shortly), the criteria for sensations (and mental states) cannot be as strong as "defining criteria" but neither can they be as weak as "symptoms." Once the criteriologist abandons the strong view of criteria, his problem is to stake out and justify such a middle ground.

If one thinks of criteria as merely sufficient conditions, then one still has a view that is strong enough to provide an answer to skepticism, for there will be numerous cases in which one can justifiably claim to know of another's mental state. The fact that there may be some such states that one cannot know of does not pose a serious theoretical threat to those who oppose skepticism. The problem remains, however, of showing that any bits of behavior, behavioral dispositions, and fully elaborated contexts in fact constitute even sufficient conditions for mental states. One has to show that there are not conceivable exceptions to any proposed criterial set of behavior and conditions; if there continue to be such exceptions, this will not prove the Argument from Criteria to be mistaken, but this argument is bound to suffer the fate rendered Verificationism: at some point, philosophers will conclude that the enterprise is hopeless, that it is the theory, not the specific applications of the theory, that is deficient.

Perhaps the wise course is, then, to abandon any claim that criteria give either necessary or sufficient conditions for mental states. This move has the merit that it avoids criticisms that center on anything like logical connections between behavior and mental states; but in so doing, it seems to abandon what was distinctive about the criteriologist's position. It becomes difficult to distinguish the weaker Argument from Criteria from the Analogy Argument; the mildness of the view seems to open the doors to skepticism once again. There is a dialectical interplay in the criteriological movement between a desire to defeat skepticism once and for all (thus suggesting a hard-line stance on criteria) and a desire to avoid a connection between behavior and mental states that is open to obvious criticism (thus suggesting a soft line on criteria). The problem of the criteriologist is to find a way of saving the virtues of either extreme without taking on their liabilities.

With the above general sketch of problems concerning criteria in mind, let us look at what philosophers have said about criteria. I have divided this section into three parts: (1) "The Strong View about Criteria"; (2) "Criteria and Conceptual Necessity"; and (3) "The Weak View about Criteria." These divisions are arbitrary in that almost any position can be placed in at least two of them; however, I think they represent degrees of emphasis that are worth noting.

THE STRONG VIEW ABOUT CRITERIA

In expounding on Wittgenstein's conception of a criterion, Rogers Albritton once believed that a criterion was both a logically necessary and a sufficient condition of something being the case, although he adds that this does not mean that criteria are rooted in the nature of things.[16] Rather, for Wittgenstein, they are based on conventions (p. 236). And although Malcolm denies that criteria "logically imply" the truth of the relevant proposition (since they hold only in certain circumstances), he does think that the pressure of criteria *settle* the correct application of words to a person (p. 84) and that "it will not *make sense* for one to suppose that another person is not in pain if one's criterion of his being in pain is satisfied."[17] Malcolm adds that one cannot formulate entailment conditions by listing all those circumstances that create exceptions to the criterion that one is in pain (one is pretending, in a play, under hypnosis, etc.) because there is no such finite list of exceptional circumstances. Nonetheless, one can be *certain* that another is in pain under certain circumstances (for genuine doubting has an end), even though one can imagine doubt in the same case (pp. 86 and 88). Malcolm concludes by saying: "The man who doubts the other's pain may be neurotic, may 'lack a sense of reality,' but his reasoning is perfectly sound. . . . His reaction is abnormal but not illogical" (p. 88).

For the moment, let me only remark that it is hard to see how a suggestion that is senseless may nonetheless be entertained with logical probity, or how one can be certain of another's pain if the criterion does not logically guarantee the presence of the sensation and if others might well have doubts in one's own situation. In another place, Malcolm seems to take a more consistently stronger line. There he contrasts effects and accompaniments with criteria, and he claims that if one rejects behavior and circumstances as criteria of mental states in others, "he ought . . . to draw the conclusions that the notion of thinking, fear or pain in others is in an important sense *meaningless*. He has no idea of what would count for it or against it."[18]

Malcolm formulates the following argument against the skeptic and his associate, the analogist. (1) You admit that you have no "criterion of verification" for "He has a pain." (2) Yet, you say that you understand the claim "He has a pain." (3) You understand "He has a pain" to mean that he has the same thing you have when you have a pain. (4) But being unable to "establish" that another has a pain, you are equally unable to "establish" that another has the same thing, and so forth. (5) Being without a criterion of "same," you agree that you do not know what you mean by "same" and, by extension, that you do not know what "He is in pain" means. (6) The conclusion ought to be that skepticism leads to solipsism and that solipsism "destroys itself"; there is no problem of other minds and no need for the Argument from Analogy.[19]

Malcolm's language here strongly suggests the following claim: if one cannot conclusively verify a statement, then one does not know what it means. If as a theoretician, one refuses to grant that any behavior-with-circumstances constitutes proof that one is in pain, one does not understand what one is saying when one says that another is in pain. But Malcolm offers no proof for what seems to be a version of strict Verificationism, and there are numerous well-known objections to that view. If, as Locke points out, Malcolm means only to claim that there must be strict criteria for the proper *use* of sensation words when applied to others, then what he says is harmless to the skeptic. For the skeptic can grant this point and only add that this is a claim about the inner structure of our language game, while his attack is on the validity of the entire structure itself. Why can it not be that one satisfies all the criteria for the proper use of "pain" and yet that the other is not in pain at all?[20]

157

Similarly, one might ask why there can not be evidence where there is no certainty? Why cannot Mill accept certain kinds of behavior as counting in favor of another's being in pain while still holding that nothing can *prove* that this is the case? If one considers the example of scientific theories, in which case there seems to be nothing that could count as a criterion (in Malcolm's sense) of the presence of an atom, then there seems to be little in favor of Malcolm's view. Mill *thought* that he knew what 'same sensation' meant, and he could give a verbal paraphrase of this concept. What, then, is the reason for thinking that he was mistaken? Again looking to science, theoretical entities could not have criteria for their presence or they would not be theoretical entities, that is, entities whose existence is postulated as part of an explanatory scheme.

Aune's defense of Malcolm does not help to make the crucial links of his argument any clearer. For example, why does it follow that if the meaning of "x and y are similar sensations" is determined without reference to behavior, "all facts about behavior, mine or anyone else's, are irrelevant to the truth of any application of the expression"?[21] Perhaps behavior could not *determine* the truth of a claim about another's pain, but why must it be excluded as evidence? Aune's assumption that on the skeptic's view it is "logically impossible to adduce even probabilistic evidence for the truth of such statements" ties meaning and verification together in a way that is highly suspect. If the meaning of a statement is not the same as its mode of verification, then why cannot one determine the meaning of "same pain" in one way and yet verify that concept in another way when other persons are involved?[22]

Once Malcolm's uniting of meaningfulness and certainty is rejected, there is little in his view that needs to bother the skeptic. Perhaps one does stop short of conceivable doubt in one's language games; perhaps one *must* do so if one is to get on with the business of communication. But none of this shows that philosophical doubt is impossible or senseless. At most it shows that *real doubt* must have a limited sphere of operation, but then the skeptic is not trying to interject real doubt into one's life. Therefore, Malcolm's statement that "it is senseless to suppose that he has this concept and yet always doubts" (*Wittgenstein*, p. 89) is either false, if philosophical doubt is involved, or at most irrelevant, if practical doubt is involved.[23]

Even more striking, perhaps, is that Malcolm admits in an offhand way precisely the point that the skeptic wishes to make. He says that such doubts are logical and conceivable but are simply not part of *our* language game. But these are no minor admissions, for all that the skeptic need show is that his alternatives are conceivable in order to make his point. And Malcolm's references to senselessness reveal, I think, a recognition that a tougher line must be taken against the skeptic. Yet the tougher line can be made plausible, if that much, by reference to the private-language argument, which we shall discuss in the next chapter.[24]

Malcolm's position gains support from a related attempt to show that there is a fundamental incoherence in the very statement of the Argument from Analogy. D. C. Long poses a dilemma for the analogy theorist:

> Either one believes that there are only material objects in the world and fails, through some defect of mind or training, even to have the concept of a person, or one has that concept and realizes that there are people, one of them being oneself. There is no middle position that can be intelligibly articulated.[25]

Long's grounds for the strong claim appearing in the last sentence are that there is no "gap" between the concept of a "living human body" and the concept of the body of a person: "Where a living human body is, there is also a person—necessarily" (p. 329). In identifying something as one, we necessarily identify it as the other. Furthermore, Long argues, any attempt to find a neutral, noncommittal word for 'body', one that will carry no connotation of its association with personhood, will inevitably result in a verifiable demarcation between the X in question and a person. For example, the term 'figure' will cover corpses, distant objects, dummies, and so forth, and these are readily distinguishable from persons (p. 327). They are also of no interest to the skeptic. The dilemma then is this: Any "thing" that is close enough to the body of a person to make skepticism interesting turns out to be identical with the body of a person; any "thing" different enough from such a body to allow of an identifiable gap between them is not in principle beyond ordinary empirical methods of testing that difference.

We will consider this approach to other-mind's skepticism in greater detail in the next section of this chapter. Let me say here that the obvious reply is that Long begs the question with the skeptic in insisting on the identity of 'living human body' and 'body of a person'. Long rejects this charge on the grounds that until the distinction is made clear there is no question before one to beg, but this reply is not convincing (pp. 326–27). Granted, anything that one would be willing to *call* a living human body one would also call the body of a person; those phrases are so used normally that one does not separate them and would not know how to understand the suggestion that they be separated. But as long as one admits a gap between mental and physical, the above is no reason for denying that one cannot come to recognize the added inference that is present in 'person's body' as contrasted with 'living body'. The former connotes the added mental dimension that the latter does not, and if one overlooks this dimension in one's daily life, there is no reason that the philosopher cannot call it to one's attention.

The skeptic could then state his starting point as follows: Is what one *calls* 'body of a person' in fact connected with those mental states that are the inner side of a person? Just because one so identifies a thing before one, it does not follow that one must on reflection accept the commitments that are implicit in that identification. Therefore, one can perfectly well have the concept of a person and know to what kinds of things this concept is normally thought to apply, and nevertheless doubt that one can be certain that one's identification is correct. Whether there is a problem in knowing that a "thing" is a fit subject for personhood depends on whether one is adopting an ordinary stance or a skeptical one, but to suggest that there is an intrinsic barrier to picking out "human bodies that *may or may not be the bodies of persons*" (p. 325) is to simply ignore the validity of the sceptical viewpoint.[26]

P. F. Strawson's famous attack on skepticism can be interpreted either as a defense of what I have called the "strong" sense of criteria or as a defense of the "weak" sense of criteria. For the present I shall take it in the former sense and shall look at four interconnected notions in his analysis: (1) The notion of a logically adequate criterion; (2) the notion that personhood is a primitive notion; (3) the presuppositions of ascription; and (4) the incoherence of skepticism.

1. If taken in its strong sense, a logically adequate criterion would be one whose presence logically entails the presence of the thing signified. And while one need not accept Ayer's claim that this could not be the case unless the "mental state" as well as the behavior were physical, the objections to this notion are the same as those applied to Malcolm's claims about criteria.[27] The difficulties in making this notion a clear and acceptable one are seen in Strawson's discussion of depression. According to Strawson, "X's depression *is* something, one and the same thing, which is felt, but not observed, by X, and observed, but not felt, by others than X."[28] This would make it intelligible that behavior (Strawson's M-predicates) is not merely a "sign" but a logically adequate criterion of depression qua feeling (Strawson's P-predicates). For the concept of depression covers both experiential and behavioral aspects; what I see in another *is* (part of) his depression.[29] Thus, "the concept of depression spans the place where one wants to drive it in" (p. 108).

However, on reflection, things are not as clear as they might at first seem. To be sure, in Strawson's view, behavior is not merely a sign of a depressed feeling. But how does this fact help one to be certain that the complex thing called depression is present merely because one observes that one of its parts or aspects is present? Perhaps one does not have depression without both, but cannot one have a single part without the other?

The case of depression seems particularly favorable to Strawson, I suggest, for the following reason. One can grant that a person may *be* depressed without *feeling* depressed; if one has any feelings, one may not notice them. In such cases, one can be certain that another is depressed on the basis of his behavior. This may lead one to think that one can be certain of the feeling component of depression on the basis of behavior. But the certainty in the first case is not transferable to the second case. If one takes the case of pain and pain behavior, one sees that the latter is not part of the concept of the former at all. And it is

161

impossible for me to understand what one might mean by saying that the feeling and the behavior are one and the same thing. In this case, the pain clearly *is* the feeling, however it may be connected to its expression. As C. W. K. Mundle points out, " 'John *is* depressed' does not, surely, entail 'John *feels* depressed'."[30]

2. In Strawsonian ontology there are entities—namely, persons—to whom both behavioral and psychological predicates may be properly applied, whereas in Cartesian ontology there are no such entities. This means, for Strawson, that 'person' is a primitive notion in that it is not a composite of entities each of which is properly characterized by only one of the kind of predicates mentioned above.[31]

Insofar as Strawson's case for the primitiveness of persons rests on his requirements for ascription, we shall wait until point three to discuss it (p. 102). For the moment, I shall remark only (a) that even if persons are primitive, it does not follow that in particular cases of ascribing P-predicates one is better off than if they were not, and (b) that the idea of one thing having two such diverse characteristics (Spinoza's substance in miniature) is one that is logically difficult and cannot be assumed as being obviously without problems. Merely to give the strange thing a name is to label, not solve, a problem.

A similar point about persons is made by John Cook in a recent analysis of Wittgenstein. He interprets the latter's message to be that

> the philosophical idea of a 'senseless body' must be dropped. But in that case we must also reject the idea that when we look at another person we see only a 'body', i.e., something which is no more a possible subject of pain or thinking than a stone would be. And finally, in rejecting *that* idea, we eliminate the only grounds of scepticism with regard to other 'minds' and in this way eliminate, too, the only source of the plausibility of behaviourism.[32]

Wittgenstein is said to want to restore 'human being' to is usual place in our language game, to "make the concept of *human beings* primary in any account of mental predicates" (p. 128). And this is said not to be question-begging because one has only to accept the common language game (p. 144). This is enough, since skepticism arises only through a false account of our language game.

But the question-begging and the mistake enters in the assumption that all that philosophers should be doing is presenting our language game and that skepticism arises from a mistaken conception of what it is. Skeptics need not assume that children see others as "bodies," for they do not present their ideas as our natural ones, ones with which we begin and operate. Therefore, even if 'human being' is a primitive notion in our language game, this does not show that the philosopher must accept it as primitive. His task seems to me, contrary to Wittgenstein, to evaluate that scheme and to accept or reject its elements according to whether they seem defensible or not. If one accepts 'human being' at face value, then skepticism cannot obtain a foothold but why need one do that?

3. Strawson mentions what he calls "a very central thought":

> It is a necessary condition of one's ascribing states of
> consciousness, experiences, to oneself, in the way one
> does, that one should also ascribe them, or be prepared
> to ascribe them, to others who are not oneself.[33]

For Strawson, this means both that the meaning of P-predicates ascribed to others is not different from those ascribed to oneself merely because one ascription is not done by observation and the other is done by observation of behavior *and* that self-ascription must be understood on the model of other-ascription, not vice versa. And since one cannot ascribe P-predicates to others without being able to identify *them*, one must be treating them as Strawsonian persons and behavior as a logically adequate criterion of those P-predicates. One must then ascribe these predicates to oneself qua person not qua Cartesian ego. The result is that the problem of other minds is incoherent, for it presupposes the very knowledge that it then calls into question. The skeptic has failed to notice that in starting with self-ascription, one begins with the notion "me" or "mine," which makes sense only if one can distinguish subjects of experience from one another. And this cannot be explained except by beginning with the concept of person as a primitive notion.

If, as Strawson asserts in a footnote (p. 99 n.1), this is the purely logical point that a predicate must in principle be applicable to more than one case, I do not see that the skeptic need bother with it. For, as Strawson also says, this affirmation need not be true, and truth is all that concerns the skeptic. It seems to me that the skeptic might well adopt the following scenario. It is true that in order to come to a recognition of what I am (a Cartesian ego), and in order to realize that there is a problem about one's knowledge of other minds, one must begin by learning other-ascription on the basis of behavior and only slowly come to the stage of self-ascription.[34] But what I am prepared to do, even when required by the logic of the situation to do so, and what is done truly are two distinct things. Strawson has not shown that other-ascriptions cannot be systematically mistaken; yet, only this will defeat the skeptic.[35]

Otherwise, Strawson's remarks amount to an investigation of the logical structure of our conceptual scheme, and since the skeptic wants to question the scheme as a whole, he can allow Strawson any logical requirements within the structure. As Ayer points out, it is not enough to show that self-ascription is based on other-ascription; one must in addition show that when self-ascription has been achieved, it cannot be detached from its base and used as a weapon to criticize the truth of other-ascription. That is, although the notion of another person as a fit subject for both M- and P-predicates be more logically primitive than the act of self-ascription, must the entity to which one self-ascribes be understood on the model of another person? Why cannot one discover in self-ascription the real self to whom P-predicates alone are applicable, and then consider one's concept of a person to be questionable and to conceal philosophical problems?[36]

4. Perhaps Strawson's strongest point against skepticism is a claim that he feels arises out of the above considerations. His reasoning is hard to follow on this point, but I will attempt to reconstruct it. (a) Our conceptual scheme is one in which persons are primitive; (b) a condition of such a scheme is that we unhesitatingly accept behavior as a logically adequate criterion for the ascription of P-predicates to others; (c) without point b we could not ascribe states of consciousness at all. (d) The skeptic accepts our conceptual scheme, and his doubts make sense only within it. (e) At the same time, he rejects b and thus the con-

ceptual scheme that it makes possible. (f) There is then an internal defect in skepticism which can be stated in different ways: either (1) the skeptic fails to realize that in rejecting our conceptual scheme he is rejecting the framework within which his doubts make sense, or (2) in accepting d he implicitly accepts b, and the skeptic's doubts cannot arise in this framework. (g) The alternative suggestion that one should not have the conceptual scheme that one has is absurd because "the whole process of reasoning only starts because the scheme is as it is; and we cannot change it even if we would."[37]

Let us grant Strawson points a–c and assume that c explains the sense in which skeptical doubt needs our conceptual scheme. Only if one can ascribe P-predicates at all, can one doubt that ascription; and the former requires our conceptual scheme. But this does not mean that the skeptic must accept the preconditions of the system within which his doubts arise. It does not mean that he is inconsistent in calling into question this conceptual scheme, even if his doubts could not have arisen without it. Nor does it mean that he accepts the conceptual scheme in a way that prevents skepticism from arising. Recall that his doubts are not real doubts within that scheme but are philosophical doubts about the ultimate justification of the scheme as a whole. Qua human being, the skeptic really does accept our conceptual scheme; qua philosopher, he calls its foundation into question. Thus the certainty and the doubt are not in conflict, and the skeptic is absolved of inconsistency. Turning on what nurtures one may be bad manners, but it is possible all the same. (The point is similar to the one made about self-ascription above.)

Point g involves an interesting distortion of the skeptic's position. The skeptic does not assert that we should not have the conceptual scheme that we have. He is not suggesting that we change the conceptual scheme that we have. He *is* suggesting that there are alternative schemes which challenge the one that we have and which, thereby, undercut our certainty about the truth of our scheme. Does Strawson have an argument to show that *this* is a mistaken claim? The answer here must be no, because Strawson has undertaken what he calls descriptive metaphysics, the discovery of the "structure of our thought about the world" (p. 9). Once within this structure, one can say of alter-

165

ternatives only what Strawson says of the revisionary metaphysician: he is someone "with whom we do not wish to quarrel, but whom we do not need to follow" (p. 36). And Strawson's remarks about our conceptual scheme tend to support this stance. For example, he says that there is nothing "inevitable" in a conceptual scheme that treats persons as members of a class of natural, moving objects, even for beings "not utterly unlike ourselves" (p. 113).

Still, other remarks suggest another interpretation. Our conceptual scheme—or at least its core—has no history (p. 10); it does not seem to be a contingent matter that empirical reality forms a single spatiotemporal system (p. 29); any ontology containing particulars must have a "demonstrative element in identifying thought about particulars" (p. 119). And his critique of skepticism at points suggests that it does not pose a genuine alternative to our conceptual scheme. His remark that "an ontology which could be taken seriously only by God is not to count as a possible ontology" (p. 126) also suggests a limitation on the meaningful alternatives to our scheme. In any case, these latter hints, even if representative of a strain in Strawson's thinking, do not constitute more than a gesture in the direction of formulating a Kantian Argument from Possible Experience.

CRITERIA AND CONCEPTUAL NECESSITY

If one were convinced that the strong view of criteria fails, that is, that in no particular case can one be certain of the presence of a mental state because of what one observes about behavior and circumstances, it might seem as if the only alternative would be to opt for a contingent connection between the two. However, an interesting suggestion of an intermediary position has been made.

One might hold only that it is *generally* true that when one behaves in a certain way, and the circumstances are "right," one is in pain.[38] One finds such a principle attributed to Wittgenstein by Albritton when he says, "That a man behaves in a certain manner, under certain circumstances, can entail that he *almost certainly* has a toothache."[39] And Shoemaker has argued that to imagine that it might be the rule that one's mental states were not connected to one's behavior in the usual way is "equivalent to the claim that one could *establish* that this had occurred in one's own case,"[40] and that there is nothing public that could be taken to show this. One's memory reports that this was so would have to be considered as dreams, not genuine memories.[41]

The first difficulty with this view lies in understanding the conditional nature of the necessary truth that is its essence. Why, when one specifies that the condition must be "right" (thus ruling out the possibility of *any* exceptional circumstances that might justify an exception), can one only be certain that the connection between mental states and behavior will hold in the majority of cases? If one has abandoned the view that behavior, plus the "right" circumstances, *entails* a given mental state, how can one justify the certainty that one is correct for any percentage of the time? There seems to be no way of justifying this much knowledge without endorsing the entailment view.

Second, it is worth noting that adherence to this principle does not amount to very much. One might well claim that most of the behavior that one has observed was an exception to the principle and still claim that this must not be the case in the majority of instances. That is, the principle would not help one to justify one's belief that in *this* case one can know that X is in pain. Similarly, one can doubt the truth of the principle without feeling any differently about most of the cases in one's experience from what one normally does. Kantian assurances that nature is law-governed do not guarantee the scientist that he will be able to master nature, which leaves him in at least the same practical situation as he was with Hume's view; and general assurances about behavior and mental states do not reduce the possibility of skepticism about mental states in every case that one encounters.

Third, there is no obvious contradiction in imagining that slowly, more and more people come to wonder about their certainty regarding mental states (perhaps under the influence of a Cartesian prophet), until it is reasonable to say that doubt is now the rule in the majority of cases. If this happened to a single person, one might well think that he did not understand our conceptual scheme, but if it attains a general frequency, a revision of our priorities may be necessary. Certainly, there is no obvious necessity in the general claim, and it is worth noting that Shoemaker has now abandoned it. He still insists that it is a necessary truth that "if someone is in mental state M, then (normally, *ceteris paribus*, etc.) he will behave in way B."[42] But obviously, this claim will not help to thwart the skeptic, and I do not see the need for it either. Perhaps it is necessary that one must *take some* behavior to be typical of pain if one is to learn how to ascribe 'pain', but that is a long way from *knowing* that, in fact, pain is so connected with behavior. Once again, how one must act if one is to learn that a language does not guarantee the truth of the assumptions reflected in that action.

Last, Shoemaker's claim that imagining that the unusual association of sensation and behavior becomes the rule in one's own case is the same thing as establishing that this occurs in one's own case is a form of Verificationism. After all, one might doubt the general principle without doubting that the usual situation obtains in one's own case; Shoemaker's formulation is unfairly favorable to his position. And even in one's own case, one can imagine pain having a bewildering variety of expressions, or expressions that one would not identify as pain behavior; and one might not have a clue as to how one might determine that this was so. But unless one can show that meaning depends on the possibility of verification, there is nothing troublesome about untestable possibilities. Recall that the skeptic need only insist on the general possibility of a break in pain and in pain behavior; he leaves to someone else the determination of how one might know that this is in fact the case.[43] None of this seems to me to touch the question of the truth of our procedures nor to justify Shoemaker's claim that "it cannot be the case that all relationships between psychological states and physical states are contingent" (p. 170).

THE WEAK VIEW ABOUT CRITERIA

There is a view about criteria that is currently in favor and that has been expressed in two related versions. According to the first version, if one correctly interprets Wittgenstein or Strawson, one will find a view about criteria in their works that avoids the overly strong claims investigated above and yet provides a sufficient answer to the skeptic. According to the second version, no matter what Wittgenstein and Strawson meant, the point that they wish to make can be stated without resting on questionable necessities. Both versions seem to agree that the search for necessities is unnecessary and smacks too much of a traditional reply to skepticism, one that is on the skeptic's own ground.

One statement of the first version is found in Albritton's Postscript to his article on Wittgenstein. There Albritton holds that behavior may be a criterion of mental states, without assuming that any proposition linking the two is anything but contingent (*Wittgenstein*, p. 247). Neither need it be possible to state anything about specific behavior that "entails" the existence of a mental state, makes it "warrantably describable" that one is in a given mental state, "or anything whatever of interest" about a mental state (p. 249). Behavior-as-criterion is a matter of definition or convention; it may change or cease entirely, and yet still be a criterion now.

A glance at the work of current writers reveals the following interpretation of the notion of a criterion.[44] (1) Criteria are linguistic conventions (Hacker, p. 286; Canfield, p. 78). (2) They justify one in using a word or in saying that another is in a certain mental state (Hacker, p. 292; Saunders, p. 111; Locke, p. 152. (3) Criteria do not entail anything (Hacker, p. 288; Canfield, p. 82; Saunders, p. 96). (4) Criteria may shift (Hacker, p. 294; Canfield, p. 74). (5) They are made for normal conditions (Hacker, p. 295), and these background conditions are not known by language users (Canfield, p. 78). (6) Criteria make it reasonable to think certain things in our language (Saunders, p. 119), and they bring "practical certainty" (Saunders, p. 97). (7) Criteria are not decisive evidence (Hacker, p. 297), and they leave open the logical possibility that the claims that one based on them may be false (Saunders, p. 119).[45]

The authors in question hold that their interpretations of 'criterion' still provide an answer to the skeptic. For Locke, once one accepts the claim that "pain-behavior, or something of the sort, must justify us in saying that another feels a pain" (p. 159), one must accept that "it is impossible to modify our talk about pains in the way that the sceptic suggests" (p. 157). His conclusion is that although one cannot prove that one's beliefs about the inner states of others are true, one can call those beliefs "knowledge," since one agrees on the necessarily evidential character of criteria (p. 68). For Saunders, the logical possibility of error in our claims about the mental states of others does not justify doubt about those states (p. 120) or doubt that one has knowledge. And Hacker claims that Wittgenstein's concept of criteria forces the skeptic to "give ground" (p. 304), for such a conception shows that "doubt presupposes the possibility of certainty." Hacker elucidates this principle as follows:

> The sceptic can only make the notion of doubting whether 'p' is true intelligible by rendering an account of the sense of 'p'. And such an account can no longer be offered in terms of the truth conditions of 'p' but must be given by specifying the criteria which would justify the assertion of 'p' and which, in the absence of specific grounds for doubting, would justify one in asserting 'p' with certainty. [P. 304]

Despite these brave pronouncements, it seems to me that the weak view about criteria is impotent against skepticism. In trying to find an acceptable view of criteria, criteriologists have so diluted the notion that it no longer stands for anything with which the skeptic need quarrel. He can perfectly well grant that certain judgments are reasonable in our language, that they are justified or warranted; for what is so characterized within our conceptual scheme may fall short of guaranteeing truth when our conceptual scheme itself is questioned. And in fact, the current view admits that even within this scheme, criteria are not decisive evidence and do not entail anything. Once criteria are thought of as conventional, they can illustrate only the way that we have chosen to speak; they cannot guarantee the truth of those ways, because conventions are not true or false, and they always have conceivable alternatives. If Albritton and Canfield are right, it is hard to see how the notion of criteria can have any philosophical force; it really becomes merely descriptive of the way we speak, and by itself, this says nothing that opposes skepticism.

If one wishes to call "knowledge" the beliefs about other minds that one has based on criteria thus conceived, one should by all means do so. Yet, this will in no way be a knowledge that will guarantee the truth of what is believed. "Knowledge" will amount to "necessarily agreed upon and justified beliefs," and the skeptic need only note that systematic error remains a possibility. Similarly, one might say to Saunders that the logical possibility of error does not justify real doubt but that it does justify philosophical doubt, that it does not allow one to say that one's beliefs are unjustified by normal standards but that it does allow one to say that normal justification does not amount to final justification. Skepticism need in no way cross swords with "justified belief," and it need not "repudiate" our normal criteria for other minds *as we normally use them.*

Hacker's defense of the philosophical force of criteria is more subtle, but it, too, falls short. A full discussion of the claim that "the sense of a sentence or expression is given by specifying the rules for its use" (p. 291) cannot be undertaken here. However, one can say that if this doctrine means that the meaning of an expression is determined by "the criteria justifying the application or assertion of the sentence in question," it faces all the well-known objections to the Verifiability Theory of Meaning. When one says "John is in pain," one does not mean anything other than what one says; nothing about how one might determine that this is the case enters into one's meaning. How does one know this? One knows it because one knows that one's use of such a sentence is an attempt to assert something about the world, and one knows this with enough assurance that if one is told that one must be saying something about "possible cognition," one knows that this claim is false. No theory can be more certain than one's sense of what one means when one utters perfectly ordinary sentences. The Meaning-as-Use Doctrine cannot support one's claims about other minds, for it is more implausible than they are.

Richard Rorty presents what I have called the second version of the weak view about criteria. He analyzes the argument for the strong line about criteria (that it does not make sense to suppose that certain evidence occurs in the absence of its "correlate") into the claims that probable knowledge must rest on certain knowledge and that the latter must be found in "rules of language," since it cannot arise from experience.[46] What if one now thinks of criteria as expressing principles that are established noncorrelationally but that at the same time are not necessary? They make correlation possible by making identification of the item in question possible (p. 320). (Rorty finds this to be the "cash value" of Strawson's "logically adequate criteria.") And,

Rorty adds, criteria are relative; they always refer to "somebody's procedure at a given time" (p. 321). As he says, "For any person at any time, identification of the presence or behavior of an unobservable entity will be by reference to some principle which states that such-and-such is evidence for that unobservable" (p. 321).

One result of this is that criteria do not establish the existence of their object with certainty. Probability is the most that one can expect here. One would then have a "third thing" called "noncorrelationally established relationships," which can answer the skeptic without claiming to possess strict conceptual necessity.

Rorty, turning Quinean, then argues that one ought to drop the notion of criteria altogether, since the need for criteria arises out of a division between "conceptually necessary" and "empirically contingent" which is no longer viable. And interestingly, Strawson's view of criteria can be adopted to Quineanism by simply sticking to the point that one cannot know of one's own inner episodes without envisaging that others have such episodes. One need make no reference to necessary connections between behavior and inner states in order to defend this point; one need only show that the identification of one's own inner states rests on a battery of concepts which cannot be made sense of unless one can ascribe, via behavior, such states to others. One would then have an answer to the skeptic that would rely on nothing but Humean regularities.

I see three difficulties in Rorty's view. First, his initial view of criteria is not strong enough to worry the skeptic. If criteria can change and if they do not bring certainty with them, then the way that we talk now is compatible with the falsity of what we say, and this is all that the skeptic needs. Perhaps one could not begin to discuss unobservables without taking something as a criterion in Rorty's sense of that term, but nothing follows about the truth of that necessary start from that fact. Second, similar remarks hold about Rorty's Quinean rethinking of criteria. If it is nonscientific or unintelligible to claim more than a Humean regularity between behavior and mental state, then one cannot rule out the skeptical possibility that what one considers to be probabilities, because of the coherence and predictive power of one's theories, are, in fact, falsities. And for all one knows, what is truth one moment may be error the next. This approach ignores the skeptic, rather than answering him or showing his position to be incoherent.

Third, it is not at all clear to me that Rorty is in fact limiting himself to Humean regularities. For example, his Strawsonian principle making identification and knowledge of one's own states dependent on that of others is surely not meant to be an empirical generalization. It tells one what *must* be the case, thus unearthing the error of the skeptic once and for all. The principle claims necessity, a necessity that has no place in Rorty's scheme.[47] Rorty seems to be in the same position that Positivists were in when they tried to eliminate synthetic a priori principles by means of their own preferred synthetic a priori principles. His view depends for its philosophic relevance on principles that smack of the very necessities that the view regards as mistakes. If these principles are said not to be different in kind from empirical, lawlike generalizations, then they cannot answer the skeptic; and one would be interested in knowing if they have been arrived at by accepted empirical means and if their possible falsification is envisaged. If no one had ever thought of philosophy, then one might do without its necessities, but getting rid of it (in its traditional guise) requires the very kind of activity and principles that the empiricist deplores.

8

Private Languages

We come now to philosophical doubts that are more extreme than those we have considered heretofore. The problem of one's knowledge of other minds, for example, involved no questions about one's ability to observe another's behavior. Perceptual contact with the world of physical objects was assumed as unproblematic, and doubts arose only after one left this secure base. In the present chapter, however, we are concerned with doubts that call this ground-floor certainty into question. Arguments are brought forward to show that one's normal perceptual assurance that one sees physical objects, and thereby knows of their existence and character, is unjustified, not to say unjustifiable. Intermediaries appear between perceiver and object-thought-to-be-perceived; they become the immediate objects of perception; and one is faced with demon hypotheses which make physical objects seem to be remote and ghostly entities that have nothing to do with what one sees and that might come and go without one's ever noticing this fact. Skepticism seems to be moving inexorably in the direction of solipsism.

In response to this final detachment of the self from the public world, ordinary-language philosophers have looked to Wittgenstein for a definitive reply. The attack on the possibility of a private language represents an attempt to uncover a fundamental incoherence which underlies apparent skeptical possibilities about the external world but which is also deeply involved in doubts about other minds.

Consider the latter problem. Strawson's principle, that self-ascription of P-predicates logically presupposes the ability and/or readiness to ascribe P-predicates to others, neatly reverses the order of logical dependence which the skeptic draws on in questioning one's knowledge of other minds. This principle means that there is a hidden incoherence in the (apparently plausible) idea that one's words have the meaning they have because they refer to inner, hidden, private states (at least this is supposed to hold for sensations and all "given" qualities). One knows what pain or red is because of the nonsharable experiences that one has. Once one begins with self-predication in this way, it is obvious that there is a problem of knowing that others use these words with the same meaning as one does and with being sure that one is communicating one's meaning to another when one uses one's privately, ostensively defined words. In fact, it seems as if there is no hope at all that any person can ever know what another is saying. Strawson and Wittgenstein both find the error of this position to lie in starting with one's own case and in the implied detachment of the meaning of words from the natural behavior that one ordinarily believes expresses certain states and in terms of which one learns when it is proper to say that someone is in pain, or sees red, or whatever.

In the *Philosophical Investigations*, Wittgenstein develops in greater detail the attack on the notion of a private language. Although he does not identify whose view he is attacking and does not even claim that any philosopher explicitly supported the idea of a private language, he implies that Cartesian skepticism rests ultimately on such a notion.[1] His general strategy is to show that a language that is private in a way that will give aid and comfort to the skeptic will not have the necessary prerequisites to be a language. But the skeptic needs words to have meaning to himself if he is to generate doubts about knowing whether these words with these meanings apply to others. The result is that Wittgenstein hopes to take away the starting point from the skeptic and, thereby, to return one to his natural language in which he has no trouble communicating about his own sensations to others, knowing of other's sensations, and the like. I think that it is not overstating the case if one says that this is a pivotal argument in the case against skepticism; if it fails, there is little hope that skepticism can be silenced by the methods available to the ordinary-language philosopher.

One essential ingredient in the generation of skepticism is the notion of a prelinguistic recognition of the data that are given to one in sensory awareness. One is thought to know what these qualities are in one's unmediated experience of them; one then gives them names for convenience: for example, communication or whatever. But with this starting point, the skeptic has the very gap (between one's inner experience and what one or others say) that he needs in order to make ordinary communication seem chancy and doubtful, if not downright impossible. But if it could be shown that recognition is language dependent, that the process of naming requires the very background conditions that the skeptic later wants to doubt, then the starting point of skepticism would be exposed as no starting point at all. The skeptic would have ignored what it takes for something to be a language or for someone to learn a language, and yet he uses, and needs to use, the notion of a language in ways that contradict this necessary background.

As we shall see, the Argument against the Possibility of a Private Language does not prove that there are in fact other persons with whom one does in fact communicate. All that it is designed to do is to show that because language use presupposes the *possibility* of independent checks on that use, words do not acquire their meanings from reference to inner particulars apart from any reference to what is publicly observable. Therefore, if even a Robinson Crusoe evolves a language, this very fact guarantees that what he says could be understood by a Man Friday who might happen by. In turn, this means that Crusoe, having read Descartes, could not then consistently come to doubt the reality of an interpersonal world. He could not so much as recognize his own sensations if he were not already committed to the common arena of material things in space and time.

Consider for a moment a position that attempted to mediate between the skeptic and the ordinary-language philosopher. To the former, C. I. Lewis grants that there is a given that is "ineffable, always . . . which remains untouched and unaltered, however it is construed by thought."[2] Such *qualia*, as he calls them, are "repeatable in experience and intrinsically recognizable" although they "have no names" (p. 61). In addition, he allows that one's entire sensuous spectrum might be the reverse of another's, but that this could never be known if there were no impairment in one's powers of discrimination (p. 75). On the other hand, he grants to the ordinary-language philosopher that these possibilities, as well as the impossibility of ever conveying in language the immediate feelings of the given, can safely be ignored. For

> idiosyncrasy of intuition need not make any difference, except in the esthetic quality of the experience of one as compared with that of another. . . . These, then, are the only practical and applicable criteria of common knowledge; that we should share common definitions of the terms we use, and that we should apply these terms identically to what is presented. [Pp. 75–76]

And of course, Lewis's claim that *qualia per se* never enter into one's language games is a congenial thought to the antiskeptic (see p. 62). The problem with this compromise (my characterization) is that it fails to please either extreme. The skeptic will not understand why, if there is a prelinguistic awareness of the given, and why, if one's use of concepts is characterized as *"an interpretation put upon my succession of sensory experience"* (p. 63), mere agreement in one's use of words is enough to guarantee knowledge. Surely, he will urge, what Lewis describes is a case in which one cannot know that one is failing to understand another and in which it does not hurt to fail; but it does not follow that one is even understanding another. One may be under an undetectable illusion that one understands another, but an illusion is no less an illusion because one remains blissfully ignorant of it. The strange thing is that, for Lewis, there is a given *within* one's experience, and yet it seems impotent, having no impact on one's communication or judgment. This in the face of what seems obvious: 'red' for one connotes the anticipated succession of *these qualia*, and if the *qualia* whose anticipated succession another calls 'red' are different, then the two fail to mean the same thing by 'red'.

The ordinary-language philosopher will find Lewis equally unsatisfactory. If *qualia* be ineffable, then he will want to dismiss them as needless excess baggage. As Wittgenstein said, "Always get rid of the idea of the private object in this way: assume that it constantly changes, but that you do not notice the change because your memory constantly deceives you" (*PI*, p. 207). In addition, he will find Lewis's reference to objects and other persons mystifying. If one's concepts are predictions of successions of *qualia*, then they refer to nothing public; all language is radically private, and talk of verification by oneself and others is gratuitous. Lewis does not acknowledge the conceptual dependence of talk about one's sensations on talk about public objects. If these two changes were implemented, then Lewis could be seen as a comrade in the fight against skepticism.

I have divided this subject into two basic parts. In this chapter I shall examine the Private-Language Argument. In the next chapter I shall consider three ways in which ordinary-language philosophers have tried to combat skepticism about the existence of the external world: (1) the Transcendental Approach; (2) the Elimination of Sensations and the Argument from Illusion; and (3) the Defusing of Science.

The Private-Language Argument begins with a feeling that it is strange to think of sensations as "essentially private." For

> could it be that the child who comes crying with a bumped head and who screams when it is touched is giving his peculiar expression to an itching scalp? . . . No, the idea of the private object is not one that turns up in our common thought and practice; it turns up only in those odd moments when we are under the influence of a false grammatical analogy.[3]

But even if one accepts that there is something strange in thinking of another's sensation as being detached from any natural expression, it is not so obviously strange to think of one's own sensations as being thus detached. It seems as if reference to one's own sensations is reference to a private mental state, without a commitment to any behavior that might result from it. In self-ascription, one seems to mean the inner state and nothing more. And the skeptic's case against knowledge of another's sensation is built on the assumption that one does know one's own sensations in a direct, unquestionable way.

To protect his flank, the ordinary-language philosopher has taken a bold step against this apparent reference to essentially private objects. He simply denies that they constitute assertions at all. Here he differs from Strawson, who treats self-ascription as genuine ascription, even though it occurs without the use of criteria:

> Instead of denying that self-ascribed states of conscious-ness are really ascribed at all, it is more in harmony with our actual ways of talking to say this: that, for each user of language, there is just one person in ascribing to whom states of consciousness he does not need to use the criteria of the observed behaviour of that person, though he does not necessarily not do so; and that person is himself.[4]

For the Wittgensteinian the difficulty with avowals is that (1) they do not employ noninductive grounds (i.e., criteria) for their use, and (2) they seem to exclude the possibility of doubt and, hence, of certainty (a form of the Argument from Polar Contrasts). Avowals are then construed as new pain behavior which grows out of natural pain behavior (*PI*, p. 244). They are not descriptions and do not "mean" the natural pain behavior that they replace, but they do stand for that behavior. Ironically, Malcolm connects this idea with Wittgenstein's desire not to ad-vance theories.[5] To say that one knows that one is in pain is then to say only that it makes no sense to doubt that one is in pain (*PI*, p. 247); skeptics go wrong when they read knowledge into this inability to doubt, and that, in turn, rests on their conviction that "I am in pain" is a genuine assertion. They mistake a gram-matical remark for an empirical one.

According to Cook, "I know I am in pain" can be under-stood as an expression of exasperation but not as an expression of certainty.[6] The reason for this is that for "I know" to express certainty, it must be "intelligible for someone to suppose that the speaker is not, in the particular instance, in as good a position as one could want for correctly answering a certain question or making a certain statement" (p. 291). Thus, the difference be-tween prefacing statements about objective facts with "I know" and doing so with verbal reports of sensations is that while it is senseless in the latter cases to add "I know" to my assertion, (1) it is never senseless for someone else to say that I know such and such, and (2) when asked, I may sensibly answer that I know. It is never the case that adding "I know" to a verbal expression of sensation can be understood as an expression of certainty.

This seems to be a clear case of a view seeming plausible to someone only because it forms a necessary link in a more-general position that one wishes to defend. As Ayer points out, there is no need for one to add "I know" to assertions about one's sensations, for everyone assumes that the subject does know what he claims to be the case. But this does not mean that such an addition is senseless or without justification.[7] And since one can lie about one's sensations, why cannot one use the very Polar Contrast Argument used by the Wittgensteinian to say that where lying is possible, so must truth-telling be possible? Certainly, one ordinarily would be willing to say that one knows when one is in pain; thus the fact that one does not say so seems to be a rather uninteresting remark about the frequency of word usage.

In fact, Malcolm and Wittgenstein here are clearly revisionary metaphysicians for a moment; they forget their allegiance to description and to restoration of our ordinary attitudes in order to do away with skepticism once and for all. This seems to be the obvious explanation for such moves as (1) thinking that because there are analogies between saying that one is in pain, on the one hand, and natural expressions of pain, on the other, one can be assimilated to the other, and (2) arguing that because self-ascriptions lack criteria, they must not be genuine ascriptions. In the latter case the Strawsonian move seems to be much in accord with revealing the logical grammar of our speech. Since one does take self-ascriptions as genuine, there must be such a things as criterionless assertions.

Hacker has demonstrated that there are a host of important disanalogies between avowals and natural pain expression (pp. 266–68). For example, past-tense assertions of one's pain are perfectly intelligible; self-ascriptions can contradict or imply other assertions about pain, can be used in arguments, and can be used as parts of molecular assertions. *These* traits make such ascriptions seem to be assertions in every way; the fact that they may *also* express the sensations that they report should not blind one to the fact that they are capable of truth and falsity. Hacker also argues convincingly that the private-language thesis does not require the truth of the avowal view, and indeed that it requires that it be false. For him, the former is the case because one does not have to condone the possibility of a private language merely because one believes that there is first-person knowledge of subjective experience. As long as one acknowledges the logical dependence of such knowledge on the ascription to other mental states on the basis of criteria, one can still ward off skepticism. The latter point is made by noting that Wittgenstein's famous diary example makes no sense unless one's own language permits self-knowledge of sensations, whereas such knowledge is not possible for the private-language linguist.[8]

Let me note, however, that if the Argument Concerning Criteria in the previous chapter is correct, it provides no case against the skeptic either. Thus, from this point of view, one begins the private-language argument with no convincing case either that self-knowledge of sensation is not knowledge at all, or, even though it is, that this offers no support for skepticism. And if that argument is to be successful in eliminating skepticism as a conceptual possibility, it must not rely on the notion of other-ascription by means of criteria.

What, then, is a private language and what is Wittgenstein out to refute in denying its possibility? According to Pears, a private language would be one that was "necessarily unteachable," and a "language" would have this feature if sensation talk were "removed from its circle of teaching links." Wittgenstein hopes to show that this is not a genuine possibility.[9] According to Malcolm, a private language is one that "not merely is not but *cannot* be understood by anyone other than the speaker."[10] Another sense of private language is contained in Locke's distinction between a language that only one person can understand and one "in which terms refer to 'private objects', items of which only one person is and can be aware, e.g. bodily sensations."[11] The source of the belief in one's commitment to a private language is said to rest on two mistakes: the belief that experience is private, and the belief that "words can acquire meaning by bare ostensive definition."[12] Or somewhat differently, we are told that the idea of a private language arises from the following argument: one cannot experience another's sensations; one could only know what another's sensations were if one could feel them; therefore, one never knows what another's sensations are.[13] One immediately wonders if it is *privacy of knowledge* that is the key notion in the idea of a private language, or *privacy of ownership*, or *privacy of experience*.

As there is at least a difference of emphasis among commentators about what a private language is for Wittgenstein, so there is a difference about what Wittgenstein's target is when he attacks the possibility of a private language. According to Hacker:

> One can, without undue caricature, conceive of Wittgenstein's purpose in the private language argument as being an endeavour to extend and elaborate the Kantian dictum that intuitions without concepts are blind
>
> . . . .
>
> The mistake at the root of the private linguist's troubles is to think that a sensible intuition can do the work of a concept, that—to use Kant's faculty terminology—sensibility can yield knowledge without the co-operation of the understanding. But acquaintance with an object falling under the concept does not provide one with a concept. [Pp. 216, 238]

On Hacker's view, then, the private-language argument is largely a reflection of what Strawson calls Wittgenstein's hostility to immediacy.[14]

Others, on the other hand, see the privacy of sensations as the target of Wittgenstein's criticisms. For Pitcher, Wittgenstein only wishes to deny a thesis about language, "namely that the word 'pain' names or designates this something that the person feels, in a way which is even remotely like the way that the words for publicly observable things name or designate them."[15] The cash-value of this is to be found in Pitcher's further remark that in our ordinary-language games, which one plays with the word 'pain', private sensations play no role at all. A word that denotes something only privately observable has no use in our ordinary language. As Pitcher says, Wittgenstein "only wants to reject the idea that in these language-games, when you use the word 'pain', you are referring to your sensation and telling other people that you have it—that you are talking about what is going on before your consciousness" (p. 299).

Some, who agree that Wittgenstein's target is privacy, think that Pitcher's rendering of his ideas is unduly paradoxical. Thus, Cook argues that Wittgenstein, far from claiming that sensations cannot have names because of their privacy, claims that since sensations do not drop out of our ordinary-language game, they cannot be private. Stated otherwise, "if the words by which we refer to sensations are connected with . . . natural expressions of sensation, if there is a 'grammar of the word "pain" ' which the naming of it presupposes, then in the use of this word we have no private language."[16] Since Wittgenstein accepts both antecedents, he affirms that reference to sensations does not commit one to the notion of a private language. One avoids this latter step by refraining from thinking of reference to sensations as analogous with reference to physical objects, an analogy that leads one to think that sensation words get their meaning from private ostensive definitions.[17]

In order to narrow the topic under investigation, let me rather arbitrarily eliminate two views of Wittgenstein from consideration. It seems to me that Pitcher's Wittgenstein provides an unacceptable answer to the skeptic. It surely is an unacceptable revision of our ordinary practices to be told that in speaking of one's sensations one is neither referring to them nor telling others that one has the sensation in question. One knows that one performs both functions every time one tells someone that one has an itch, pain, or whatever; only an overwhelming fear of the consequences of such a reference would cause one to deny that we do so refer. As I see it, the case here is quite similar to that of avowals discussed above: a view that is wildly at variance with ordinary practice is adopted because it seems the best, the most decisive, way of dealing with skepticism. Somewhat ironically, I shall argue, the more reasonable ways of dealing with sensations do not, in fact, provide a sufficiently strong answer to skepticism. Once reference to sensations is granted, there is no argument that is strong enough to eliminate skepticism as a conceptual possibility.

I wish also to set aside an appealing view of Wittgenstein, on the grounds that on this interpretation the skeptic need not reject what Wittgenstein says. It seems to me that one might agree with Hacker's Wittgenstein that (1) one cannot doubt whether another is in pain without the concept of pain (p. 239) and that (2) despite Locke's empiricist account of the origin of concepts, one does not acquire concepts simply by having experiences or by private operations (abstraction, comparison, etc.) on such experiences: "Acquaintance with an object falling under the concept does not provide one with a concept" (p. 238).

But the skeptic need not hold either that one acquires one's concepts through an inner ostensive definition (perhaps he thinks that one does not acquire concepts at all because they are innate and awakened in one by experience) or that one could know what words mean simply by having an experience. (The skeptic might say that a being who was capable of sensibility but not of conceptualization, if conscious at all, would know nothing about his experiences and certainly would not be capable of wondering about the sensations of others.) In fact, the skeptic might have no views on the acquisition of concepts at all. All he need affirm is that, however one has come to the stage at which one does have the concept of 'pain', one now means by 'pain' a certain kind of sensation and that each person knows directly of only one occurrence of a sensation that he has learned to label 'pain'. This rules out, for example, that one means by 'pain' "whatever sensation is caused by wounds, accidents or is expressed by grimaces, screams, and the like." It also implies that the meaning of the word 'pain' is now intimately bound up with the sensation that 'pain' refers to, even though this may not have been true when one first learned when it was correct to attribute pain to someone else or to oneself.

Thus, Hacker's claim that "what we are studying in philosophy are concepts rather than objects, and hence the use of a word rather than the object to which the word refers" (p. 238) makes a sharp division where such a division is not appropriate. One would think that philosophers study things by means of concepts, that it is the true use of words that interests philosophers, for they want to know what the world is like, not *merely* how one speaks of the world or how one thinks about it. Therefore, it is perfectly proper for the skeptic not to want the sensation referred to by 'pain' to drop out of the discussion of 'pain' and to insist that this object be the focus of the discussion. But this does not entail an identification of concept and sensation or any theory of how one comes to know what 'pain' means. Thus, when Hacker adds that "the naming relation as conceived by the private linguist has nothing to do with the explanation of what is involved in knowing the meaning of a word, or in meaning something by a word, or in understanding what someone else means by a word" (p. 238), one wants to object that there is a confusion here between how one learns to do these things and what finally becomes the meaning of a term or what is finally involved in understanding someone else. The fact is that sensations are experientially private and that criteria cannot prevent this form of privacy from leading to privacy of knowledge.

Consider Malcolm's case of the man who never felt pain. As long as he can say truly that he is not in pain, recognize the characteristic expressions of pain in others, react properly to others when they are in pain, and so forth, he will still be able to understand sentences about pain. As Malcolm says, "I have never been in Brazil, and so have never been in the position to say 'I am in Brazil,' when this was true: but of course I understand the sentence."[18] Malcolm points out (p. 49) that whereas a blind man would lack the ability to "assign the right names to colors *by sight*," the painless man lacks no verbal ability that normal persons have. Understanding a concept is to be analyzed in terms of "abilities," what a person "can do," and by this criterion, "congenital incapacity to feel pain does not logically imply any failure to understand the word, or to 'know what pain is' " (p. 50).

This seems to me to be a clear case of the confusion between meaning and verification. It is true that one would suspect that the blind man (but not the painless man) lacked a certain experience and, hence, understanding, because of the inabilities that the one, but not the other, would display. But this is no reason for identifying the ability with the understanding. And the analogy with being in Brazil is an unfair one at precisely the crucial place. One can understand sentences about Brazil because one has experienced things that are like those described and that exemplify the features of Brazil; but if one has no experience of pain, then it is hard to see what one is to make of references to pain, no matter how well one uses sensation words. One could not detect the painless man's state, but does that mean that he might not be in that state?

Let us now turn to Wittgenstein's attack on privacy and the possibility of a private language. A key notion in this attack is that of a rule. In fact, Locke refers to "the" private-language argument as that which deduces the impossibility of a private language from the claims that "a language must have publicly checkable rules" and "a private language would not have publicly checkable rules."[19] Obviously, the key to this argument lies in the initial premise. The idea seems to be that if one lacks rules for determining whether one is using expressions properly, then one lacks a means of distinguishing what seems to be a proper use of the word from what is actually so.[20] And such rules could be effective, could be genuine rules, only if one admits that there are independent checks by which one can determine whether or not one is following the rules. One's impression that one is following them does not constitute such a test. Since a private language would not have any place for such independent checks, it does not have rules. Lacking rules, it lacks the notion of correct use and is therefore not a language.[21]

Now, one might well grant that unless one can know that one is using a concept or word in a regular manner, one cannot know that what one is thinking or saying is true. But it is not at all clear that one cannot think or say things that are true, that one cannot be using a conceptual or linguistic scheme, and that one is not able to be sure that one is obeying the necessary rules. In fact, the Argument from Publicly Checkable Rules seems to be little more than Verificationism warmed over once again. The private linguist has only his memory to tell him that this is what he has always called pain, and while this leaves open the possibility that he is wrong, it does not prevent him from being correct. *Contra* Malcolm, the distinction between seeming to use a word consistently and doing so will not have collapsed and, with it, the notion of correct use; rather, there will be no final, conclusive test of consistency. But what follows from that?[22]

Even appeals to so-called objective, independent checks require that one remember correctly that they are those checks and not some others. Why should it be that merely because *only* memory is involved in the first case, there are the marks of a genuine language in the latter but not in the former case?[23] One suspects that behind this criticism of untestable rules lies an adherence to the Correspondence Theory of Truth, for it would seem that the coherence of one's memories would provide *evidence* that one was using a word consistently with previous uses. One also suspects that a version of Strict Verifiability underlies the refusal to accept this as enough for testing the corrections of a current use.[24]

But there is even a more significant criticism of Wittgenstein's claims for independent checks being essential for the possibility of a language. Let us grant that the first premise in the above argument is correct: there are no languages without public rules. But remember that these rules only tell one that one is using a word in the proper way, under the proper circumstances. They do not and cannot show that one is saying something true in speaking properly, and the skeptic need only defend the possibility of error even though all the criteria for proper use have been fulfilled. Our criticism of criteria has shown that they cannot guarantee truth; as long as sensations play a role in our language game, one cannot be assured that the move from propriety to truth is a valid one, no matter how natural it may be. I am imagining a case in which the public criteria for the use of a term do not determine its meaning. Thus, one can fulfill the public criteria but still mean a private object and not be certain that this object exists merely because what one thinks of as its natural expression exists. In this case, there is a sense in which the language that one uses is public and also a sense in which it is private; and the former does not negate the latter, nor does it avoid skepticism.[25]

A second key notion in the attack on private languages is that of "stage-setting." This idea is simply an extension of the idea that "it is an essential feature of any language that there should be effective rules which a person using the language can follow and know that he is following."[26] As Pears puts it, what prevents a private language from being a language is "the absence of teaching links, which, if they had been there, could have been used as checks" (p. 169). Now, the model of the private linguist for both a necessary and sufficient condition of learning the meaning of words is that of inner ostensive definition. One learns what 'pain' means by the direct, unmediated naming of a private experience. But, says the Wittgensteinian, ostensive definition, in general, is possible "for conveying or establishing the meaning of a word only for people already in possession of a language. . . . Private ostensive definition gives the impression of being a possible procedure precisely because we do have the concepts of the 'objects' in question . . . because we do know what 'pain' means."[27] As Pears says, "The person who has the sensation cannot be mistaken about it . . . only because he has already learned the meaning of the appropriate sensation word through the teaching links" (pp. 169–70). These links form genuine rules, which others can use to check their use of words and which drop into the background (but remain as a kind of "safety net") as one becomes a full-fledged language user. To use the metaphor of foundation and superstructure, the teaching links are the foundation of a language, not a mere frill necessary for practical communication.

Another way of stating this point is to claim that since words for sensations are part of our natural language, their use must have a public justification; and this cannot be the case with a private language.[28] Returning to Malcolm's case of the painless man, Malcolm points out that one's doubts that one could understand 'pain' rested on the assumption that this word has a common meaning, an assumption that is unjustified on the model of naming by inner ostensive definition.[29] Inward pointing cannot produce common meaning. The private object is, in Wittgenstein's words, not "part of the mechanism," for it "can contribute nothing to the understanding of a concept. It can have no significant consequences" (pp. 56–57).

On one interpretation at least, this view has the following consequences. In understanding one's normal use of sensation words, one can get rid of the private object in the following sense. Since 'pain' must have a public meaning, while it still refers to a private object, it names "the sensation, *whatever it may be like*, we feel in certain circumstances. . . . *It does not matter what the object is like 'in itself'*. It does matter that some object exist."[30] Private reference is compatible with public meaning and knowledge; in order to understand another's use of 'pain', one has to know only that one is using it to refer to an inner thing and does not have to know what the quality of that thing is. This move against the possibility of a private language might be summed up by saying that Wittgenstein's primary goal is to show that a private language is unintelligible to the speaker himself and not merely that it cannot be understood by others or taught to others (although if all three failings can be traced back to a lack of independent checks, it does not seem important which failure is thought of as Wittgenstein's prime target).[31]

The major way that this is to be shown is to argue that linguistic references to sensations presuppose the very acknowledgment of public criteria which are made to seem doubtful by the skeptic. But this doubt is incoherent if one realizes that the private language is always parasitic on the public language and that one forgets this when one tries to make the private language foundational and to construe public references in terms of this base. The private-language theorist is ungrateful to public language in the same way that a rebellious child is ungrateful to the parents who have nurtured him and made his rebellion possible.

Let me say right off that the above argument has shown how absurd it is to believe that one actually does learn the meaning of words in a way that is supportive of the private-language advocate, and if Locke believed that he was describing an actual process of learning, he was very wrong indeed. It has also all but destroyed the hope of some sense-data theorists to show that a sense-datum language "could stand alone as the foundation of all factual discourse, even if no superstructure were added to it."[32] I take it that Wittgenstein has shown that natural languages are not logical constructions out of a sense-data base.

I am even willing to go further and to agree that one *could not* learn the meaning of words in a Lockean way and that no natural language *could* be constructed out of a sense-data base. Certainly Robinson Crusoe could teach himself a language that no one else understood (because he was alone on his island), and he could keep a diary of his thoughts long before the arrival of Man Friday. But none of this would mean that his language was private in a way that would be bothersome to the Wittgensteinian, for there is seemingly nothing to prevent Man Friday either from learning Crusoe's language when he appears on the scene or from checking his use of words. The interesting question from the point of view of skepticism is whether, as Ayer thinks, Crusoe could make undetectable mistakes: "To say that nothing turns upon a mistake is not to say that it is not a mistake at all,"[33] or whether there could be portions of his language—those parts that refer to sensations without any natural expressions—that he *could not* teach to Man Friday but that would still have a use for Crusoe (p. 47). And in turn, these questions rest on the question of whether the possibility of public checks is a necessary requirement for one to be able to make meaningful statements, even silent ones or ones intended only for oneself. As long as the latter remains a possibility, public checks will tend to fall into the category of a convenience, and skepticism will have its toe hold in language.[34]

In this regard I am puzzled by Ayer's further claim that Man Friday could understand Crusoe's statements about his own sensations and could know what Crusoe's sensations were "even though the experience which he rightly ascribes to Crusoe is unlike any that he has, or ever has had, himself" (p. 48). After all, how could Man Friday rightly ascribe a sensation to Crusoe and understand Crusoe's sensation words if he had no idea about what kind of sensation Crusoe felt when he said 'pain'? Man Friday might have all the linguistic abilities that one might imagine, but he would only be under the illusion that he understood Crusoe and that he knew Crusoe was in pain. At most, he would know when Crusoe was having a sensation that Crusoe called pain, but that would leave both understanding and meaning open to question.

In essence, I am willing to grant that references to sensations presuppose the application of public criteria for teaching and communication. But I do not see that this point should worry the skeptic. To begin with, the skeptic need have no commitments as to how one learns words. He may leave that subject to the linguists; Locke's a priori linguistics plays no essential role in his skepticism. Nor, I think, need the skeptic believe that reference to sensations is anything but parasitic on public references. Let the skeptic agree that one does, and must learn how to, use words in a public context; let him agree that one comes to know what the sensation of pain is only because one first speaks of pain in connection with wounds, gestures, and so forth. Still, once one has achieved an awareness of the sensation that one has when it is appropriate to say one is in pain, one realizes that the built-in criteria for pain do not have the theoretical claim on one's allegiance that one had assumed all along.

The sensation is the pain, and the behavior is something else whose relation to the pain is not problematical. (One cannot claim to "see" that the two must go together, even in one's own case.) I see no reason that, even if references to sensations are in a sense epiphenomenal, they need be impotent. One may recognize what public references have built into the notion of pain and still reject that underpinning as being logically conclusive. Just as Bradley argued that the highest achievement of thought was to recognize that its fulfillment meant its destruction, so one might say that a public language finally results in the realization that its very publicity may be a sham.

The attempts of Malcolm and Locke to show that this cannot be the case, or that one does not need the qualities of sensations in one's talk about them, seem to me to lead to begging of the question, on the one hand, and absurdity on the other. Malcolm's remarks assume that there is genuine agreed-upon use for 'pain', and not the mere illusion of one, and that inner ostensive definition fails because it cannot, as it intends to, produce this common reference. Yet, the issue with the skeptic is precisely whether there is such a common meaning; to assume its reality is to beg the question. Nor does the skeptic think that he can produce this meaning from inner ostensive definitions. Indeed, the very statement of the skeptic's doubts about the painless man's knowledge of pain assumes that he lacks a knowledge of the same thing that one knows when one knows that one is in pain, but this is because our common language has that feature built into the meaning of its words. Surely, the point being made in this alien context is that unless a person experiences the same sensation that one has when one says one is in pain and that one identifies as one's pain, then one does not understand the other one and does not know what pain is, as the other one uses that term. And since these words also presuppose a common meaning, perhaps it is best to say that language points to what the skeptic wishes to say without ever quite being adequate to that task.

Locke's version of what our public talk about sensations pre-

191

supposes about sensations themselves is even more objectionable. He says that when one believes that another is in pain, it does not matter what the quality of the feeling is, as long as the circumstances are right. Of course, this is just another way of saying that the public criteria for the use of 'pain' determine its meaning. But this seems clearly false. The quality of the sensation means everything in one's reference to another's pain. If this quality were different from what one believes it to be, then one would withdraw one's claim that he is feeling pain, could think that one's compassion for him was misplaced, and so forth. One not only refers to the sensation, but the word one uses connotes or means a sensation of a certain kind. Perhaps this may tie privacy of meaning to privacy of reference in a way that bothers Locke's compromise between a Pitcher-like view of Wittgenstein and subjectivism, but to deny it is to fly in the face of the most elementary facts of ordinary belief.

One begins to wonder if Wittgenstein's claim that the private object is useless in establishing the meaning of words merely points out an obvious fact which no skeptic need deny. For example, Hacker says that the famous "Beetle in the Box" metaphor shows that

> on the private linguist's conception of the relation between a name and the object it refers to, then, *if communication is possible*, the private object allegedly referred to is a piece of idle machinery and plays no part in the mechanism of communication, and conversely *if the private object does play a part*, then communication is impossible.[35]

But unless one can *show* that communication does take place (assuming that it does would be to beg the question), these remarks are harmless to the skeptic. That communication may be an illusion is what he argues for, and this conclusion holds no terror for him. And the fact that 'pain' is a word in English proves nothing about communication.

A similar point about the "Beetle in the Box" metaphor is made by Cook in criticizing Pitcher. According to Cook, in order to avoid paradox, we must read Wittgenstein as saying, not that sensations drop out of the language game, but that since the view that sensations are private "makes it impossible to give any account of the actual (that is, the 'public') use of sensation words, we must, if we are to give an account of that language game, reject the view that sensations are private."[36] Such an interpretation suggests that one's goal is to give an account of the ordinary-language game, and it assumes that one must accept at face value the connection between behavior and sensation that is part of that game. I suggest that to begin here is to beg the question against the skeptic.

A third criticism of the private linguist is that he thinks that "'pain' is the name of what it denotes in much the same way that 'red' is the name of what it denotes."[37] The mistake here is to assume that the fact of the privacy of the pain makes no essential difference in the denoting relation. But I think that the skeptic might make the following rejoinder. First, sensations *are* objects of awareness, even if they are not *merely* such objects. (Perhaps they are states as well.) Second, the disanalogy between the two cases stresses such things as how one *learns* the meaning of words, how one *teaches* this meaning to others, what is necessary for *communication*, and how one cannot be certain of the correctness or incorrectness of usage pertaining to inner objects, as one can be with usage directed to public objects. But we have seen that these disanalogies do not show that sensation references do not refer to inner states whose connection with public expression and circumstances is less certain than one normally assumes. Thus, there is no mistake in treating sensations as special kinds of objects in whose qualities one is interested and to which one refers. This is not a self-defeating move, and it seems to be in accord with what finally emerges as what one means by 'pain', even if one does not normally follow up the skeptical consequences that are latent therein.

A fourth argument against the possibility of a private language emerges from the Ascription Argument considered in the previous chapter. According to it, a private linguist can ward off the criticisms that his language cannot be governed by rules, but he must assume that he has the notion of *himself* as thinking, remembering, believing, and so on. But since the Ascription Argument shows that he can have this notion only if he is first committed to the existence of other persons whom he is willing to recognize as such, and thus to the public domain, he must withdraw even this notion if his language is to be fully private:

> But then, bereft of a notion of *myself*, or of any persons, he cannot be said to live up to rules, to check—in a word, to speak a language. Neither the earlier nor the later assaults, by themselves, quite manage to overcome traditionalism. But together they vanquish it utterly.[38]

The point is not merely that without the notion of oneself one could not know that one was doing these things, but that one could not be doing them at all. For they are activities that cannot be done unless one realizes that one is doing them (p. 186). This argument fully expresses the parasitic dependence of private-language terms on the battery of terms that refer to interpersonal items.

My point here is the same as it has been before. Let us grant the principle that consciousness implies self-consciousness or, at the very least, the possibility of self-consciousness.[39] Let us assume, further, that consciousness of one's sensations, thoughts, and so forth can be achieved only through a medium of concepts such as 'thing' or 'person' and through the reference to public criteria that this implies. Still, the necessity that one use such notions, that they form a basic part of our conceptual abilities, says nothing about their truth. It only says something about the way in which one must take one's experience, about the distinctions that one must make within it if one is to achieve full self-awareness. For once the conceptual framework has made possible one's awareness of one's sensations and of their distinctiveness from anything bodily, the commitment to that categorical scheme ceases to have sufficient theoretical justification. In short, one can have the concept of oneself because of the contrast with other persons, and statements about oneself and others can be judged to be proper or correct by public criteria; and yet, one can still find that references to others are uncertain in ways that references to oneself are not. Even if one *must* take things in this way, one is not thereby guaranteed that this "taking" leads to truth.

9

Transcendentalism, Sensations, Science, and the External World

THE TRANSCENDENTAL APPROACH

A transcendental argument is one in which it is argued that so-and-so must be the case, because something else surely is also the case. Obviously, such an approach will carry conviction only if it spells out the "must" and specifies something to which one really is committed. The hope is equally clear: to prove the existence of whatever is in question and, thereby, to eliminate skepticism as a genuine possibility.

The Transcendentalist must, however, keep a proper distance from the Humean; for the latter is willing to grant the former any number of principles of organization (he calls them principles of "feigning"), and he will also concede that these principles are necessary for life itself. Thank goodness, says Hume, nature has made one as ready to believe as she has made one ready to breathe. There is a sense in which our commitments beyond what we see are necessary; certainly they form the basis of our conceptual scheme. The Transcendentalist, eschewing Dogmatism on the one side, must not fail to distinguish himself from Skepticism on the other. His principles must bring truth with them as well as commitment, or the Humean will welcome him to the fold as a brother skeptic, albeit one who dresses his ideas in the clothing of knowledge.

The ordinary-language philosopher might well look for the basis of a transcendental argument in the fact that we do have certain concepts, that our conceptual scheme is as it is. This is something that we might all agree upon. He might then try to show that presupposed in the very existence of this scheme is the commitment to the independent, common physical reality that the skeptic finds doubtful. But he should not be content to show merely that the Cartesian notions that one has require a commitment to physical categories, for this is compatible with that commitment's making self-experience possible without requiring that things really are as we (must) take them to be. If after our transcendental argument is over, the thing-in-itself remains undetermined, all that we will have accomplished is a more accurate mapping of the "logic" of our subjective point of view. And while this does reveal the iceberg beneath the exposed tip, it does not silence the skeptic. Even a Kantian "Who cares?" approach to things apart from our conception of them will not do the job, for skepticism does care about precisely this gap.

Of course, Strawson has made just such an attempt. He argues that: (1) Identification requires "location in a unitary spatio-temporal framework of four dimensions" (p. 39).[1] (2) We can identify particulars and they would not be a part of our ontology if they could not be identified (p. 16). (3) We do have the idea of a "single spatio-temporal system of material things" (p. 35). (4) This presupposes "unquestioning acceptance of particular-identity in at least some cases of non-continuous observation" (p. 35). The last point means that in order to have the system that we have, we must be able to reidentify particulars when they have been out of sight. Now the skeptic insists that if one is going to be strict in what one claims to know, perhaps one can claim in such situations that the thing before one is qualitatively the same as the thing that one saw a while ago but not that it is numerically the same entity. Strawson here is saying that one *must* be able to make this distinction if one is going to explain the conceptual scheme that we do have. (5) Reidentification in turn presupposes that there are basic particulars, that is, entities that make identification of other things (sensations) possible but need nothing in order to make their own identification possible (p. 39). Strawson makes clear that this is to follow simply from the "general character" of the conceptual scheme. (6) Material bodies are basic particulars; indeed, they must be our basic particulars, given our conceptual scheme (p. 39).

This last point is a significant one, for it rules out options that philosophers have found attractive. For example, it means that the entities of physics must necessarily suffer "identifiability dependence" in relation to ordinary material bodies. As Strawson says: "We must ultimately identify them, or groups of them, by identifying reference to those grosser, observable bodies of which perhaps, like Locke, we think of them as the minute, unobservable constituents" (p. 44). Such dependence Strawson is willing to call ontological (p. 17). The disturbing thing about this view is that it conceives of microscopic particles as literally parts of the framework of ordinary physical objects. Since they are unobservable parts, naturally they seem to have a status secondary to observable bodies.

But on one view, at least, this interpenetration of the scientific view into the common-sense view leads only to confusion, the confusion of thinking that ordinary things are mostly empty space, discontinuous, and the like. Rather, one might think of one framework as a possible replacement for the other, in which case the ontological roles now associated with them would be reversed.[2] Since Strawson does not show that this reversal cannot occur, his view of the order of dependence risks being reduced to a remark about our current attitudes, thus losing its sense of necessity. Indeed, in his discussion of "process-things" he explicitly says that the dependence of processes on the things that undergo them reflects our actual distinction and the categories that we actually possess (p. 57).

One need not argue with this bit of conceptual description, but it is worth noting that Strawson here explicitly limits himself to the investigation of "the relations of identifiability-dependence between the available major categories, the categories we actually possess" (p. 57). If so, then nothing that Strawson says about the priority of identification of physical objects can constitute a proof that such objects exist, for the skeptic can well grant that this is a feature of our current conceptual scheme and merely insist that there are alternative conceptual schemes in which this need not be the case. As long as Strawson is merely describing the features of our conceptual scheme, he is not entitled to rule out questions about the validity of the framework as a whole; the "could" in the sentence "We could not speak of sensations unless we were already committed to material objects" becomes very dubious indeed.

Let us assume that Strawson has shown that as we ordinarily operate, there are, in fact, criteria for the numerical identity of objects not continuously observed and that these criteria are at times fulfilled. This need not worry the skeptic. He is at liberty to say that the fulfillment of such criteria only indicates our way of taking experience and that it proves nothing about the truth of that outlook. It is perfectly possible that the criteria are fulfilled and that the judgments that we make on this basis are false.[3] Even Strawson's own language of "unquestioning acceptance" leaves room for this interpretation.

Strawson apparently then relies on his claim that the skeptic inconsistently accepts our conceptual scheme but also rejects it. He accepts it because his doubts about numerical identity make sense only if A and B are parts of the same system, and in this system, numerical identity is justified on many occasions. In turn, this is true because if "we were *never* willing to ascribe particular-identity . . . we should, as it were, have the idea of a new, a different, spatial system for each new continuous stretch of observation" (p. 35). And doubts about the identity of items in such different systems makes no sense. In summary: the ability to doubt presupposes that the doubt has limitations.

But Strawson does not explain why the skeptic should not be willing to ascribe particular identity in the ordinary way. He treats the skeptic as if his skepticism will be put into practice, but there is no reason for thinking that this will happen. The skeptic does not claim that his alternatives will be, or even can be, adopted for general, everyday use. As Plantinga points out, to show that the skeptic's doubts are empty is not to show that skepticism is incoherent.[4] Perhaps skepticism can occur only if one has both the notion of numerical and of qualitative identity and if those are features of our conceptual scheme; but this shows neither that the skeptic must accept these distinctions as equally valid or that in rejecting one, he must cease to use it in the ordinary way. Thus the skeptic is not guilty of any inconsistency even if he agrees with Strawson that "the whole process of reasoning only starts because the scheme is as it is; and we cannot change it even if we would."[5]

A fall-back position against the skeptic is suggested by Richard Rorty. He accepts the criticism that in order for terms to have meaning (and thus to make even doubts possible), one must be willing to identify some things as X, but that this cannot show that there are X's; it can only show that we must take things as X, that there must seem to be X's. But he then argues that a Wittgensteinian-Strawsonian "parasitism" argument remains. To wit: if the skeptic suggests a new and better way of describing the world (in terms of sense data, perhaps), then it can be shown that "your new way of describing the world would not be intelligible to someone who was not familiar with the old way."[6] At the same time, Rorty agrees that the skeptic can avoid this argument by insisting only that there are no conclusive reasons for thinking that material objects exist and that a better way of describing the world may come along which will make no use of 'material object'.

But then, skepticism as we have characterized it does remain intact, for parasitism as described by Rorty does not allow for a definitive proof in favor of any ontological notion. In addition, the point that it does make against skepticism seems to be a harmless one about the order of knowing or of learning. Even if it be true that one could not understand alternative languages without a base in ordinary speech, this would not show that the latter had any prior call on one's philosophical allegiance. It might well be that the languages that emerge only later and that are in this sense "dependent" on ordinary speech can be shown to reveal the nature of things more fully than one's common base. The most dependent form may nonetheless be the highest and the most revelatory.[7] The lack of ontological punch in the fall-back position can be seen in Rorty's formulation of a Verification Principle which avoids committing one to the claim that current methods of confirmation are sound: "All he has to say is that there has to be a situation which present practice would call 'a man's having accepted a method of finding out whether something is a K' if there is to be a situation which present practice would call 'a man's thinking a thing is of the kind K and its not being so' " (*VTA*, p. 9). But now our necessities are completely *within* language, leaving it an open question whether the "finding out" proves anything about the world or not. Things cannot be constrained by what one must say if one is to say something else.

In another place, Rorty reformulates the Argument against the Possibility of a Sense-Datum Experience, that is, "an experience such that no concepts are used in it save those of sensory qualities."[8] He says:

> To use a concept is to be able to make a judgment, which involves having a thought expressible by a complete sentence; but if all one has are names for sensory qualities, one will not be able to construct sentences. . . . For one is not yet, lacking substantives, in a position to use these adjectives to form a judgment, and if one cannot form judgments, one does not possess concepts. [*SOA*, pp. 219–20]

There is an identification of concepts and judgments, on the one hand, with words and sentences, on the other, in this quotation, which forms a crucial but very questionable link in the Argument against a Private Language and for the parasitic character of sense-data languages on ordinary discourse. For one thing, it smacks of Verificationism (*SOA*, p. 222); for another, it restricts the use of concepts in a way that other behavior suggests to be overly restrictive. I will have more to say about this point later. For the present, let me simply point out that even if it is true that one cannot use 'red' as a word unless one can know what kinds of things are red (that is, unless we have the concept of a red thing), it does not follow that one can know that there are things in the world. It *may* only mean that one needs a contrast with the notion of a quality in order to be able to speak of qualities at all; for all one knows, this is merely a remark about the conditions of speaking about what there is, not about the reality of the conditions themselves. Rorty makes a similar point about knowing what a K is. If all one knows is "that there is a K if and only if a man believes there is, then we don't know *anything* about K's, not even that."[9] Without the proper correlations, 'there is a K' or 'red' amount to parroting or ejaculation, not speech. Rorty would admit this, for he says that it cannot be shown conclusively that new, nonparasitic, but nonobject, languages cannot be formulated (*SOA*, p. 223); but then no transcendentalist can find solace in parasitism.[10]

It is important for our later discussion to catch the drift of Rorty's argument here. To clarify and firm up transcendental arguments, Rorty thinks that they must be interpreted as showing that "*if* you have certain concepts you must have certain other concepts also" (*SOA*, p. 231). This means that it no longer makes any claims about the order in which experiences come, about the regularities that are required if there is to be experience at all (*SOA*, p. 230). The conditions for the employment of concepts rest in relations between concepts (one can have the notion of 'seems' only if one has the notion of 'is', and vice versa) and not in a relation between concepts and something else, say, intuitions. The notion of an experience to which one *could not* apply physical-object concepts is incoherent; one cannot imagine and cannot make sense of an experience that resembles that of a preconceptual infant. And not being able to make sense of this notion, one can in turn make no sense of the claim that experience requires that there be a certain regularity among our intuitions (*SOA*, p. 231).

Rorty's challenge to the skeptic thus comes in the form of a challenge to show that some judgment could be made by a being who lacked both "experience concepts" and "physical-object concepts" (*SOA*, p. 235). But this means nothing less than that for the purposes of transcendentalism, "only the concepts and the judgments matter; the intuitions drop out" (*SOA*, p. 227). The truth of the concepts that require one another (Language is an organic, not an atomic, notion) is no longer required or provable, and it is not required even that the person be aware of the sensuous. As long as concepts entail one another, "it does not even matter that the man is stone-deaf and his language-training is done by inserting electrodes in his brain. In the only relevant sense of 'had in his experience' he will still have had the appropriate correlation in his experience" (*SOA*, p. 227).

Rorty's next step is to characterize an intuition as "a dispositional state—a state apt, given the fulfillment of certain other conditions, for making a given assertion" (*SOA*, p. 242). Intuitions are noncognitive states of an organism which help in the production of assertions. And concepts are to be understood as dispositions to behave, much in the pattern set by the *Concept of Mind*. But now one must ask not only how this can any longer constitute an answer to skepticism. After all, skepticism consists, not of the claim that one can have certain concepts without having others, but of the claim that one can *doubt* the truth of judgments employing one kind of concept in a way that one cannot doubt judgments that employ another kind of concept. Rorty still seems to hanker after a proof of knowledge, for he says that in order to defeat the skeptic, one must show that "you can't know about your experience without knowing about something else" (*SOA*, p. 236). But it is hard to see how his formulation of the answer to skepticism entitles him to the guarantee of any *knowledge* claims—unless, I suppose, he thinks he can explicate "knowledge" without bringing in the world that he has dismissed from philosophic concerns.

One must ask whether the price one is asked to pay for this answer has reached the point that it constitutes a *reductio* against the Linguistic Turn. What has happened to the sensuous side of experience? It seems to have been relegated to the category of the ineffable and, thence, to nonexistence. But this is absurd. No matter what the difficulties in speaking of the sensuous apart from categories, it forms an undeniable ingredient in one's experience. Lewis had the final word when he said:

> In a sense the given is ineffable, always. It is that which remains untouched and unaltered, however it is construed by thought. Yet no one but a philosopher could for a moment deny this immediate presence in consciousness of that which no activity of thought can create or alter.[11]

Once again, expression in a language—that is, communication and verification—has been given such prominence in philosophic discussion that one is encouraged to turn away from the most obvious experiential facts. Progress with philosophical problems simply is not worth the price of Wittgenstein's transformation of Kant.

THE ELIMINATION OF SENSATIONS

The introduction of talk about sensations or sense data into discussions about perception is an important source of skepticism about the existence and nature of physical objects. For if one is willing to grant that in cases in which two persons see the same object, but in which it looks different to one than to the other, it is correct to say that each "directly" sees something different from the other; and if one is inclined to think that in all cases of perception there is a subjective side stemming from conditions in the perceiver and in the world, then one is liable to conclude, as Moore did, that in no case can the sense datum that one directly sees be identical with the surface of the seen object.[12] Sense data, which at first seemed to be part of an explanation of seeing, now seem to form a barrier to visual contact with physical objects. The obvious next step is to wonder whether the thing seen is like the thing directly seen or whether there is any reason to think that there is such an indirect object at all. Demon hypotheses become possible as soon as physical objects retreat to the other side of the visual screen.

In order to combat such skepticism, ordinary-language philosophers have attacked the notion of a sense datum in two general ways. First, they have tried to undermine arguments or claims about perception that suggest that there are such things as sense data. Both the claim that perception involves inference and the Argument from Illusion fall into this category. Second, they have tried to show that the notion of a sense datum is a theoretical one, having no hard and fast foundation in experience. As such, it is, in principle, eliminable. Rorty's Eliminative Materialism is a case in point here, and it reflects the attack on the notion of a given that we encountered in the last chapter. If one cannot legitimately appeal to a given in experience, then at least the kind of skepticism that arises through a contrast between the known quality of the given and the chanciness of the inferred will disappear.

Perception and Inference

In *Sense and Sensibilia*, J. L. Austin attacks the idea that, in perception, one always makes inferences or assumptions; he claims

that whether one does or not "depends, not on the form of words
I use, but on the circumstances in which I am placed."[13] Thus, to
use Austin's example, if one has only a sound to go on, then one
can say that one makes certain assumptions in saying that one
hears a car:

> But what if I already know that there is a car just out-
> side? What if I can actually see it, and perhaps touch
> and smell it as well? What would I *then* be 'assuming,'
> if I were to say, 'I hear a car'? What 'further investi-
> gation' would be necessary, or even possible? To make
> the form of words 'I hear a car' look *intrinsically* vul-
> nerable, by implying that their utterance *can only* be
> based on just hearing a sound, is little better than a
> frame-up. [Pp. 137–38]

Ordinary assertions are not per se chancy.

Similar remarks apply to 'evidence'. Austin says:

> The situation in which I would properly be said to have
> *evidence* for the statement that some animal is a pig is
> that, for example, in which the beast itself is not actu-
> ally on view, but I can see plenty of pig-like marks on
> the ground outside its retreat. . . . But if the animal
> then emerges and stands there plainly in view, there is
> no longer any question of collecting evidence; its com-
> ing into view doesn't provide me with more *evidence*
> that it's a pig, I can now just *see* that it is, the question
> is settled. [P. 115]

And he adds, "But how absurd it is, really, to suggest that I am
giving a verdict when I say what is going on under my nose!" (p.
141). For Austin, the question of how talk about sense data is
related to talk about material objects is a "quite unreal question"
which one should not get "bamboozled" into asking at all (p.
142).

Austin makes two main points against the notion that perception involves inference by its very nature and thus that notions
such as 'evidence', 'verdict', and the like apply to it in every case.
The first is that notions that have a use in a limited area are thus
extended to cover an entire region. The result is absurdity.
Second, and a corollary of this point, is the claim that there are

quite ordinary cases in which perception is conclusive. Incorrigibility is itself a matter of circumstances, not of the kind of sentence that one uses in order to express one's judgment (p. 114).

Both points seem to mark distinctions that we make in ordinary speech, but neither seems decisive against the skeptic. Take perceptual certainty, for example. Austin says that after perceiving, using, and even dismantling a telephone, "I *do* make sure; what more could possibly be required? This object has already stood up to amply enough tests to establish that it really is a telephone; and it isn't just that, for everyday or practical or ordinary purposes, enough is *as good as* a telephone; what meets all these tests just *is* a telephone, no doubt about it" (p. 119). But it surely is too strong to say that *is* what a telephone is, for one can imagine all of the above experiences apparently occurring and yet being convinced by the testimony of others, and one's own further experience, that there was no object before the one at the time or that there was, but that it was not a telephone. The more experiences one has, the more certain one feels of one's judgments; but at no time can one say that one is more than practically certain, for the possibility of error still exists. The ordinary circumstances that allow for ordinary certainty simply do not guarantee that one is right in what one says. What one takes for certainty in one's ordinary framework is one thing; what certainty is, is quite another. The latter requires a kind of justification that is not envisaged in the former.

Austin is right that collecting evidence is normally contrasted with seeing; to incorporate the former notion into the latter is thus to cross established boundaries. But one can show that such a maneuver is not absurd by producing reasons for thinking that a perceiver is not in the direct contact with physical objects that the ordinary distinction assumes. Such an argument might start from the claim that all perceptual claims admit of the possibility of error and that, at the same time, they start from something in the perceptual field that does not admit of doubt of the same kind as the doubt that I might not be seeing a so-and-so. This type of argument must be shown to be radically mistaken if one is to be assured that the expanded use of inference, evidence, and so forth is itself mistaken. Austin's statements to this effect do not constitute such an argument. If one takes Austin's remarks here in the spirit of his famous statement in "A Plea for Excuses," then one has no quarrel with them. Ordinary language has no claim to being the Last Word; its distinctions tend to be practical, but "likely enough" not the best way of dividing things "if our interests are more extensive or intellectual than the ordinary."[14] But his language in *Sense and Sensibilia* suggests a stronger view, one in which philosophical theses are undercut by references to ordinary practices.

Gilbert Ryle has attempted to provide just such an account. He claims that philosophers are committed to sense impressions because they are deductions from a theory. One concludes that because some observers seem to report what they see more fully than others, this extra knowledge or belief indicates the presence of inference. In turn, inference requires some immediate data, and this is what one identifies as sense data. But this reasoning is questionable for two reasons: not all thinking is inferring, and the fuller description of a perception need not indicate the presence of thinking at all. Perception involves the "possession and exploitation of knowledge previously acquired. But this exploitation is not thinking."[15]

Ryle supports his claim that sensations are theoretical entities by noting that "we have, in fact, no special way of reporting the occurrence of these postulated impressions; we are, therefore, without the needed marks of our being conscious of such things at all" (p. 195). In *The Concept of Mind* he makes the same point by saying that "we do not employ a 'neat' sensation vocabulary. We describe particular sensations by referring to how common objects regularly look, sound and feel to any normal person."[16] And if one asks about the notion of 'looks', Ryles is quick with an answer: "In saying that the plate looks elliptical, he is not characterizing an extra object, namely 'a look', as being elliptical, he is likening how the tilted round plate does look to how untilted elliptical plates do or would look" (*COM*, p. 217). Thus, on Ryle's view, Moore's appeal to experience as a justification for one's belief in the existence of sense data actually represents a misinterpretion of the meaning of ordinary statements about how objects look; in fact, all that such statements report is how objects that really had the properties that one

senses would look under standard conditions to properly constituted observers (*COM*, p. 220).

Since Ryle has already made the claim that one cannot 'witness' his sensations (although one can be said to feel them, have
them, and even notice them) and since he denies that sensation
words stand for "any sort of a *thing* or 'term'" (*COM*, p. 209)
and cannot be spoken of sensibly in the language of "internal-
external" or "hidden-unhidden," he moves to the bold but natural conclusion that "to have a sensation is not to be in a cognitive relation to a sensible object. There are no such objects.
Nor is there any such relation" (*COM*, p. 214).

But I think that Ryle's remarks do not constitute a sufficient
answer to Moore's question. Surely Ryle does not mean to claim
that what one *means* when one says that something tastes bitter
or looks greyish is that it looks like an object that actually had
this characteristic would look under normal conditions to a normal observer. One surely means to describe the quality of the
taste or of the color expanse and, if the emphasis is on "tastes"
or "looks," to retreat from the claim that this is a genuine feature
of the object. But then, there must be something before one
which one is describing. One's terms may not be "neat"; they
may be all borrowed from the qualities that one normally at-
tributes to objects. But this does not show that in using those
terms, one is actually talking about the normal properties that
objects display under normal conditions. Our sensation words
may all be parasitically derived from talk about public objects,
but that does not mean that they cannot be used in speaking
about private objects.

It is a mystery to me why Ryle thinks that one could not be
conscious of sensations unless one had a special vocabulary with
which to speak about them. All of this seems not to affect the
seemingly obvious fact that when objects appear to have qualities
that they do not have, or appear to be two when they are one,
there is a sensory object before one, not part of the public world,
which is of a certain quality. Whatever the squinter is saying
about what he sees,[17] what is Ryle going to do with the two
candlelike shapes that are in the squinter's visual field?

Nor does Ryle's point about witnessing carry any weight.
Although one does not normally witness one's sensations, one

may do so. Under a doctor's orders, one may record the intensity, and so forth of a pain, and one may do so carefully, sloppily, and so forth. But even if this not be possible, it does not follow that sensations are not objects at all; it only follows that they are not merely objects, or not objects precisely like physical objects; but one knew this all along. If all that Ryle can do is to point out some disanalogies between sensations and public objects, his conclusion that sensations are not objects at all is much too strong.

But if Ryle has failed to undermine the Cartesian's claim that sensations are objects of experience, his remarks about inference are correspondingly weakened. One need not rely on some general identification of thought and inference in order to claim that perception involves inference, for one will have found the data or premises that justify the claim that perception does use inference. That there is thought at all present in perception, rather than a mere response conditioned by previous learning, is shown by one's admitting on reflection that one was wrong (or could have been wrong) in *thinking* that something was red or round. One's unquestioning acceptance that what seemed to be the case was the case cannot contain so much as the possibility of error if it is a mere response to a stimulus. Such responses can lead to difficulties, but they cannot be false or true. In a way, Ryle's use of 'pondering' in this context comes close to question-begging, for no one claims that perceptual inference is equivalent to deliberation or to drawing conclusions in an explicit way. The claim is only that perception does involve a claim about the world, a claim that is based on an immediate presentation; and that there is such a claim seems amply testified to by our acknowledgment of actual or possible error.

This point about inference has important implications for the extent of sense data in perception. For if it is granted that there are sense data in *some* perceptual situations and that they are *sometimes* different from the qualities we believe the objects to have, then one wonders if there is any reason for thinking that sense data are present in *every* perceptual situation, even cases of what one calls veridical perception. Two considerations weigh in favor of a positive answer. First, the argument for sense data rests, not on actual error, but on the possibility of error. But if all perception involves inference because it involves the possibility of error, then it should also involve the presence of sense data. One might buttress this point by adding that there is nothing so experientially different in cases of perceptual error and truth that it justifies limiting sense data to only the former case. Second, perception always functions in a medium; if in extreme cases one recognizes that the medium presents sense data that do not accord with the object, why should one think that in more ordinary situations it gives one the object directly? At what points does one get, not the appearance, but the real thing?[18] Once sense data intrude themselves into perception as the primary visual objects in some cases, there seems to be no preventing their becoming omnipresent. Of course, this result supports perceptual skepticism.

ELIMINATIVE MATERIALISM

Cartesian skepticism about the external world rests on knowledge of the inner world, particularly perhaps on knowledge of one's own sensations. One is thought to have a certainty about one's own pains that cannot be present either in one's beliefs about another's pains or in one's beliefs about the existence and character of physical objects. If it could be shown that one's so-called knowledge of one's own sensations amounts to nothing more than a view about something whose nature is capable of alternative descriptions, then at least the contrast between inner certainty and external uncertainty would have been eliminated. Doubt would still be possible about *any* view, inner or outer, for no view could claim certainty; but in being totally general, it would be less interesting, for the contrast between inner certainty and outer uncertainty is what has provided the framework for replies to skepticism at least since Descartes. And if this idea is applied to visual sensations, it would undercut the defense of skepticism that treats such sensations as experiential items whose known character makes the inferential leap to physical objects seem chancy.

On the view of Richard Rorty, to defeat the Cartesian, all one needs to do is to show that there is nothing that prevents ordinary sensation talk from being replaced *in toto* by a more adequate scientific mode of speech. Our ordinary talk about sensations is comparable to talk about demons. Once they were thought to explain (particularly strange) events and were even thought to have been observed, but now one regards such reports as mistaken and considers demons a poor mode of explanation. Rorty imagines "two sets of people, one raised to speak conventional English and the other raised to use only neurological predicates in the place of those conventionally used in introspective reports."[19] Both vocabularies are answers to the question, "What do you experience under the following conditions?" Which is to be preferred? The one that passes the (pragmatic?) test of survival.

Rorty is suggesting that one might come to say that one's "sensations" have radically different properties from those that one now says they have. The new words would not simply be verbal substitutes for the old ones. On Rorty's view, we shy away from this market-place conception of sensation vocabularies only because we still believe "that there is a sort of prelinguistic givenness about, e.g., pains which any language is to be adequate must provide a means of expressing."[20] In fact, "there is no criterion for the adequacy of a bit of language to a bit of non-linguistic awareness. Indeed, the notion of a non-linguistic awareness is simply a version of the thing-in-itself—an unknowable whose only function is paradoxically enough, to be that which all knowledge is about."[21]

This attack on the Myth of the Given seems to me to be sound insofar as it suggests that one's claims about the world, including one's perceptual claims, involve an element of interpretation or inference. None is sacrosanct. But I do not see that this carries with it the result that one must abandon the notion of prelinguistic givenness and the attendant notion that one has a direct grasp of the qualitative side of experience. C. I. Lewis was right to say that this qualitative character cannot be spoken of, but he was equally right to say that it is an "identifiable constituent in experience." It is what makes an awareness of green visually different from an awareness of red.

Consider Rorty's example of pain. Is it convincing to say that what one experiences when one feels pain is totally dependent on the linguistic scheme that one employs to describe that experience? Does neurological man not feel the same sensation that I do merely because his language is different from mine?

Never have words been accorded more magical powers than in Rorty's view of sensation talk! To think that experiences are created by one's talk about them is to rob 'experience' of its meaning. The qualitative feature of the pain lies within one's experience. And does the experience of children have no qualitative distinctness to it? Or, perhaps, are they to be denied experience altogether, as I suppose dogs must be, on this account? I am more certain that neither alternative will do than I am of the philosophic theories in whose name they are proposed.[22]

Rorty tells us that our intuitions are baffled when we are asked to identify the "same thing" described by the two languages, but I find no such difficulty. The "same thing" is the feeling that we call pain, with its characteristic features, and that the neurophysiological language does not describe at all.

Even if one grants that one's ordinary view of the world is in some sense a construction and, therefore, is in principle replaceable by an alternative conception, there are still the qualities of experience to contend with. Rorty seems to deny that there is any such dimension to experience at all. It is hard to know what to say other than to point out that Linguistic Idealism simply ignores the world experienced when it comes to characterize that experience. There certainly may be alternative ways of describing what one sees or feels, but these alternatives must occur within the limitations that the sensed qualities present to one. *These are not the creation of language.*

Rorty makes a final point which, if valid, would tend to undermine the sharp distinction between the "made" and "found" elements in sensation reports that I have endorsed. It goes as follows. (1) One can imagine a situation in which one would no longer rely on first-person reports, honestly made, as the criterion for the occurrence of the items so reported. (2) Thus, the private-public distinction should be regarded as a relative one. (3) But then the certainty that now goes with a private report may be transferred to a public report. That is, our criterion of the occurrence of pain may become a public one. (4) But then the irreducible mentality of the events reported privately and certainly may reflect only our creation of special objects for our reports to be about. (5) Finally, there is no reason not to

211

think that what one reports noninferentially and (one now thinks) certainly are brain processes.[23]

It seems to me perverse to argue that one must postulate the mentality of sensations in order to explain their privacy, for their mentality is not a theoretical postulate. It is just as much an experiential feature of sensations as are their other qualitative characteristics. More of this later. Second, the privacy argument could not refute my claim even if it went through. Let us grant that in the future a split occurs between a first-person sensation report and a highly confirmed theory linking sensations and brain processes. In such a situation, one would not be able to know whether one simply was not using 'pain' as others use it, or whether one was using it as others do but simply wasn't feeling pain. Rorty is right here; unless one first assumes that one knows how to use words correctly, one will not be able to distinguish between misnaming and misjudging.

Ordinarily, one assumes a "natural" connection between inner state and outer expression. If this breaks down, one no longer knows how to make judgments in this area. In such a situation, people might override one's reports when these reports conflict with public evidence. But this would in no way mean that there was not something of which the person was aware and of whose features he was certain. It would not mean that pains are in fact public occurrences. When Rorty says, "Pains will be (but are not now) what the Standard 'Pain'-Training Program calls 'pain',"[24] he identifies the thing, pain, with the way we use 'pain'. But this is mistaken if pain is an identifiable item in experience, and that seems undeniable to me. If, in the situation imagined, others do not believe our reports and we ourselves are unsure about our use of language, this does not show that we are unsure about the character of what we experience when we are in pain.

Rorty thinks such authority pays one an "empty compliment," but then he gives undue emphasis, in my view, to the public acceptance of what we say. Thus, he states that our inability to be mistaken is *no more* than having our fellows accept what we say if they think we are sincere and know how to use the language.[25] But surely it is more than this; knowledge can be useless and still be knowledge for all that. My conclusion is that there is no conceivable confusion about criteria that could force us to admit that what we now call 'pain' is in fact something quite different from what we take it to be. The attempt to neutralize the content of sensations fails, and so—to the extent that knowledge of this content (of the "what" of sensations as well as of the "that") lies at the heart of skepticism about other minds and about the physical world, by supporting the notion of a given, privacy, and the like—one seems to be stuck with the problems that this knowledge engenders. At least, one cannot dissolve them by the means that Rorty suggests.[26]

Another kind of attack on the notion of a prelinguistic experience is offered by J. O. Urmson in his discussion of recognition. H. H. Price had suggested that both primary recognition (recognition *of* signs) and secondary recognition (recognition *by* signs) might well be nonverbal or preverbal.[27] One sense given to this claim by Price need not trouble the ordinary-language philosopher: namely, that one can recognize something, after one has learned a language, without having a word for that thing. For his point is not that we have words for everything that we experience, but that experience cannot happen unless one has linguistic skills, unless one has acquired a language. But the ordinary-language philosopher is opposed to Price's claim that animals, prelinguistic children, and presumably adults who are without language are capable of recognitional experience. For him, this is another form of the Myth of the Given.

Urmson argues that although animals without language can properly be said to recognize things, recognition still is dependent on language in the following sense: "It is simply that we may be trained to follow the rules constituted by linguistic use without learning the language. . . . But that recognition can be pre-verbal in the sense of being independent of the logic of language we have not admitted and must not admit."[28] One thing this means is that the naturalist can recognize a beast without having learned the "logically arbitrary rules enshrined in the correct use of the name" only because "he has a wide experience of the language of zoological classification; he knows the principles on which names are given, what sort of criteria are used for classifying beasts of this type" (pp. 268–69).

The case of the zoologist is uninteresting, because he does

possess a classificatory scheme into which he fits unusual observations. But what reason is there for thinking that a being without language, whether child, higher animal, or adult, cannot recognize recurrent features of experience? No doubt, such recognitional abilities would be greatly reduced by the absence of language. Thus, as Urmson points out, if experience were more complex, creatures would react similarly to animals that *we* would classify separately (p. 270). Thus, it would be difficult to say that they recognize *this* creature as a *dog*, for example. But surely, they would be reacting to observed similarities in what they saw or smelled, and this is a form of recognition. Their classes would be broad and clumsy by our standards, but similarity of reaction to similar creatures would still be an indication of a recognition of similarities.

Nor does the teaching of recognition depend on language, as Urmson asserts. A human who is without language might well teach another human, also without language, to recognize a fruit that is good to eat, merely by example: each time he sees one, he takes it and eats it. His comrade might soon be on the lookout for something looking like this fruit in order that he might eat also. And even if it were true that only a language-user could teach recognition to a non-language-user, I do not see that this fact should be of much comfort to the ordinary-language philosopher. It would still be the case that a non-language-user could perform recognitional acts; the teaching connection with language would not be strong enough to prevent the reappearance of a private, given experience and the problems that it engenders. At least the Rorty version of Linguistic Idealism could not go through if nonlinguistic experience is possible in any circumstances.

THE DEFUSING OF SCIENCE

One of the disturbing developments to philosophers over the past few hundred years has been the extent to which the scientific approach to knowing what the world is like has seemed to call into question our ordinary conception of things, reducing it to the level of "appearance" or of prescientific mythology. One thought that scientists were going to tell us how we perceive the world around us, and in so doing, they seem to have told us that we don't perceive it at all and, anyway, that the world we *thought* we perceived isn't the real world after all. In this section I want to examine not only two kinds of skepticism about the normal Aristotelian world which arise from the apparent conflict of science and common sense but also some examples of how ordinary-language philosophers attempt to combat such skepticism. First, I shall consider the so-called Time-Lag Argument and then the view that science is a kind of metaphysics, telling one what things are really like and subordinating the world as one ordinarily thinks of it and encounters it.

One obvious tack to take in rendering harmless the developments in science is to insist that the causal language of science be carefully separated from the ordinary language appropriate to perception. Thus, according to Ryle, one runs into trouble when one gives causal answers to noncausal questions; ordinary questions about technique are of a different type from the kind of questions appropriate in science.[29] Similarly, Frank Ebersole states: "Puzzles arise from a crossing of pictures. Put the troubling phrases back in the language game of which they are a part. We must learn to leave everything as it is. Learning a language is learning a way of life."[30]

This applies to the Time-Lag Argument as follows: to think that one does not see stars because the light from them takes time to reach one (and by extension, that one does not see any physical object; one only fails to note the disparity in the case of objects closer to us) is to think of seeing stars on the analogy with receiving a letter that tells of the past (p. 62). Yet, when one sees stars and speaks of what one sees, one is not thinking that "information came from the star faster than it did. I am not thinking of information at all" (p. 63). The analogy with the postal service mixes two areas of discourse and thereby creates needless puzzles.

It is an attractive way of handling scientific accounts of human actions to isolate them in a different sphere where they cannot harm one's ordinary conceptions. However, the problem with this maneuver is that the scientific account continues to pose as an alternative, complete account which pushes to replace the way that one normally conceives of seeing, acting, or whatever. It seems to be a competitor and, as such, will not be put off by remarks about two languages, two types of questions, or the like. No doubt, Eddington was mistaken in the way he mixed the two languages ("Tables are mostly empty space"? Nonsense!), but this does not show that one can ignore the scientific account. It only means that the latter, taken as a whole, offers itself as a better account of what needs explanation than the common-sense account, also taken as a whole. If one does not ordinarily regard common sense as an account, this is because it is our "form of life"; but this does not show that the scientific account cannot become a better form of life with time. Just as one is left with a haunting feeling that causal considerations *do* threaten ordinary ideas about free action, so we may have to rethink seeing stars once we have to consider the underlying conditions of perception.

Another way of dealing with the Time-Lag Argument is as follows. The skeptic suggests that there is a conflict in the ordinary meaning of 'see'. On the one hand, one can be said to see things only "when they happen, and not later."[31] On the other hand, one can be said to see physical objects, and stars are certainly physical objects. But if the first component of 'see' is emphasized, it becomes puzzling that one sees physical objects, and so the skeptic argues that one sees only one's own brain. For it seems that one can never see anything distant from the brain when it happens.

But Henson says that if there is no such conflict in the ordinary meaning of 'see', the skeptic's case will have rested on a "misconstruction" of ordinary usage, "and the ordinary language philosopher would be quite right in saying that the sceptic has misunderstood and misused ordinary expressions and is wrong" (p. 29). Wrong, presumably, *because* he has misused ordinary expressions. Henson then argues that to "see it [something] when it happens" is ordinarily contrasted with seeing it (or hearing it) later (via reports, newsreels, and the like); therefore, that expression ordinarily means "seeing on the original occasion." Given this meaning, there is no reason to think that one cannot see things when they happen even though they are distant from us (so long as one is present); and therefore the skeptical argument collapses. In essence, the skeptic's claim is one about language, and he is wrong about the way 'see' is ordinarily used.

But the skeptic does not think that he is trying to represent the ordinary sense of 'see', nor need he think that there is a hidden conflict in the ordinary use of that term. Rather, the conflict for the skeptic is between the scientific account of perception, which suggests that one does not see things in the state that they apparently have when one sees them (at best, one sees their state of a moment ago), and the ordinary assumption behind the ordinary use of 'see', which is that seeing is the visual awareness of the present. But is this conflict genuine? At least, Henson's argument does not show otherwise. For we surely think *not merely* that to see something happen means being present as contrasted with learning of it indirectly; no doubt, this is a minimum condition for seeing something happen. But in addition to presence at the occasion, we think that seeing something happen requires the presence of the object or event seen, where 'presence' means that the seeing and the state of the object seen are not earlier or later than one another. The two are copresent. It is only with the advent of science that one has reason to think that the spectators in a stadium may not be visually present to the events they witness, as they assume they are.

That is, underlying the kind of contrast that Henson thinks sets the meaning of "see when it happens" are assumptions that go beyond this contrast and that explain (and make reasonable) why the scientific account of perception does (and *should!*) seem to conflict with common sense. The rather superficial distinction between present and absent does not bring out the full meaning of 'present' that is packed into our ordinary views about perception. Thus, I disagree with Henson when he says: "One need not surrender any feature of the ordinary use of 'see' in order to accommodate the empirical facts cited in the argument" (p. 31). To say that the question is about how language ought to be used, not about nonlinguistic facts, is to draw a sharp distinction which the debate tends to fudge. For how one ought to use 'see' does depend on how one thinks of the nonlinguistic world; facts can impinge on the criteria for the proper use of expressions. It is then that our ordinary conceptions begin to look like theories themselves and to be susceptible to criticism from new facts or interpretations of facts. I conclude that the above ordinary-language attempts to dissolve the apparent conflict between common sense and science have not shown that the conflict is merely apparent. For all we have seen, skepticism about ordinary conceptions is the reasonable outcome of the impact of science on common sense.

The second kind of challenge that science seems to offer to common sense is that of an alternative conception of the kinds of things there fundamentally are in the world and the parallel reduction in the ontological status of the world as ordinarily conceived. The interpretation of science that suggests this conflict is clearly stated by Wilfrid Sellars when he says: "To have good reason for holding a theory is *ipso facto* to have good reason for holding that the entities postulated by the theory exist."[32] According to this view, science seeks truth; truth requires correspondence with objects; the kind of objects that especially physics employs requires that common sense and science be thought of as self-contained competing views of the world; therefore, one must be considered inadequate as an account of what there is.

But there is another approach to science which suggests that we are led to think that there is a conflict only because we have misunderstood what science is all about. Gilbert Ryle tells us that it is misleading to speak of a conflict between two theories because "it suggests, for one thing, that in using his eyes and ears the child is after all taking sides with a theory, only with a popular, amateurish and unformulated theory; and this is quite false. He is not considering any theoretical questions at all."[33]

He depicts the relation between common sense and science in several typical, catchy analogies. The physicist's account is like the economic conception of man in that the latter is not a "general diagnosis of people's motives and intentions" (p. 69). The economist does not characterize or mischaracterize my brother; he offers an account of "certain marketing-tendencies" (p. 70) which cover all persons engaged in this activity. Alternatively, the physicist's account is like the auditor's account of a college's activities, which uses colorless, precise terms. Such accounts "cover" but neither characterize nor mischaracterize the persons and activities so covered. The accountant gives one the arithmetical relations between bills and receipts; he is simply silent about the contents of books and lectures. Thus, "it is not a question of two rival libraries, or of two rival descriptions of one library, but of two different but complementary ways of giving information of very different sorts about the one library" (p. 78). Physics and common sense are not rivals because "a statement that is true *or* false of the one is *neither* true *nor* false of the other" (p. 79). Finally, the physicist is like the geologist who tells one about the geology of the hills that the painter depicts. Both are concerned, in their respective ways, with the same hills.

Ryle states that he hopes his analogies have shown that there is "no general logical objection" to his conception of the relation between science and common sense. Certainly, they could do no more than this, for they presuppose, rather than argue for, a "calculational" view of science. Thus, they beg the question with the Scientific Realist. Second, they could accomplish this modest goal only if there were an accompanying commentary which would explore the conception of science that they embody in order that one might see that such a view contains no serious difficulties. Otherwise, one simply cannot judge whether this view is a logical possibility.

But have Ryle's analogies worked? I think not, for they distort the scientific enterprise. The analogy with the economist will not work for a reason that Ryle himself concedes: the physicist's account is all-encompassing, whereas the economist's is not. Thus, the former cannot be eased out of its apparent role as a competitor to common sense in the way that the latter can. It cannot be thought of as an ideal account of one facet of the world precisely because of its wholistic character. But neither is the physicist's account like that of the accountant, for the latter clearly covers its "world" from only one point of view, while there is no such obvious, self-imposed limitation on the scope of physics. And what reason is there for thinking that physicists give us the relations between ordinary things? They have their own entities in whose relations they are interested. Ryle says many times that physics is not descriptive, yet the physicist does describe his theoretical entities in whatever terms are available to him and in ways that will help him to explain the behavior of ordinary things.

Ryle's view of science misses the essential role that theoretical entities play in it; because the physicist finds it necessary to postulate certain entities in order to explain the behavior of ordinary things, his view clashes with our ordinary one.[34] Our ordinary conception of the world does have the methodological or epistemological priority that Ryle stresses, but that is no reason for thinking that the scientific account lacks ontological priority. Recall here our remarks about whether a parasitic language of the inner could nevertheless cause one to question elements of the basic objective language on which it was dependent.

Last, Ryle seems to think that common sense could be theoretical only if children consciously mulled over theoretical questions as they made observations. But if these children are language-users, it seems fair to say that their observations already embody the point of view of ordinary speech. The mere fact that children do not explicitly theorize when their eyes are open proves nothing interesting. Since there are alternative languages, it seems reasonable to speak of language as embodying a point of view; it is theoretical in this sense.

If physics did not have its own entities, then it could be thought to be describing ordinary things, albeit abstractly; and if it were not apparently all-encompassing, then it might be thought to represent merely a perspective on the ordinary world. Ryle's account of science does not dissolve the conflict with common sense precisely because he does not cope effectively with these features of physics. At least we can say that he has not *shown* that metaphysical skepticism induced by scientific theories is mistaken.

10

ALTERNATIVE CONCEPTUAL FRAMEWORKS
AND THE
PROPER TREATMENT OF PHILOSOPHICAL ISSUES

In the previous chapters of this book, I have defended the skeptic by arguing that ordinary-language methods have failed to show that our ordinary claims to know about the past, other minds, physical objects, and so forth can withstand his argument that they are overblown and cannot provide a justification for their truth, which is commensurate with the confidence that a knowledge claim implies. As long as doubt remains a possibility, the skeptic wins the battle, even though this doubt is purely intellectual and lifeless. When more sophisticated replies to the skeptic took the form of insisting that skepticism is an extreme form of bad faith or ingratitude, in that it refuses to acknowledge the conditions of the very language or conceptual scheme that make its very statement possible, my argument was that these frameworks may indeed provide a context within which skepticism can flourish, but that once the skeptic comes upon sensations, appearances, and so forth, there is nothing inconsistent in his questioning the strength of the bonds that tie subjective inner states to outer, publicly shareable objects. As long as there are meaningful alternatives to "our conceptual scheme," the skeptic can look down on that scheme and wonder about the connections that constitute it and that we of course take for granted.

Skepticism may take the form of actually proposing alternatives and of treating our own scheme as of merely practical value (as Hume did in his treatment of 'physical object'), or it may consist only of arguing that alternatives are possible, thereby reducing knowledge claims to merely spelling out the commitments of a single categorical scheme. There is nothing in this to bother the skeptic.

But what if it could be shown that there is something fundamentally wrong with the notion of an alternative conceptual framework? Then it would seem that although any particular judgment about the world might be false, it could not be the case that the majority of our claims could be false; for if to have a concept is to be able to use it correctly in most cases and if there is no sense to a skeptical claim that there might really be no physical objects even though they form part of our framework, then the mere having of such concepts would guarantee their truth (at least in the sense that their existence was unquestionable). According to this interpretation of skepticism, the skeptic suggests that "our entire belief structure might dissolve, leaving not a wrack behind, to be replaced by a complete but utterly dissimilar alternative."[1] One might say: If the skeptic be right in a single case, the ramifications would be so horrendous that nothing of our conceptual scheme would be left standing after we realized what they were in all their detail. The skeptic need not suggest such a framework, but his criticisms of ordinary convictions at least require that alternative frameworks be conceptually possible; if not, there must be something wrong with his criticisms.

But before one evaluates the attempt to undercut the notion of alternative frameworks, one must be clear about what an alternative framework would be, and this point proves to be a difficult one. In *Individuals*, Strawson rejects the notion of "process-things" as "one we neither have nor need."[2] His remarks there suggest that Broad's conception, in *Scientific Thought*, of the Cliffs of Dover as a slow, complex event represents an alternative scheme to the one that we have in which processes are dependent for their identification on things, which are the primary occupiers of space.[3] Yet, Broad's view is certainly not unimaginable and has been suggested by Sellars as the "true" view of what there is toward which science seems to be tending.

However, in our current discussion, this different version of things would not count as an alternative conceptual framework, for Rorty states that as soon as one can describe "alternative" frameworks, they become "merely alternative theories within a common framework" (p. 656). Presumably, Hume's reconstitution of things out of impressions counts merely as an alternative theory, not as an alternative framework, for we understand him when he questions the identity and continuity of physical objects. This is where the difficulty begins, for we seem stuck on the horns of a dilemma. The notion that there are not any alternative conceptual frameworks is supposed to show that skepticism cannot get off the ground, while the kinds of alternatives that skeptics envision or even suggest as possible are not extreme enough to be considered alternative conceptual frameworks. Thus, it seems that the skeptic has all the possibilities that he needs, whether or not there can be such things as alternative conceptual frameworks.

Perhaps we can work our way out of this dilemma by looking more closely at what lies behind the issue of alternative conceptual frameworks. As Rorty states it, the possibility of them rests on the prior notion of a conceptual scheme, the latter necessarily correlating with the notion of a given that one spontaneously interprets. And we know that Rorty opposes the notion of a given and of the incorrigibility that is associated with it because of the interminable skeptical issues that it engenders. For example, Rorty introduces the Principle of the Relativity of Incorrigibility, namely, that to be incorrigible means only that questions about justification for a belief are at present inappropriate and that doubts about this belief have no accepted procedures for their solution.[4] This means that what counts as incorrigible at present "is a matter which is subject to revision in the course of empirical inquiry" (p. 286). Thus, there are no "natural explananda," and in a change in language (e.g., from phenomenalistic to scientific), "no knowledge would have been lost, nor would any realm of being be lost to human sight" (p. 286). If Rorty is right that behind psychophysical dualism lies epistemological dualism and the skepticism that results from it, one can see what a powerful solvent this principle might be.

If there be no given, then there is no "constitution of ex-

223

perience"; if there is no constitution of experience, then there are no conceptual frameworks and, hence, no alternative conceptual frameworks. What remains are alternative empirical theories, whose merits are to be decided by the power to predict and control and which permit only of the uninteresting skeptical observation that any theory can be replaced by another and better theory. One will no longer be faced with the specter of the possibility that some may experience and speak of the world in ways that are not like ours at all, on the one hand, and the resulting permanent skepticism that this possibility suggests, on the other. All that will be left are competing theories about the world and recognized means of deciding between those theories.

The result is that "most of our beliefs . . . simply *must* be true—for what could count as evidence that the vast majority of them were not?"[5] Without Cartesian incorrigibility, "we shall automatically be 'in touch with the world' (most of the time)" (p. 661), for there are no "coherent global sets of beliefs" (p. 660) that differ radically from ours. According to this view, "the world" becomes whatever is caught up in our judgments about it, "whatever that vast majority of our beliefs not currently in question are currently thought to be about" (p. 662). Modifications of this view are permitted, of course, but one's beliefs will tend to reinforce most of its essential elements. Any other notion of "the world," one that conceives of the world as independent of one's thought about it and, hence, capable of being totally unlike any of one's (current) ways of thinking of it, is "the notion of something *completely* unspecified and unspecifiable— the thing-in-itself, in fact" (p. 663). This "world," which a Cartesian, such as Bradley, thinks is given as a whole in immediate feeling, can play no role in our explanations. So we are left with the following easy choice: " 'The world' is either the purely vacuous notion of the ineffable cause of sense and goal of intellect, or else a name for the objects that inquiry at the moment is leaving alone: those planks in the boat which are at the moment not being moved about" (p. 663). In one fell swoop the independent world, the given, and all constitutive principles are dismissed with ourselves being none the worse for it. The independent world of the realist, which keeps skepticism alive as a possibility, arises, Rorty suggests, only because we think of ourselves as interpreting a given (p. 664). Relinquish this conception, and we have no need for a world other than the one contained in our present thoughts.

One thing clearly emerges from this discussion. Although the drift of Rorty's argument is heavily negative (against alternative conceptual frameworks and not in favor of a single such framework), it carries implications for the permanency of the one view that we now have. This view may be amended to improve prediction and the like, but this correction is described as "slight" and certainly cannot extend beyond certain limits (those that would turn it into another conceptual scheme). Second, we can be sure that "we shall *always* be holding mostly true beliefs and, thus, presumably be 'in touch with the world' the vast majority of the time" (p. 660). This suggests that while we can repair and replace *some* of the planks in our ship, we cannot countenance the idea of completely replacing our ship with totally different parts. Global skepticism is rejected ("the notion of 'people who speak our language but believe nothing that we believe' is incoherent"; p. 653), thus leaving our conceptual scheme in an unquestioned and unquestionable position.

Third, this argument apparently does not count against the skeptical alternatives to our ordinary beliefs that are suggested by Hume and Descartes; the latter are to be interpreted as offering differing theories of what a cause or thing is, not as delineating alternative conceptual frameworks. This is because they accept the notion of 'cause' or of 'thing'; they would agree with us in our talk about causes of things, attribution of personhood, talk about objects, and so forth. And even though this arrangement might be merely verbal (does Hume *really* agree with us when he also says that friction causes heat?), it would be enough so that we could understand what Hume was saying when we learned how he disagreed with common sense.

What reason is there for thinking, then, that this most radical of all skeptical possibilities is not a genuine possibility after all? It will not be enough to point out, as Rorty does in another context, that a language is a "form of life" that cannot be transcended at will.[6] For in the situation imagined, one is wondering whether one might be confronted with another, completely alien, form of life. One major argument, developed by Davidson and

Stroud, "is verificationist, and turns on the . . . unrecognizability as a *language* of anything that is not translatable into English."[7] The argument has two steps. (1) If we find that a translation of another language yields mostly false beliefs in our language, then we must conclude that we have failed to translate the other language properly. And nothing in one's nonlinguistic behavior would induce us to call it evidence that the "person" held fantastic beliefs generally (p. 655). (2) If one allows that a good translation might result in generally false beliefs, then anything at all might count as a language or a language-user. Since this is absurd, one would do better to treat the untranslatable "language" as mere sound and the "language-user" as a mere cause of that sound.

Let me begin by saying that I do think that one kind of global skepticism is incoherent. If in the translation situation imagined above, the sentences of the foreign "language" were to turn into logical contradictions in English, one would be forced to regard the "language" as meaningless noises. But this has nothing to do with Verificationism. We know that we cannot make sense of contradictions; they convey nothing. And any attempt to think of this as a mere limitation of our faculties requires us to admit that we *can* make sense of the very thing we admit that we cannot make sense of. There are no meaningful alternatives to the laws of logic, no genuine alternative logics that operate in opposition to the law of contradiction. What prevents this from turning into a "logico-centric" predicament, similar to the "egocentric" predicament, is that in the latter case one has the feeling that one's inability to *tell* how things are "outside" of one imposes no limitations on how things "outside" of us *are*. On the other hand, in the former case, there is nothing conceivable as a meaningful outside; testing is not the question, but conceivability is. Without logic, the skeptic cannot so much as conceive of his case, let alone state it coherently. Logical coherence forms a base beyond which any meaningful thought, the skeptic's included, cannot go.[8]

But short of such skepticism, I do not see how one's inability to recognize an alternative conceptual framework when confronted with one can possibly eliminate the possibility that there are such alternatives. Let us assume both that one would not

226

count a translation as successful if the translated sentences were mostly false and that even the addition of nonverbal behavior would not be counted by us as evidence for the presence of an alternative conceptual framework. To say that this limits what could be the case seems to be yet another tiresome confusion between one's knowledge and the way things are (or may be). Of course, if the Verificationist is right, then there would be no reason for the linguist to be interested in "signals" from outer space which one can only turn into false sentences in English. The mere possibility that noises and impulses might be messages cannot justify his investigating and classifying all sorts of noises as languages in alternative frameworks. *His* inquiry needs some limiting conditions, and perhaps the condition of truth sets the boundaries of what one should count as a language in order that investigation can have some sense of direction. But why should philosophers not be concerned with conceptual possibilities if it can be shown that they are relevant to issues surrounding skepticism?

To show that there is an incoherence in the notion of an alternative conceptual framework (one that when "translated" into English yields mostly false beliefs), one would have to show that no amount of nonlinguistic behavior could justify the claim that there are beings who have a language that one simply cannot translate into English. But such stories do not seem to be absurd on the surface, especially if what these Galactic Beings do and have done is so remarkable that one continues to think that they *must* be intelligent beings and therefore their noises *must* constitute a language. This move also marks a kind of distinction between Galactics and butterflies or stars, although it seems to me that there is no absolute way of ruling out the *possibility* that there are languages there too.[9]

Thus, I cannot accept Rorty's "don't care" attitude toward the debate between the global skeptic and the opponent of alternative conceptual frameworks. First, Rorty's own admirable statement of the dispute (pp. 654–55) seems not at all a stand-off to me. The burden of proof seems to be clearly on the one who thinks that because global alternatives are not statable or verifiable, there cannot be such things. As I have argued above, the mere possibility of their existence, although this is not enough to justify ordinary inquiry, is enough to undercut knowledge claims about our own conceptual scheme. And I would say the same thing about Rorty's dismissal of the realist's conception of the world and of the Kantian notion of an intuition. No doubt, as inquirers, we are interested in the world under some theory, and the world that we speak of is already so structured. However, this does not prevent one's finding in experience an admittedly ineffable something that one's conceptions are about and that does not change (the given), nor does it prevent one's commitment to a world that is always beyond one's conception of it and that cannot be reduced in a Peircean manner to what we will all agree on in the long run.

Empirical inquirers can well lose this world, but philosophers cannot, for their conceptions of truth will suffer without it, and they will ignore troublesome radical skeptical possibilities if they try to ignore it. We can extricate ourselves from philosophical difficulties by reconceiving or eliminating the notions that seem to cause these problems, but this will constitute intellectual progress only if these notions can be shown to be racked with confusion as they now stand and/or if they play no role in *philosophical* debates.[10] Rorty's emphasis on what is effable, and so has an explanatory function, constitutes a begging of the question with the skeptic, unless one can be convinced of the *general* uselessness of such notions and of their impossibility.

Of course, views that involve a given—a world beyond knowledge, and the like—involve serious problems. But then, Rorty's view that the "world" is well lost bears the burden of explaining sensuous experience without a given and of showing that the world is not needed for truth. Not caring about debates with the skeptic and moving on to a different conception of things that avoids these debates is not enough to dissolve the puzzles in which philosophers are entrapped.

As an additional remark, let me raise the question of what follows if Rorty is right and there are not (cannot be) such things as alternative conceptual frameworks. If one does not admit the possibility of such an alternative, could one know that this was the case? One thinks of the Hegelian point that to come up against a boundary is already to have passed it; if one is truly confined to a conceptual scheme, can one have a sense that there are limitations to what counts as such a scheme? In short, if one has not glimpsed unrealized possibilities, then one will not have found any boundaries to one's outlook; yet, once one has glimpsed such possibilities, one can no longer hold that only his outlook is possible. If Rorty's claims are true, then he could not know that they are true.

Let me put the difficulty in another way. How is one to take the argument that shows that we must reject the notion of alternative conceptual frameworks? One might take it (whatever form it takes) merely as a reflection of the conceptual scheme in which we all operate. According to this reading, the argument amounts to no more than a self-congratulation. And this reading is not a far-fetched one, for Rorty's view smacks too much, I feel, of the self-satisfied person who is sure that his way is the only way. Short of outright logical contradiction, attempts to delimit what is possible inevitably sound like defenses of the status quo. Looking out on the world from one's goldfish bowl, things look a certain way; therefore, one cannot conceive of them being radically different. But why should one care about the limitations of one's vision? I do not suggest that Rorty argues this way; I only suggest that this pastiche of his views is too close to make one feel fully comfortable with the genuine thing.

On the other hand, one might interpret Rorty's argument as reflecting a neutral stance from which our conceptual scheme might be placed in perspective. Certainly, it does not mean to give us anything but the objective truth. But the question then presses itself: If there is only one conceptual scheme conceivable, how can one obtain even this much distance from it? How can one be "outside" it enough to know of its uniqueness if there is no "outside" at all? And if one can view it from above, then why cannot there be alternative possibilities to it which find their place in the space beyond our scheme? Limitations of knowledge and of possibility seem to be caught in the same self-referential predicament.

This brings us, finally, to an extreme but understandable conception of the best way to treat philosophical puzzles, in general, and skeptical puzzles in particular. Imagine that one is determined to take seriously Wittgenstein's assertion that "we may not advance any kind of theory. There must not be anything hypothetical in our considerations. We must do away with all *explanation,* and description alone must take it place."[11] Other commentators have tended to stress this aspect of Wittgenstein's philosophy in one breath, while talking of what Wittgenstein has shown or argued in the very next breath (Pitcher is a good example of this). So by "taking seriously," I mean thinking of Wittgenstein's assembling of reminders as the key to his thinking; I also mean self-consciously refusing to think of him as engaging in the argument that is typical of the philosophical tradition.

Obviously, this is not an easy position to maintain, because, as Pears has pointed out, "If citing a fact about language corrects a false generalization, it surely must also suggest truer ones."[12] One is tempted to ask how examples can do anything, how they can bear on philosophical claims in order to deflate them, unless they embody and implicitly suggest the better view from whose stance criticism of other views makes sense. This line of thought leads ultimately to the charge that Wittgenstein would be guilty of bad faith if he simply refused to disclose his own philosophical stance, hiding it behind examples, suggestions, and the like. Such an approach may make criticism difficult, but only by concealing the true philosopher behind the descriptive mask.

However, such remarks are premature. Let us for the moment concentrate on understanding the force behind this reading of Wittgenstein. Rorty presents a dialectical move that is characteristic of philosophic controversy. One can show that an opponent's position is bankrupt if one can expose it as being self-referentially inconsistent. Rorty characterizes this fault as "a set of categories which he takes as ultimate is, in some sense, inadequate to cover the case of his own arguments for the ultimacy of this set."[13] Of course, a prime example of such inconsistency is found in the philosophic attempts to finish off speculative philosophy in favor of some preferred form of knowledge, which one finds in such writers as Hume, Kant, and the Logical Positivists. About their claims, one always wants to know: How could they be true or even meaningful if knowledge and meaning are restricted in the way that they say? What they do is clearly not science; it seems to be philosophical by any standards; but how can philosophy do away with itself?

Rorty recognizes that the other dangerous extreme lies in

circularity, in "having formulated a criterion for the ultimacy of categories which presupposes the ultimacy of the very set of categories which he wants to propose as satisfying this criterion" (p. 312). Appeals to the self-evidence of one's categories are not likely to impress one's opponent either. The way out that Rorty suggests for the claim that language cannot be transcended (common ground for both ideal and ordinary-language philosophers but particularly emphasized by the latter) is to think of the proposal of categories, not "to offer a description of a non-linguistic fact, but to offer a tool for getting a job done" (p. 313). The job in question is to be able to propose categories without falling into the self-referential-circularity impasse. The solution is to judge such proposals by whether or not they aid in this task and not from some external standpoint. If roadblocks to discussion are overcome by adopting an approach as well as the categories that go with it, then it is good for so much. For the moment, let me remark only that this seems to beg the question with the metaphysician who wishes his categories to be true and who wishes philosophical controversy to "advance" only if truth is not ignored. This conception of the "job" rejects the internal method of evaluation suggested by Rorty.

In a recent paper, Rorty puts the dilemma somewhat differently. Wittgenstein's attempt to bring philosophy to an end seems to fail if one regards him as proposing yet another philosophical theory. He must then be interpreted as continuing philosophy in his own works and merely objecting to the way that philosophy has been practiced before him, or (although Rorty does not say this) he is being self-referentially inconsistent in denying the validity of the very categories that he uses to end philosophy. On the other hand, one might think of Wittgenstein as not doing philosophy (perhaps he is doing linguistics, albeit unsystematically), in which case it is hard to see how what he says can bear on philosophical issues.[14]

As long as one thinks of Wittgenstein as having located necessity within language (instead of within the world or within our minds), one will be viewing him in the first guise and will be stuck with trying to understand how this fits with his attacks on theorizing.[15] Thus, Rorty grasps the other end of the dilemma. Let us think of Wittgenstein as "the satirist who suggested that

231

we get along without the concept of necessity" (p. 346). Let us regard the *Investigations* as a mixed work, containing old-fashioned positions or theories and also numerous attempts to show

> by examples, how hopeless the traditional problems are —how they are based on a terminology which is as if designed expressly for the purpose of making solution impossible, how the questions which generate the traditional problems cannot be posed except in this terminology, how pathetic it is to think that the old gaps will be closed by constructing new gimmicks. [P. 354]

We are then left with three questions. (1) How can "pure satire" be an effective and fair weapon against philosophical difficulties? (2) What will it mean to say that philosophy has ended? (3) What will be left after philosophy has ended? Skipping the first question for the moment, Rorty tells us that the end of philosophy will consist in people's simply finding the picture of the relation of man and the world, which generated traditional philosophical puzzles, to be quaint, boring, a waste of time, or the like. It will simply cease to be a subject of interest, as Rorty thinks is the case with theology, and not because it has been refuted by the analysis of language or because its confusions have been exposed by linguistic techniques. In Rorty's terms, people will stop thinking of "the standard list of Cartesian problems as a *Fach*" (p. 352).

Once this shift has occurred, it will still be possible to study the circumstances and attitudes that characterized the Cartesian period. That is, the history or sociology of philosophy will replace philosophy as we have known it. One can see that making fun of the belief that philosophy has something to explain might be an appropriate means for philosophers to make a contribution to this "paradigm shift," and one can also see how this approach to Wittgenstein would avoid having his thought dragged back into the philosophical arena and thus would perpetuate philosophy instead of ending it. A Wittgenstein purified of all philosophical elements can remain above the conflict while putting an end to it.

My difficulties with Rorty's sense of what such a Wittgenstein could accomplish emerge when one looks at the sense in which he might end philosophy. Effective satire can reduce one to embarrassed silence, and the constant bickering of philosophers may well lead to a wholesale dismissal of the entire enterprise, even by philosophers themselves. Certainly, it might be said that philosophers avoid certain philosophical issues now, not because they have been solved, but because after lengthy discussion, one simply could not face another article or book rehashing the same old material.

But this kind of an end to philosophic dispute does not make Wittgenstein-the-satirist an effective critic of philosophical issues. Only if his satire conceals a truth could he end philosophy in a way that should interest philosophers; but if this were the case, then his humor would conceal an argument, and we would be back on the philosophical treadmill once again. The fact that people may lose interest in philosophy altogether (except as a subject for historical study) says nothing at all about the worth of philosophy, the meaningfulness of its problems, or the viability of the solutions to those problems. In the same way, people may lose interest in the arts and simply cease to care about Shakespeare or Beethoven; but this will be their loss, not a sign of progress. To be the latter, one must know that what has been left behind *ought* to have been left behind, and the only way that one can do this is to do philosophy in a better, more fruitful manner than it has been done in the past. To think that *pure* satire can be a *fair* weapon against philosophical *issues* is to blur the distinction between rhetorical persuasion and reasoned argument without showing that philosophy consists only of the former or something of the kind.

And so, I believe, ordinary-language philosophy—in its quest against philosophy generally, and skepticism in particular—ends in a *reductio ad absurdum*. A new game is invented, which in some strange way is to do away with the old game without participating in the old game. Yet, as long as the members of the old game retain their poise, there is no reason whatever for paying the slightest attention to satirical remarks by participants in the new game. All the weight of the new game is placed on the shoulders of fashion, as if philosophy were similar to styles in clothing. And yet, if one makes fun of philosophy, how can that be justified unless one claims to have *seen* the absurdity of the philosophical enterprise, and what can this "seeing" be but a *philosophical* insight? Rorty's own account of Wittgensteinian satire contains the germ of arguments and theories that stand behind the satire and make it seem reasonable (p. 346). So, perhaps nothing at all should be said in explanation of the satire, and the satirist himself must refrain from anything smacking of understanding the object of his humor. Then what does one have except mindless fun-making, and why should anyone care about this?

Rorty suggests in another place that philosophical choices may be like "the practical disagreement between a man who refuses to invest further in the development of a promising but never perfected mechanical device, and the man who persists in investing, in the conviction that the machine will some day function."[16] If so, one must show it by reasoned argument, thus continuing the same game. And if one refuses to do so, then while one may abandon particular issues, or indeed philosophy as a whole, because of fatigue or a desire to try one's hand at something else, one can say that this move, no matter how wide-spread, will leave philosophical issues right where they were: alive and crying out for light. Philosophy will not have ended; it will merely have been passed over until such a time as the interest in theoretical reason revives. Bradley, I think, was wiser than Rorty when he said: "If a theory could be made by the will, that would have to satisfy the will, and, if it did not, it would be false. But since metaphysics is mere theory, and since theory from its nature must be made by the intellect, it is here the intellect alone which has to be satisfied. . . . For we may feel as we please about the intellectual conclusion, but we cannot, on such external ground, protest that it is false."[17]

ORDINARY-LANGUAGE ANALYSIS
AND SKEPTICISM: A FINAL EVALUATION

The purpose of this book has been to show that the appeal to ordinary language fails to undercut philosophical skepticism. This is not to deny that we have learned a great deal about skepticism and its conceptual surroundings because of the arguments that ordinary-language philosophers have brought against it. But to the extent that skepticism remains a real conceptual option (if one of interest only to philosophers), there is no compelling reason to abandon those philosophies that depart from our common framework and to adopt the investigation of ordinary language as the only appropriate method of philosophizing. Austin's dictum that ordinary language gives the first word but not the last one remains valid; no one need object to the claim that knowing "what we should say when" forms an important first step in philosophizing.[1]

In trying to explain why arguments based on ordinary language do not silence skepticism, let me begin by observing that there is a genuine conflict between skeptical or revisionary philosophies and the ordinary-language account of what words mean. If one thinks that the skeptic is using ordinary words in unusual or esoteric language games, it becomes impossible to explain why the skeptic and his opponent *think* that the former is challenging ordinary conceptions. As Stanley Cavell points out, the attitudes of Descartes and Hume about their own thoughts are inexplicable on the assumption that they have merely introduced some new technical terminology in the guise of ordinary words.[2]

Still, the conflict engendered by the skeptic is not all that direct or simple. The skeptic is not reporting how we actually use terms such as 'illusion', 'real', 'know', and the like, nor is he urging that we use these terms differently from the way we now use them. He is not saying simply that we are wrong to identify certain states of affairs as real, or nonillusory, and to identify certain claims as knowledge, or certain. If he were, then one could easily show him that we do not use words as he says we do. (This in itself is a mystery, since the skeptic is every bit as much a speaker of a natural language as is his opponent.) Or to take an example from Moore, who himself grants that the skeptic's meaning overlaps with the ordinary meaning, one could refute the skeptic's claim that "time is not real" simply by pointing out that this implies the obvious falsity that nothing happens before or after anything else.[3] But neither of these moves hits the mark. Unless the skeptic has lost his senses, he cannot be denying something that he knows as well as anyone else.

What the skeptic does in fact, I think, is to find a central or core meaning for a word that is present in the multitude of ordinary uses of that word but not fully represented in all of those uses. Thus he claims that knowledge involves certainty but that we use 'know' much more widely than this link with certainty would permit. Or the skeptic finds that our ordinary ways of distinguishing dreaming from waking, which are justified or reasonable from their opposites, are not as definitive as we normally take them to be. Certainly *some* distinction is marked by these terms, but the skeptic insists that this will not suffice to demonstrate the existence or character of the items in question. Our implicit belief that we *know* certain general things about the real world never seems fully reflected in the methods that we use to support those claims. And so our use of terms seems loose and without *final* justification to the skeptic.

The reason that the skeptic's position seems invulnerable to appeals to "what we should say when" is that he is really challenging the framework within which our ordinary beliefs occur

236

and within which our ordinary use of words makes sense. Even when he seems to be challenging a particular area of belief, he is doing more than this, for the kind of challenge that he poses threatens to disorient anyone who tries to make sense of the world and his experience of it. If one could not begin with the "absolute presuppositions," to borrow Collingwood's phrase, that the past exists, that I can know in principle of the existence and character of other minds, or that I can know when I am awake and really seeing something, then the entire enterprise of knowing anything in particular at any time seems to have lost the ground on which it rests. Thus I agree with Cavell when he says that "this is why the sceptic's knowledge, should we feel its power, is devastating: he is not challenging a particular belief or set of beliefs about, say, other minds; he is challenging the ground of our beliefs altogether, our power to believe at all."[4]

Here we have the reason that the appeal to ordinary language against the skeptic, when that appeal is supposed to result in a convincing refutation of the very intelligibility of skepticism, seems so feeble and beside the point.[5] The ordinary-language philosopher describes the language games that together express our form of life, whereas the skeptic says that he knows all of this but sees no final justification, much less necessity, for accepting the divisions and certainties that are integral parts of this scheme. In fact, he produces reasons for doubting the face-value validity of what our words normally lead us to accept, and he challenges the person who uses ordinary language as a final court of appeal in order to show that our conceptual scheme is capable of rational justification.

At this point the ordinary-language philosopher seems to have two choices. First, he can put forth arguments that try to set limits to meaningful utterance or that purport to give the conditions for the very existence of a natural language. These arguments will obviously involve principles about traditional philosophical issues, and only if one both accepts them as true and acknowledges their relevance to philosophical skepticism will one be inclined to feel the weight of such argument forms as the Paradigm Case Argument, the Argument from Meaningful Contrasts, and so forth. Arguments against the possibility of alternative conceptual frameworks are precisely designed to cut off at ground level the questioning of our ordinary-language framework. They try to show that with our conceptual scheme we have a genuine case of "this or nothing."

The difficulty with this approach to skepticism lies in the philosophical claims that these principles express. As I have tried to show above, these principles are question-begging; they show, perhaps, how we *do* function linguistically, but they do not show how we *must* or *should* function conceptually. And apart from the detailed criticism of such principles, there is a more serious general difficulty. What can the status be of such principles from the perspective of the ordinary-language philosopher? If he can engage in something like a transcendental defense of ordinary language as one's only available reference point, then he surely must admit the possibility of philosophy as a legitimate mode of knowledge. To admit this, however, is to undercut the very raison d'être of his enterprise, namely, that the philosopher must engage in description and must shun philosophical theory at all costs. Once the appeal to necessities of a philosophical kind about language is made, the skeptic may either claim that the limits of language are not the same as the limits of thought, or he may try to show piecemeal that such principles lack the kind of justification that is necessary in order to refute skepticism. And the ordinary-language philosopher will find himself engaged in the very enterprise that he wants to dissolve. There is nothing special about philosophical principles regarding language once they are advanced against an opponent.

Pears's account of Wittgenstein is a good case in point. He tells one that Wittgenstein's later philosophy is a kind of "linguistic naturalism" which can respond to a request for a justification of these forms "only by a careful description of the language in which they find expression."[6] In another place, Pears wavers between saying that there can only be one theory and saying that there can be no theory, only description; he adds, "But perhaps the best way to put it is that the only possible theory is the theory that there are only the linguistic facts" (p. 139). That is, when the philosopher seeks for independent backing outside of language for the necessities within it, "the pointing is deceptive and the idea that the backing is independent is an illusion" (p. 145).

238

But how can Wittgenstein, as conceived by Pears, have it both ways? Not only are the principles as stated highly suspect (what does it mean to say that there can only be one theory?), but more importantly, they are clearly in conflict with the program of linguistic naturalism. On the other hand, if linguistic naturalism is a philosophic program, how can it avoid having its own philosophic principles and necessities?

This brings us to the second path that the ordinary-language analyst might follow in his response to skepticism, namely, the one that emerged in our discussion of Rorty's interpretation of Wittgenstein in chapter 10 of this book. What if one made a Herculean effort to put behind one all references to necessities of the philosophical variety? At the same time, imagine that one thought that the skepticism formulated to date, notably Cartesian skepticism, seemingly was forgetful of the conditions of the linguistic practice of the skeptic himself. In addition, say that one limited oneself to making the grounds of this practice evident and, by so doing, forced the skeptic to become aware of them, putting him on the defensive until he could explain how he could square his theory with his linguistic practice. Cavell states: "My interest, it could be said, lies in finding out what my beliefs mean, and learning the particular ground they occupy. This is not the same as providing evidence for them. One could say it is a matter of making them evident."[7] We need diagnoses that show the possibility of either agreement or disagreement, "not as if the problem is for opposed positions to be reconciled, but for the halves of the mind to go back together" (p. 241).

Two remarks seem appropriate here. One possibility is that the ordinary-language philosopher, so conceived, is guilty of bad faith. That is, the very fact that he finds something troublesome about skepticism indicates that he has adopted some kind of implicit meta-theory about philosophy, the limits of meaningful discourse, and the like. Yet, merely because he refuses to disclose the philosophical base from which he operates does not free him from the burden of both revealing and defending that base. He refuses to be explicit about his commitments, but he has them all the same.

A second possibility is at least worth entertaining. The ordinary-language philosopher is merely interested in exhibiting the fact that skeptical discourse is parasitic on ordinary discourse and in raising a question mark about the possibility of any skepticism that can be so characterized. Here no final refutations of skepticism are envisaged, no attempt in the tradition of Kant to put skepticism to rest once and for all. Add to this the practical desire simply to put skepticism behind one, regardless of any final questions about its validity.

If this be the purpose of the true Wittgensteinian, then I think that he has succeeded very well. Skepticism seems to be much harder to understand and defend as the result of many linguistic treatments, and for many philosophers, the issue has become something that one would rather not discuss. But then, nothing that I have said has denied either that this has happened or that it has been healthy. My only point throughout this book has been to point out that ordinary-language methods have failed to show conclusively either that skepticism is not a viable philosophic position or that metaphysical theories in general can be known in advance to be without merit. In addition, however, I have tried to provide additional reasons for thinking that skepticism can overcome the questions that have been raised by the display of the parasitic character of skepticism. Thus the so-called Private Language Argument, interpreted in this way, merely displays a linguistic fact that I think the skeptic can handle without undue effort. Beyond this, the mapping of the internal geography of ordinary language leaves skepticism untouched.[8]

Ordinary-language philosophy then faces this dilemma: The closer it remains to what seems distinctive and original about it, the less it is able to constitute a refutation of skepticism (and the more it suggests an element of bad faith); the further it strays from this distinctive nature, the more it perpetuates the very kinds of argument it wishes to set aside, and the more its principles seem either question-begging or open to the kind of criticism that sent Positivism to an early grave. Until a way can be shown out of this dilemma, the philosophical merit of ordinary-language methods remains, at best, very much in doubt.

12

EPILOGUE:
TWO RECENT DEFENSES OF SKEPTICISM

In the previous chapters of this book, I have been concerned to show that ordinary-language philosophers have failed to undermine philosophical skepticism. Even after their attempts to neutralize the force of skepticism, it remains a theoretical or conceptual possibility. Rather like an unwanted relative, it will not go away.

Since the Wittgensteinian treatment of skepticism is the most powerful and thorough that I know, its failure raises the question of whether skepticism can be defended in its own right. That is, one wonders whether it can be shown not simply to survive ingenious attacks but to be, in light of all the available evidence, the rational attitude to take toward knowledge claims. One wonders, further, if skepticism can be defended (for philosophical purposes), should it range over *all* knowledge claims or only over many more claims than we normally think can or should be questioned?

This last question is particularly relevant, since we have seen that Cartesian and Humean skepticism arises out of a solid basis of certainty. Because Descartes and Hume take some things to be known or certain, they are able to question other claims that we normally leave undisturbed by doubt. Certainty in one area, and concerning a particular subject matter, provides an achieved standard which claims in other areas, and involving other subject matters, cannot match. For them, skepticism has limits, and their means of showing that skepticism is a real option require that it be limited.

Nonetheless, there have been two recent and significant attempts to argue in favor of total skepticism. According to both of these views, no one knows anything at all.[1] If this is correct, then all of our knowledge claims are overblown; we at most attain only highly confirmed beliefs, and these, of course, are necessarily less than certain. Such skepticism about knowledge cuts far more deeply than anything considered heretofore, but it might be thought to be a natural extension of Cartesian skepticism, much as Cartesian skepticism might be thought to be a deepening of the normal range of doubting. Therefore, it is important to see if total skepticism seems to be the defensible result of a thorough critique of knowledge claims.

According to Lehrer's brand of skepticism, "the contention is that no one knows anything, not even that no one knows anything" (p. 284). The latter clause is intended to protect Lehrer from the circularity apparently inherent in claiming to know that one knows nothing, while still allowing the position to have force against those who claim knowledge. For, after all, they are said to lack knowledge as much as does the skeptic. Furthermore, skepticism may be defended through what the skeptic believes to be true, as long as he does not lapse into thinking that his beliefs are in fact bits of knowledge. For Lehrer, the skeptic needs to know neither that the one claiming knowledge is wrong nor even that there is evidence to support his conclusion. As Lehrer puts it, "He affirms that we know nothing, but he believes most of what most men believe" (p. 284).

Lehrer argues that such skepticism is both logically consistent and meaningful. It is the former because there is nothing inconsistent in doubting the character of one's sensations (p. 287), and to argue that one cannot be mistaken in believing a necessary proposition to be true does nothing to show that one knows such a proposition to be true. Since, in both areas, mistakes are logically possible (with the exception that if I believe that I believe something, then I cannot be mistaken that I believe something), knowledge claims short of "complete justification" are unwarranted.

Skepticism is meaningful because "we can tell that he has denied what we have affirmed" (p. 290). We can understand both what the skeptic is saying and why he says it: "He said it because he is a sceptic showing his agnoiological goods" (p. 289). Nor can skepticism be rendered harmless by arguing that it involves a special use of 'know'; rather, the skeptic believes something different from the rest of mankind, namely, that there is no knowledge.

Are there any good reasons for denying skepticism? Not, says Lehrer, if one accepts the "agnoiological principle of impartiality" (p. 293). No side in the dispute is to assume the burden of proof; none is to be judged guilty or innocent without proof. But then, one's most fundamental beliefs—for example, those of common sense—cannot be accepted without justification (in the form of arguments either for them or against skepticism); if this is not forthcoming, knowledge will not have been demonstrated on either side. Yet, such a seeming stalemate favors skepticism since it claims only that we *know* nothing. Skepticism does conflict with one's ordinary attempts to explain things and to order one's affairs in a productive manner, but this shows only that skepticism cannot be (or should not be) believed, but not that it is false.

Insofar as Lehrer's position allows for the achievement of knowledge about at least some mental states, I do not wish to take issue with it here. However, I take it that the main thrust of his position resides in his opening claim that there is a universal lack of knowledge. If so, there remain two significant claims against his version of skepticism: his skeptic does not have a position that threatens one who claims knowledge, and his principle of impartiality should in fact be called the principle of partiality.

Consider the first point. Lehrer's skeptic cannot know that he is correct. Presumably, the most he can do is believe that he is correct. And, Lehrer acknowledges, he cannot know that there is evidence in favor of his position. Again, he can only believe this to be so. Further, he cannot know that he believes in skepticism, although he can know that he believes that he believes in skepticism.

But then the skeptic loses all purchase on those who are committed to knowledge. His argument can amount only to an expression of his belief that knowledge claims are always over-extended, and he cannot know that it is even as much as this. In such a case, it seems to me that the one who claims knowledge may simply ignore the skeptic until such time as he can *show* that no one knows anything. And it seems that his position prevents him from ever doing this, for an argument in which *nothing* is claimed to be known turns out to be nothing more than a bit of autobiographical reporting.

After all, the skeptic cannot claim to know that his view is either consistent or meaningful, or that claims to knowledge cannot be defended. On the other hand, the one who claims knowledge can honestly say that his opponent's position is not a genuine possibility since he knows it to be false. This would mean that Lehrer's principle of impartiality could never get off the ground, since from the perspective of one side there need be only one candidate in the field. The situation would be very different if the skeptic thought that he could *prove* that there is no knowledge, for then his claim would be on a par with that of his opponent. Unfortunately for the skeptic, this would reduce the skeptic's position to the apparently absurd claim that he knows that there is no knowledge.

Of course, one can harbor doubts about the truthfulness of present and future knowledge claims in various areas; and after one states a position, one can wonder if one's claims really con-stitute knowledge; but how can it be built into one's position that it is not knowledge and still claim that this position is on sounder ground than one that claims knowledge? There seems to be no middle ground for an all-embracing skepticism to occupy between inconsistency and harmlessness. I might add the *ad hominem* point that when Lehrer argues for skepticism and against defenses of knowledge, he gives every indication that he thinks that he knows which position is superior. And it is only natural that this should be so.

Let us now consider the principle of impartiality. Lehrer derives it from an analogy with the law: all are innocent until proven guilty. Now I agree that, on the above assumption, skepticism will win out. Either the person defending knowledge will simply assert that he knows certain things, thus begging the question against the skeptic; or he will try to justify his claims to knowledge. However, these justifications will have to rest on principles that are unjustified within the argument; and since they seem to be bits of assumed knowledge, the defender of knowledge begs the question here, too, if somewhat more subtly.

The problem is that the principle of impartiality is far from impartial. Under the guise of fairness, it awards the argument to the skeptic. That is, it begs the question in his favor by making a defense of knowledge impossible. We certainly think that every hypothesis deserves a hearing and that none should be ruled against without a fair hearing. And in the normal case, when one is considering two alternative ways of explaining something, this is a productive attitude. But if one knows something, then one is justified in rejecting the skeptic's position on the basis of that knowledge. Sooner or later the one who claims to know something will have to rest on some knowledge claim that he cannot further justify. At that point, either one is justified in claiming that one knows that skepticism is false, or the rules of the game have made it impossible for one side ever to succeed.

Thus, to the charge of arbitrary dogmatism, one can reply that any other course forces one to doubt or deny what one knows, thus unfairly undermining one's position and awarding the prize to the skeptic before the race begins. "Innocent until proven guilty" is a happy maxim to follow in all those cases in which there can be a reasonable doubt about the outcome. But the knowledge-claimer cannot be asked to forfeit his claims as a precondition of entering the debate. There is a real problem of finding a neutral starting point from which this philosophical issue might begin with fairness to both sides, but the principle of impartiality does not provide it. Under its reign, the skeptic will win only an empty victory, for the ground rules will have made defense of the opposing view impossible.

Lehrer is then faced with a dilemma. Either he knows the principle of impartiality to be fair and knows what follows from it, or he does not. If he does, then his skepticism is less than total. If he does not, then what he believes may be false (as I think it is), and it does not provide a suitable foundation from which to argue against one who thinks that we do know that something is the case.

In his recent book *Ignorance: A Case for Scepticism*, Peter Unger has worked out in great detail a view that "no one ever knows anything to be so" (p. 93). As he also states his thesis, ignorance is both inevitable and universal. His basic plan of attack is disarmingly simple. First, argue that one is concerned only with the ordinary sense of 'know' and 'certain', not with some special, philosophical, or technical sense of those key terms. Second, argue that although one speaks loosely and carelessly in our ordinary exchanges with others, one finds that knowing requires being certain. Further, demonstrate that 'certain' is an "absolute" term, a term, namely, that sets an absolute limit, which is approached to the degree that the relevant relative properties are absent (p. 55).

Armed with this strict sense of 'certain', Unger then tries to show that none of our claims can pass this strict test. Once again, his method of showing this is simple. Take any claim to know anything at all; indicate possible experiences that would (or should) make one less certain than one needs to be if one is to be justified in claiming to know, for being less certain, in fact, is not to be certain at all but to be less than certain; then, conclude that one didn't know what one originally thought one knew. It is uncontroversial, Unger thinks, to say that certain conceivable experiences "ought" to make us wonder to some small degree about our previous knowledge claim (p. 127). But if so, then we cannot have been truly certain at the time, for true certainty involves not only the absence of any actual doubt but also the absence of "any *openness* on the part of the man to consider new experience or information as seriously relevant to the truth or falsity of the thing" (p. 116).

To sum up: since possible future hesitancy is enough to warrant the claim that one does not know now and since there is no claim for which some degree of hesitancy cannot be imagined in the future, there are no cases of knowing.[2] This means that all claims for certainty must be rejected as dogmatic and, hence, as wrong (p. 105). In saying that one knows, one commits oneself to future attitudes that one cannot be certain that one will have and that if one does have, one ought not to have.

But Unger's skepticism cuts even more deeply than his categorical denial of knowledge would indicate.[3] He argues that if no one ever knows anything, then "it follows that it is also true that nobody is ever (even the least bit) reasonable or justified in anything, in particular, in believing anything to be so" (p. 198). And by an analysis of 'truth', Unger reaches the conclusion that truth and falsity are *impossible*, that no one can ever believe anything to be the case, and that states of affairs are contradictory (see pp. 308–13). Unger does not take these results as constituting a *reductio ad absurdum* of his position. Rather, he takes them to be disturbing results which we must face up to and somehow acknowledge.

Before attempting some general comments about Unger's position, let us consider a difficult test case for his skepticism. Even if one grants that no one has produced a perfected analysis of the notions 'I' and 'exists', cannot one claim to know that one exists at the moment that one thinks one exists? In this case, thinking seems to make it so. Attempts at doubting this result presuppose the existence of what one is attempting to doubt. In this case, Moore seems to be correct. We can know something to be so without waiting for philosophers to produce an analysis of the concepts involved.

Not at all, says Unger. Imagine a voice that tells one that one confuses the meaning of 'exist' with 'persist'. One will then become less than certain that one *exists*, even if one continues to believe that one does (see p. 132). Doubts about verbal matters, which are appropriate in this case, undermine one's certainty. As we know, this means for Unger that one never was truly certain in the first place.

But now I have trouble understanding what one must show in order to convince someone that he never really knew. In some cases, what I show is that certain situations may obtain and that if they do, I do not know what I claim to know. I do not ordinarily take such logical possibilities into consideration, but when I do, I find that they cannot be ruled out on the basis of the evidence before me.

In the present case, however, all that happens is that one is caused to become confused over one's use of words. If all that has to be shown in order to prove a lack of knowing is that some circumstances might arise in which someone might become confused about what he meant, then no one can say that this cannot happen. A blow on the head might serve, as would an inner voice. What one ought to show, it seems to me, is that when one is perfectly clearheaded, one can still see one's way open to entertain doubts of an unusual and impractical nature. By this test, the person who claims to know that he exists at the moment of believing it seems to be correct in his claim. One may be caused to become disoriented and thereby be caused to become unsure of even the most obvious things; but this does not mean, as Unger says, that it is "proper" for one to become unsure. Rather, one's unsureness is, in such circumstances, irrational and can be dismissed as such.

Interestingly, Unger does not say that people *would* become unsure in the situations that he imagines. Instead, he says that it would be "proper" or "right" for them to do so, or that they "ought" to do so. But what can he mean by these words? They suggest that it would be justified or rational for one to lose one's grip on certainty upon hearing the inner voice or upon thinking of the world as wildly different from the way we normally treat it. At the same time, he tells us that no one is to any degree justified about anything. Worse still, if no one believes anything, then what are we to understand by the original claim to know and by the suggested recanting of that claim? These seem to be at least changes in belief. In order to make out that his case is reasonable, Unger must employ the very notion that he later discredits.

These remarks lead me to some general comments about Unger's case for skepticism. I do not quarrel with his assertion that 'know' carries with it the sense of 'certain' and that this linking makes philosophical skepticism possible. Much of what I have said in the earlier chapters of this book is based on precisely this notion.[4] But I do quarrel with his attempt to show that *no* uses of 'know' in this strict sense are legitimate uses and that no such uses *could* be legitimate.

It is apparent, for example, that Unger knows the premises of his argument to be true. Or at the very least, he knows that it is rational to believe them, that they are substantiated by relevant evidence. He knows that certain conclusions follow from these premises, or at least he claims to know this. Otherwise, his refusal to renounce his skepticism in the face of its results could only be viewed as dogmatism of the highest order. Surely, he knows that he believes what he says to be true. Yet, on his own view, not one of these implied claims to knowledge can be justified. How, then, is his argument to have any force against the person who claims some minimal kind of knowledge?

Ordinary-language philosophers often charge skeptics with setting the standards of knowledge so high that nothing can count as a case of knowing. I think that this charge is usually made unfairly, for there was implicit in the skepticism presented earlier in this book a standard of knowledge that could be met, and was met, in some restricted cases. It seems to me, however, that Unger is open to this charge. The claim that someone might feel less certain about an assertion in the future and under unspecified conditions is so unspecific that one cannot deny it. But if one bases a denial of knowledge on the claim that this proposition cannot be known to be false, one has ruled out the possibility of knowledge by fiat. On the other hand, if one takes ordinary-language claims one at a time and shows that there are conditions under which theoretical doubt is reasonable, all the while allowing for the possibility of knowledge in some imaginable or real cases, one avoids the charge of victory by arbitrary exclusion.

Unger does make a rather brief attempt to argue that it is all right if, by his own beliefs, his view cannot be considered to be true. He says: "But even if what I have placed before us is not true [because it cannot be true!], it may well be worth your while to focus on it, to be influenced by it, and even to be guided by it in the construction of some new, better intellectual approach to the world" (p. 310). But this will not do. Recall that, for Unger, what he says cannot be false either. Neither can it be believed by Unger, so one is not faced with simply the possibility that his false beliefs may be of some utilitarian value. Even if they could be so regarded, however, it would be necessary to explain the theoretical nature of Unger's account of knowledge. The dilemma is this: if Unger wants his argument to have force against one who claims knowledge, then he must claim truth for his position. Yet, his own position prevents him from claiming even this much.

This brief examination of two recent defenses of a skepticism that has no limits prompts me to make the following summary observation. Skepticism is a reasonable possibility for theoretical purposes in contexts that are normally thought to be free from doubt. One can show this in a piecemeal fashion by revealing the logical possibility of error in the contexts being considered. But if one tries to promote a theory of unlimited skepticism, thus generalizing the results obtained one at a time, one fails to express any position at all. This is because any skepticism takes place within a context of at least the possibility of knowledge. To then rule this out as a possibility is to remove the foundation that makes a deepened skepticism a reasonable, imaginable possibility. We may know far less than we think we know, but we cannot meaningfully assert the total absence of knowledge, much less of truth. Skepticism must be limited.

NOTES

Within any one chapter, full references will be made when a work is first cited; subsequent page references within any one section will be given either in parentheses or in brackets.

INTRODUCTION

1. J. L. Austin, *Philosophical Papers*, ed. J. O. Urmson and G. J. Warnock (Oxford: Clarendon Press, 1961), pp. 129 and 133.
2. I might add that even Austin's practice is not always in accord with his methodological pronouncements. In *Sense and Sensibilia* the analysis of what we would say is used to show the mistaken character of certain theories of perception and of associated notions such as 'real'.
3. Ludwig Wittgenstein, *Philosophical Investigations*, trans. G. E. M. Anscombe (Oxford: Basil Blackwell, 1958), § 109.
4. Norman Malcolm, "Moore and Ordinary Language," in *Ordinary Language*, ed. V. C. Chappell (Englewood Cliffs, N.J.: Prentice-Hall, 1964), p. 15.

CHAPTER 1

1. A. J. Ayer, "Philosophical Scepticism," in *Contemporary British Philosophy*, ed. H. D. Lewis (London: George Allen & Unwin, 1956), p. 48.
2. Ibid., pp. 52–53.

3. George Edward Moore, *Philosophical Papers* (New York: Collier, 1962), pp. 43–44.

4. For a radical change in Ayer's attitude as to whether Berkeley and Hume can be considered merely as analysts, see first *Language, Truth, and Logic* (New York: Dover Publications, 1946), pp. 53–54, and then "Berkeleianism and Physicalism as Constructively Critical," in *The Nature of Philosophical Inquiry*, ed. Joseph Bobik (Notre Dame, Ind.: University of Notre Dame Press, 1970), pp. 132–48.

5. See Ayer, "Philosophical Scepticism," p. 56. Ayer goes further than I would when he says, "Experimental reasoning may carry us along at a given level, from actual to possible sense-data, from observation to prediction of overt behaviour: but it can never enable us to jump from one level to another." For one thing, I do not see how inferences to unobservables in scientific reasoning can meet this conception of experimental reasoning. However, I think the point is well taken that the lack of direct verification does mean that the Argument from Analogy cannot capture the immediacy that is characteristic of our ordinary attitude about other minds.

6. Charles S. Peirce, *Values in a Universe of Chance*, ed. Philip P. Wiener (Garden City, N.Y.: Doubleday Anchor Books, 1958), p. 99.

CHAPTER 2

1. P. F. Strawson, "Carnap's Views on Constructed Systems versus Natural Languages in Analytic Philosophy," in *The Philosophy of Rudolph Carnap*, ed. Paul Arthur Schilpp (La Salle, Ill.: Open Court, 1963), p. 503.

2. Norman Malcolm, "Philosophy for Philosophers," *Philosophical Review* 60 (July 1951): 340.

3. J. N. Findlay, "Time: A Treatment of Some Puzzles," in *The Philosophy of Time*, ed. Richard M. Gale (Garden City, N.Y.: Doubleday & Co., 1967), p. 145.

4. Apparently, the reason that one can speak about "momentary presents" or Zeno's "infinite happenings" in a way that is satisfactory is that these are new, out-of-the-ordinary uses which one does not need to treat as having the same meaning and implications as ordinary notions have.

5. Terence Penelhum, "Hume on Personal Identity," *Philosophical Review* 64 (October 1955): 579.

6. See Roderick M. Chisholm, "On the Observability of the Self," *Philosophy and Phenomenological Research* 30 (September 1969): 9–12.

7. Max Black, "Making Something Happen," in *Determinism and Freedom in the Age of Modern Science,* ed. Sidney Hook, Proceedings of the First Annual New York University Institute of Philosophy (New York: Collier Books, 1961), p. 32.

8. W. E. Kennick, "Philosophy as Grammar and the Reality of Universals," in *Ludwig Wittgenstein: Philosophy and Language,* ed. Alice Ambrose and Morris Lazerowitz (London: George Allen & Unwin, 1972), p. 142.

9. Brand Blanshard, *Reason and Analysis* (London: George Allen & Unwin, 1962), p. 269.

10. George Edward Moore, *Philosophical Papers* (New York: Collier, 1962), p. 37. Referred to hereafter as *PP.*

11. See Blanshard, *Reason and Analysis,* pp. 267–68, for a good discussion of the claim that necessary statements are conventions.

12. Ludwig Wittgenstein, *The Blue and Brown Books* (Oxford: Basil Blackwell, 1958), pp. 135 and 55.

CHAPTER 3

1. Norman Malcolm, "Certainty and Empirical Statements," *Mind,* n.s. 51 (January 1942): 21 ff. Referred to hereafter as *CES.*

2. Norman Malcolm, "The Verification Argument," in his *Knowledge and Certainty* (Englewood Cliffs, N.J.: Prentice-Hall, 1963), p. 38. Referred to hereafter as *VA.*

3. "Ordinary Language *is* correct Language." Norman Malcolm, "Moore and Ordinary Language," in *Ordinary Language,* ed. V. C. Chappell (Englewood Cliffs, N.J.: Prentice-Hall, 1964), p. 15. Referred to hereafter as *MOL.*

4. See also ibid., p. 20.

5. J. L. Austin, *Sense and Sensibilia,* ed. G. J. Warnock (Oxford: Clarendon Press, 1962), p. 119. Referred to hereafter as *SS.*

6. Norman Malcolm, "Knowledge and Belief," in *Knowledge and Belief,* ed. A. Phillips Griffiths (Oxford: Oxford University Press, 1967), pp. 72–73. Referred to hereafter as *KB.*

7. Norman Malcolm, "On Knowledge and Belief," *Analysis* 14 (March 1954).

8. Bertrand Russell, *An Outline of Philosophy* (New York: W. W. Norton & Co., 1927), p. 7.

9. A. C. Ewing, "Knowledge of Physical Objects," *Mind,* n.s. 52 (April 1943): 109–11.

10. George Edward Moore, *Commonplace Book, 1919–1953*, ed. Casimir Lewy (London: George Allen & Unwin, 1962), p. 187.
11. George Edward Moore, "Four Forms of Scepticism," in his *Philosophical Papers* (New York: Collier Books, 1962), p. 216. I have restated Moore's point for my purposes.
12. See René Descartes, "Meditations on First Philosophy," in *The Philosophical Works of Descartes*, trans. Elizabeth S. Haldane and G. R. T. Ross, vol. 1 (New York: Dover Publications, 1955), pp. 145, 147, and 189.
13. See Ewing, "Knowledge of Physical Objects," for this point.
14. George Edward Moore, "Certainty," in his *Philosophical Papers* (New York: Collier Books, 1962), p. 245.
15. See also *MOL*, p. 20.
16. O. K. Bouwsma, "Descartes' Evil Genius," in *Meta-Meditations*, ed. Alexander Sesonske and Noel Fleming (Belmont, Calif.: Wadsworth, 1965).
17. Gilbert Ryle, *Dilemmas* (Cambridge, England: Cambridge University Press, 1960), pp. 94–95.
18. C. K. Grant, "Polar Concepts and Metaphysical Arguments," *Aristotelian Society Proceedings* 56 (1955–56): 88 and 93.
19. See John A. Passmore, *Philosophical Reasoning* (New York: Charles Scribner's Sons, 1961), pp. 112–13.
20. Anthony Flew, "Divine Omnipotence and Human Freedom," in *New Essays in Philosophical Theology*, ed. Anthony Flew and Alasdair MacIntyre (London: SCM Press Ltd., 1955), p. 150.
21. Bertrand Russell, *An Inquiry into Meaning and Truth* (London: George Allen & Unwin Ltd., 1940), p. 119.
22. Susan Stebbing, "The Furniture of the Earth," in *Philosophy of Science*, ed. Arthur Danto and Sidney Morgenbesser (Cleveland, Ohio: World Publishing Co., 1962), p. 70.
23. See *MOL*, p. 13, for Malcolm's defense of Moore's "linguistic" reply to skepticism.
24. See A. G. N. Flew, " 'Farewell to the Paradigm-Case Argument': A Comment," *Analysis* 18 (December 1957), for this point.
25. J. W. N. Watkins, "A Reply to Professor Flew's Comment," *Analysis* 18 (December 1957): 42.
26. See Passmore, *Philosophical Reasoning*, p. 115, for a good criticism of Malcolm's distinction between what can be learned descriptively and what ostensively.
27. Flew, *New Essays*, p. 150. Also quoted in "Farewell . . . A Comment," p. 37.
28. In fairness, one must mention that Flew now says that the Argu-

ment from Paradigm Cases was never meant to be more than a first step. But this more modest claim does not represent the use to which both Malcolm and Flew put the argument when they were doing philosophy, not talking about how to do it. See Anthony Flew, "Again the Paradigm," *Mind, Matter, and Method*, ed. Paul K. Feyerabend and Grover Maxwell (Minneapolis: University of Minnesota Press, 1966), pp. 264 and 271.

29. Norman Malcolm, "On Knowledge and Belief," *Analysis* 14 (March 1954): 97.

30. In a similar vein, Professor Ambrose neglects this very point when she claims that criticism of ordinary language that is aimed at its defectiveness is empty or spurious because "no complaints over failures to overcome shortcomings are real complaints if success is ruled out by logic" (Alice Ambrose, "The Problem of Linguistic Inadequacy," in *Essays in Analysis* [London: George Allen & Unwin, 1966], p. 165). If there is a contrast with language—say, Bradleyan or Bergsonian immediate experience—then the fact that the difficulties with language know of no solution is not a good reason for thinking that the claims are empty. See Grant, "Polar Concepts," p. 102, for a similar point regarding Descartes's criticism of the senses.

CHAPTER 4

1. Arthur C. Danto, *Analytical Philosophy of Knowledge* (Cambridge, England: Cambridge University Press, 1968), p. 197.

2. Danto earlier has asserted three interlocking theses which explain his stand here. (1) "To understand a sentence *s* is to understand a *rule of meaning* for *s*"; (2) "To understand a rule is in principle to be able to apply that rule," i.e., to be able to tell when *s* is true; (3) "The rule of descriptive meaning for *s* specifies a set (*k*) of conditions under which *s* is true." Ibid., p. 185.

3. The descriptive meaning for a sentence gives a "definition of truth" and that for a term gives its "definition." Danto makes it clear that loss of descriptive meaning is not the same as meaninglessness or nonsense. Ibid., pp. 162 and 161.

4. I say "almost" because no one has yet shown convincingly that we do not understand words such as 'God' or 'particles too small to observe' or 'underlying ego', and yet, how does one specify the conditions under which it would be true or false to say, "This is God?" Perhaps one could grant that these terms lack descriptive meaning but are still meaningful in some other sense(s) and, hence,

are understood. Then it need not bother the skeptic that his theory makes terms descriptively meaningless.

5. Thus I reject Danto's claim that there is no epistemological problem concerning illusions and that they should be considered a fit subject only for the empirical scientist. *Analytical Philosophy of Knowledge*, pp. 200–201.

6. For example, see Moore's assertion (partly supporting Malcolm) that one should not know what to think if startling things happened to one when one went to test one's observations. He says that "such experiences wouldn't *prove* that it wasn't a dog. But they would give me some reason to think that it wasn't." George Edward Moore, *Commonplace Book, 1919–1953*, ed. Casimir Lewy (London: George Allen & Unwin, 1962), p. 176. And this is a difference with Malcolm.

7. G. E. Moore, *The Philosophy of G. E. Moore*, ed. Paul Arthur Schilpp, 3rd ed. (La Salle, Ill.: Open Court, 1942), p. 668.

8. George Edward Moore, *Philosophical Papers* (New York: Collier Books, 1962), p. 233.

9. Norman Malcolm, "Moore and Ordinary Language," in *Ordinary Language*, ed. V. C. Chappell (Englewood Cliffs, N.J.: Prentice-Hall, 1964), p. 8.

10. See Alice Ambrose, "Moore's 'Proof of an External World,' " in *Essays in Analysis* (London: George Allen & Unwin, 1966), pp. 214–32, for the case that the skeptic is making disguised linguistic proposals and that Moore's quasi-empirical argument does not work because it does not relate to what the skeptic is doing. For Ambrose, Moore does show that it makes sense to say that "I know there is a dime in the box" and, hence, that this is logically possible. The skeptic thinks that this is logically impossible. Moore is said to implicitly reject the skeptic's linguistic proposal. See Moore's reply to Ambrose in *The Philosophy of G. E. Moore*, especially pp. 671–73.

11. Moore, *Philosophical Papers*, p. 43. Referred to hereafter as *PP*.

12. G. E. Moore, "Some Judgments of Perception," in his *Philosophical Studies* (London: Routledge & Kegan Paul, 1951), p. 228.

13. In my judgment, however, there are numerous instances in which Moore's bare assertions are so briefly stated that they may well constitute a serious begging of the question. I refer to his statements in "A Defense of Common Sense" to the effect that there are *no good reasons* for holding that all physical facts are logically or causally dependent on some mental facts, that God exists, that there is life after death, etc. (see *PP*, pp. 45 and 52). These claims

do seem to be in need of defense in a more immediate way than do Moore's claims about the existence of physical objects.

14. Really, the issue is whether Moore claimed to *know* for certain that there was a window, for one can *feel* certain about that which he does not know for certain. See *PP*, p. 234, for this point.

15. See Moore's *Commonplace Book*, p. 175, for the example of dinosaur marks: "There is *no doubt whatever* that they were made by the foot of an animal: this is *known*: but it is certainly a case of inference—inference by *analogy*."

16. Of course, the ordinary-language development from Moore denies that there is *a* correct analysis of a term, seeking for the meaning in the use of the term. Then there is no vantage point from which the skeptic can try to correct common sense. Moore seems to expose the flank of common sense and then to deny that he has done so.

17. See A. J. Ayer, *Russell and Moore: The Analytical Heritage* (Cambridge, Mass.: Harvard University Press, 1971), p. 177.

18. John A. Passmore, *Philosophical Reasoning* (New York: Charles Scribner's Sons, 1961), p. 79.

19. See Ayer, *Russell and Moore*, p. 169, for this point. However, Ayer does hold that Moore's attempt to show that skepticism is self-refuting works against those philosophers who "dispense with space and time" (p. 186). Then, however, it is an argument that works against certain metaphysical suggestions and not against skeptical beliefs about knowledge.

20. Norman Malcolm, "Defending Common Sense," *Philosophical Review* 58 (May 1949): 219. Hereafter referred to as *DCS*.

21. C. D. Rollins makes this point in "Ordinary Language and Procrustean Beds," *Mind*, n.s. 60 (April 1951): 225.

22. Norman Malcolm, "Moore's Use of 'Know'," *Mind*, n.s. 62 (April 1953): 241–42.

23. Ibid., p. 243.

24. For a good discussion of the paradoxical consequences of Malcolm's view, those that revolve around knowing something versus saying that one knows, see Max Black, "On Speaking with the Vulgar," *Philosophical Review* 58 (November 1949): 616–21. There Black says: "But Moore's utterance is not pointless—he uses it, in its ordinary sense, for an unusual philosophical purpose. He thinks that the truth of 'That is a hand' is incompatible with the truth of the philosophical assertion, 'There are no external things.' His purpose is to use the common-sense assertion to *prove* that the philosophical thesis is false. And if we understand this, we can see the point of what he is doing" (p. 621).

25. Ludwig Wittgenstein, *On Certainty*, ed. G. E. M. Anscombe and G. H. von Wright (New York: Harper & Row, 1969), § 521. Referred to hereafter as *OC*.

26. As far as I can see, the teacher's reaction to the schoolboy's doubts (§§ 310–15) does not show that the latter cannot have a meaningful doubt in mind.

27. Wittgenstein's examples in which mistakes are said to be impossible lend credence to the view that skepticism is possible even where it may at first seem absurd. For Wittgenstein claims that it is certain within our system that "no one has ever been on the moon," for "our whole system of physics forbids us to believe it" (§ 108). Yet, science-fiction stories are perfectly plausible and require no movement outside our normal scheme. And when he says that it would be madness to doubt that my friend does not have sawdust in his head or body, he seems to overlook Moore's distinction between finding something doubtful and being in (real) doubt (§ 281). A similar remark applies to Wittgenstein's statement that "it is imaginable that my skull should turn out empty when operated on," although I cannot doubt that this is not the case (§ 4).

28. Ewing puts the case nicely when he says: "But if there are cases of apparent perception in dreams which exactly resemble internally the kind of experience I now have when I seem to perceive the chair, it is very difficult to see how I can possibly know in the strictest sense of 'know' that I am perceiving a physical chair." A. C. Ewing, "Knowledge of Physical Objects," *Mind*, n.s. 52 (April 1943): 111.

29. Austin's Argument from Meaningful Contrasts in *Sense and Sensibilia*, pp. 48–49, is an example of this.

30. O. K. Bouwsma, "On Many Occasions I Have in Sleep Been Deceived," *Philosophical Essays* (Lincoln: University of Nebraska Press, 1965), p. 164.

31. Frank B. Ebersole, "De Somniis," *Mind*, n.s. 68 (July 1959): 338.

32. Norman Malcolm, "Dreaming and Scepticism," in *Descartes*, ed. Willis Doney (Garden City, N.Y.: Doubleday & Co., 1967), p. 60.

33. For amplification of the senselessness of trying to determine whether one is awake or asleep, see Norman Malcolm, *Dreaming* (London: Routledge & Kegan Paul, 1959), pp. 108–13.

34. Malcolm, "Dreaming and Scepticism," p. 74.

35. Malcolm, *Dreaming*, p. 60.

36. On Ayer's interpretation of this connection: "The existence of the waking impression is at any rate a necessary condition for one's having had a dream." A. J. Ayer, "Professor Malcolm on Dreams," *Journal of Philosophy* 57 (4 August 1960): 525.

37. He says that this is his meaning, but words such as 'claiming', 'asserting', and 'affirming' obscure the point. See Malcolm, "Dreaming and Scepticism," p. 59.

38. On the extent of the departure of Malcom's view of dreams from our ordinary one, see Hilary Putnam, "Dreaming and Depth Grammar," in *Analytical Philosophy*, ed. R. J. Butler (Oxford: Basil Blackwell, 1962), p. 125.

CHAPTER 5

1. Bertrand Russell, *The Analysis of Mind* (London, George Allen & Unwin, 1921), pp. 159–60.

2. I assume here that attempts by Dewey and Ayer to construe statements about the past as really about the future are implausible.

3. A. J. Ayer, "Statements about the Past," in *Philosophical Essays* (London: Macmillan & Co., 1965), p. 190.

4. Marcus G. Singer, "Meaning, Memory, and the Moment of Creation," *Aristotelian Society Proceedings*, n.s. 63 (1962–63): 189.

5. Norman Malcolm, "Memory and the Past," *Monist* 47 (Winter, 1963): 263. Malcolm goes so far as to question the logical possibility of Russell's hypothesis on the grounds that nothing could support it. Since by 'nothing', Malcolm's examples show that he means 'nothing empirical', one can only conclude that he is implicitly appealing to a version of the Verifiability Theory of Meaning. Otherwise, his remarks are puzzling, for Russell surely does argue for his possibility by showing that it cannot be disproved. This work is referred to hereafter as *MP*.

6. Frank B. Ebersole, "Of All My Fallacious Memory Represents," in *Things We Know* (Eugene: University of Oregon Books, 1967), p. 192.

7. For example, see Malcolm, "Memory and the Past," p. 251.

8. Edward J. Bond, "The Concept of the Past," *Mind*, n.s. 72 (October 1963): 535.

9. Arthur C. Danto, *Analytical Philosophy of History* (Cambridge, England: Cambridge University Press, 1965), p. 84.

10. Sydney Shoemaker, "Memory," in *The Encyclopedia of Philosophy*, ed. Paul Edwards, vol. 5 (New York: Macmillan Co. and The Free Press, 1967), pp. 273–74.

11. I am here interested only in occurrent beliefs and not in dispositional beliefs.

12. Sydney Shoemaker, *Self-Knowledge and Self-Identity* (Ithaca, N.Y.: Cornell University Press, 1963), p. 229.

13. A good discussion of this issue can be found in John Turk Saunders and Donald F. Henze, *The Private-Language Problem* (New York: Random House, 1967), pp. 48–65.
14. See James W. Cornman, "Malcolm's Mistaken Memory," *Analysis* 25 (April 1965): 166, for this point.
15. See also Don Locke, *Memory* (Garden City, N.Y.: Doubleday & Co., 1971), pp. 122–23, for more examples of situations in which error might be more common than truth.
16. See ibid., p. 125.
17. See Cornman, "Malcolm's Mistaken Memory," pp. 162–64, for a thorough discussion of the weaknesses in Malcolm's chess analogy.
18. For a good discussion of the reliance of Shoemaker's argument against memory skepticism on the Verification Principle, see Barry Stroud, "Transcendental Arguments," in *The First Critique: Reflections on Kant's "Critique of Pure Reason,"* ed. Terence Penelhum and J. J. MacIntosh (Belmont, Calif.: Wadsworth Publishing Co., 1969), p. 63.
19. John O. Nelson, "The Validation of Memory and Our Conception of a Past," *Philosophical Review* 72 (January 1963): 36.
20. See H. H. Price, *Thinking and Experience* (London: Hutchinson's University Library, 1953), pp. 78–79.
21. For this point see Locke, *Memory*, pp. 118–19.
22. Ibid., p. 131.
23. For a similar claim, see John Turk Saunders, "Skepticism and Memory," *Philosophical Review* 72 (October 1963): 485.

CHAPTER 6

1. David Hume, *Enquiries Concerning the Human Understanding and Concerning the Principles of Morals*, ed. L. A. Selby-Bigge (Oxford: Clarendon Press, 1957), p. 26.
2. Brian Skyrms, *Choice and Chance* (Belmont, Calif.: Dickenson Publishing Co., 1966), p. 23.
3. For this view of Hume see A. J. Ayer, *Probability and Evidence* (New York: Columbia University Press, 1972), pp. 3–6.
4. Hume, *Enquiries*, p. 37. My emphasis.
5. David Hume, *A Treatise of Human Nature*, ed. L. A. Selby-Bigge (Oxford: Clarendon Press, 1955), p. 89, stress added.
6. Hume, *Enquiries*, p. 35; *Treatise*, p. 89.
7. Bertrand Russell, *The Problems of Philosophy* (London: Oxford University Press, 1956), p. 62.
8. Donald Williams, *The Ground of Induction* (Cambridge, Mass.: Harvard University Press, 1947), p. 20.

9. A. C. Ewing, *The Fundamental Questions of Philosophy* (London: Routledge & Kegan Paul, 1951), p. 47.

10. A. C. Ewing, "Causality and Induction," *Philosophy and Phenomenological Research* 12 (June 1952): 482.

11. Ewing, *Fundamental Questions*, p. 47.

12. See A. C. Ewing, *Idealism: A Critical Survey*, 3rd ed. (London: Methuen & Co., 1961), pp. 176–77.

13. See Ewing, "Causality and Induction," pp. 483–84.

14. Margaret MacDonald, "Induction and Hypothesis: I," in *Knowledge and Foreknowledge, Aristotelian Society Proceedings*, supp. vol. 16 (1937), p. 24.

15. Frederick L. Will, "Generalization and Evidence," in *Philosophical Analysis*, ed. Max Black (Ithaca, N.Y.: Cornell University Press, 1950), p. 410.

16. Alice Ambrose, "The Problem of Justifying Inductive Inference," in *Essays in Analysis* (London: George Allen & Unwin, 1966), p. 199.

17. Max Black, "The Justification of Induction," in his *Language and Philosophy* (Ithaca, N.Y.: Cornell University Press, 1949), p. 62. See also p. 85.

18. Ibid., pp. 62 and 76–77.

19. Will, "Generalization and Evidence," pp. 403–4.

20. Black, "The Justification of Induction," p. 67. See also p. 74.

21. Paul Edwards, "Russell's Doubts about Induction," *Mind*, n.s. 58 (April 1949): 146–47.

22. P. F. Strawson, *Introduction to Logical Theory* (London: Methuen, 1952), p. 250.

23. This material is covered in ibid., pp. 258–63.

24. Wesley C. Salmon, "Should We Attempt to Justify Induction?" *Philosophical Studies* 8 (April 1957): 39.

25. P. F. Strawson, "On Justifying Induction," *Philosophical Studies* 8 (January–February 1958): 20–21.

26. Alice Ambrose, "The Problem of Justifying Inductive Inference," pp. 201–2.

27. Morris Lazerowitz, "The Problem of Justifying Induction," in his *Philosophy and Illusion* (London: George Allen & Unwin, 1968), p. 225.

28. Recall Edwards's "high" and "low" redefinitions.

29. See also pp. 117 and 214–15 for the application of this claim to other philosophical issues.

30. Frederick L. Will, "Will the Future Be Like the Past?" in *Logic and Language*, first and second series, ed. Anthony Flew (Garden City, N.Y.: Doubleday & Co., 1965), p. 266.

31. See ibid., pp. 262–63.

32. See Donald Williams, "Induction and the Future," *Mind*, n.s. 57 (April 1948), for a similar criticism of Will's attack on skepticism.

33. Casimir Lewy, "On the 'Justification' of Induction," *Analysis* 6 (1938/39): 89.

34. The formulation of Lewy's conclusion apparently reflects his stated purpose to concern himself only with inductive arguments whose conclusions are of the form "Probably A and B are *always* associated," p. 87.

CHAPTER 7

1. I assume for the moment—an assumption that will become an issue in the next chapter—that skepticism about other minds is compatible with direct, unquestioned perception of the physical world.

2. Austin makes the point that "the man doesn't 'know his pain': he feels (not knows) what he recognizes as, or what he knows to be, anger (not his anger), and he knows that he is feeling angry." J. L. Austin, "Other Minds," in his *Philosophical Papers*, ed. J. O. Urmson and G. J. Warnock (Oxford: Clarendon Press, 1961), p. 65. But even if one distinguishes between having a sensation and knowing that one is having a certain sensation, the source of the latter knowledge is different in one's own case than in the case of knowledge claimed about another. This is all that the skeptic about other minds needs to claim.

3. Bruce Aune, "Feelings, Moods, and Introspection," *Mind*, n.s. 72 (April 1963): 201.

4. Don Locke, *Myself and Others* (Oxford: Clarendon Press, 1968), pp. 34–35.

5. For a first step, however, see my article "Scientific Materialism," *Idealistic Studies* 6 (January 1976): 1–19.

6. Don Locke, *Perception and Our Knowledge of the External World* (London: George Allen & Unwin, 1967), pp. 155–56.

7. In a similar vein, Austin claims that we are (sometimes) perfectly justified in saying "I know" even if things turn out badly for us and we must retract the claim to have known. See *Philosophical Papers*, pp. 66 and 69. He further claims that if something outrageous happens in the future, we may not know what to say, instead of retracting the claim that the thing is a real so-and-so (pp. 56 and 63). I see no reason that the skeptic cannot accept this and simply disclaim any interest in the normal constraints on the use of 'know' and 'real'.

8. Ludwig Wittgenstein, *Philosophical Investigations*, trans. G. E. M. Anscombe (Oxford: Basil Blackwell, 1958), p. 178. Referred to hereafter as *PI*.

9. Norman Malcolm, "Wittgenstein's *Philosophical Investigations*," in *Wittgenstein: "The Philosophical Investigations,"* ed. George Pitcher (Garden City, N.Y.: Doubleday & Co., 1966), p. 91.

10. See *PI*, par. 654 and p. 226. See also *Philosophical Papers*, where Austin states that "believing in other persons, in authority and testimony, is an essential part of the act of communicating, an act which we all constantly perform. . . . We can state certain advantages of such performances. . . . But there is no 'justification' for our doing them as such" (p. 83).

11. See Locke, *Myself and Others*, pp. 83–85.

12. There is a good discussion of the so-called Attitudinal Objection in Alvin Plantinga, *God and Other Minds* (Ithaca, N.Y.: Cornell University Press, 1967), pp. 233 ff.

13. Stuart Hampshire, "The Analogy of Feeling," in *Freedom of Mind* (Princeton, N.J.: Princeton University Press, 1971), p. 118.

14. Norman Malcolm, "Knowledge of Other Minds," in *Essays in Philosophical Psychology*, ed. Donald F. Gustafson (Garden City, N.Y.: Doubleday & Co., 1964, pp. 367–68.

15. Hilary Putnam, "Other Minds," in *Logic and Art*, ed. Richard Rudner and Israel Scheffler (Indianapolis, Ind.: Bobbs-Merrill Co., 1972), pp. 83–84.

16. Rogers Albritton, "On Wittgenstein's Use of the Term 'Criterion'," in *Wittgenstein: "The Philosophical Investigations,"* ed. George Pitcher (Garden City, N.Y.: Doubleday & Co., 1966), p. 235.

17. Norman Malcolm, "Wittgenstein's *Philosophical Investigations*," p. 85. My emphasis.

18. Norman Malcolm, "Knowledge of Other Minds," p. 372. My emphasis.

19. See ibid., pp. 366–67 and 372–73.

20. See Locke, *Myself and Others*, pp. 122–24.

21. Bruce Aune, "The Problem of Other Minds," *Philosophical Review* 70 (July 1961): 324.

22. See Malcolm's discussion of this point regarding J. S. Mill in Norman Malcolm, *Problems of Mind* (New York: Harper & Row, 1971), pp. 20–23.

23. Norman Malcolm, "Wittgenstein's *Philosophical Investigations*," p. 89. Even in the latter case, I see no reason that a person could not become so involved in philosophical doubt that he would practice it and reject any suggested behavioral criterion of pain.

24. On Malcolm's criticism of skeptical doubt (treating it as practical doubt and then calling attention to the wreckage that this would cause to one's ordinary conceptions if put into everyday use), Plantinga notes that there is no reason that the analogy theorist may not, qua practical man, accept behavior as a criterion of pain. All he need claim is that this certainly needs a justification; he need not claim that his argument describes the way in which we learn to say that another is in pain. Malcolm's emphasis on how one learns concepts (see "Wittgenstein's *Philosophical Investigations*," p. 83) distorts the nature of philosophical argument by putting it to a test that it need not meet in order to be effective philosophically. See Alvin Plantinga, *God and Other Minds*, pp. 218–19.

25. Douglas C. Long, "The Philosophical Concept of a Human Body," *Philosophical Review* 73 (July 1964): 337.

26. I might add that Long's implicit assumption that skepticism is obviously incoherent once one identifies 'living human body' with 'body of a person' constitutes another begging of the question. For the skeptic does not need the concept 'living human body' at all. He can perfectly well wonder if what one calls a 'person's body' is in fact only a 'material entity', even though when one calls it the former, one commits oneself to the mental side as well. Why does Long assume that the skeptic must accept this commitment?

27. A. J. Ayer, *The Concept of a Person* (London: Macmillan & Co., 1963), p. 95.

28. P. F. Strawson, *Individuals* (London: Methuen & Co., 1959), p. 109.

29. Austin does not employ Strawson's terms, but two things that he says support Strawson's position. First, he points out that natural behavior is an expression or display of pain, not a symptom of pain. This allows one to say that he knows that another is in pain and not merely that he believes it. Second, he claims that 'being angry' is a "description of a whole pattern of events," not merely a single item in that pattern; and similarly with 'being in pain'. The pattern allows us to know that another is in pain even when we have observed only a part of the pattern. See *Philosophical Papers*, pp. 75–78.

30. C. W. K. Mundle, *A Critique of Linguistic Philosophy* (Oxford: Clarendon Press, 1970), p. 143.

31. Strawson, *Individuals*, pp. 102–5.

32. John W. Cook, "Human Beings," in *Studies in the Philosophy of*

Wittgenstein, ed. Peter Winch (New York: Humanities Press, 1969), p. 127.

33. Strawson, *Individuals*, p. 99.

34. Since Strawson denies that he is doing "*a priori* genetic psychology," perhaps I should say: Other-ascription must be thought of as basic if one is to grasp self-ascription.

35. See Ayer, *Concept of a Person*, p. 105–6, for this point. Locke makes the same point in *Myself and Others*, pp. 146–47.

36. See Ayer, *Concept of a Person*, p. 101.

37. Strawson, *Individuals*, p. 35. The above summary is my reading of passages found on pp. 35 and 106 of *Individuals*.

38. The necessity here would directly parallel that attributed to the general truth of sincere memory reports by Sydney Shoemaker, *Self-Knowledge and Self-Identity* (Ithaca, N.Y.: Cornell University Press, 1963), p. 229.

39. Rogers Albritton, "On Wittgenstein's Use of the Term 'Criterion'," p. 246.

40. Sydney Shoemaker, *Self-Knowledge and Self-Identity*, p. 190.

41. See ibid. for this discussion. Plantinga also discusses this claim in *God and Other Minds*, pp. 226–27.

42. Sydney Shoemaker, "Critical Study: *Myself and Others*," *Philosophical Quarterly* 19 (July 1969): 273.

43. See Shoemaker, *Self-Knowledge and Self-Identity*, pp. 168–70, for the Argument from the Possibility of Having a Word for Sensations in One's Language.

44. I refer here to P. M. S. Hacker, *Insight and Illusion* (Oxford: Clarendon Press, 1972); Don Locke, *Myself and Others*; J. T. Saunders, "Persons, Criteria, and Scepticism," *Metaphilosophy* 4 (April 1973): 90–123; and John V. Canfield, "Criteria and Rules of Language," *Philosophical Review* 83 (January 1974): 70–87. Page references to these works are indicated in the text by reference to the author's last name.

45. Canfield and Saunders seem to disagree as to whether criteria can logically guarantee their evidential strength. Is it necessary that criteria justify belief? But this dispute is of no importance in the evaluation of the weak view of criteria.

46. Richard Rorty, "Criteria and Necessity," *Nous* 7 (November 1973): 319.

47. For example, what does the 'can' mean in "One can ascribe states of consciousness to oneself only"?

CHAPTER 8

1. P. M. S. Hacker, *Insight and Illusion* (Oxford: Clarendon Press, 1972), pp. 224–31, shows that Locke's views about language can serve as a paradigm for the view that Wittgenstein is attacking.
2. Clarence Irving Lewis, *Mind and the World-Order* (New York: Dover Publications, 1956), p. 53.
3. John W. Cook, "Wittgenstein on Privacy," in *Wittgenstein: "The Philosophical Investigations,"* ed. George Pitcher (Garden City, N.Y.: Doubleday & Co., 1966), p. 323.
4. P. F. Strawson, *Individuals* (London: Methuen & Co., 1959), p. 134.
5. Norman Malcolm, "Wittgenstein's *Philosophical Investigations*," in *Wittgenstein: "The Philosophical Investigations,"* ed. George Pitcher (Garden City, N.Y.: Doubleday & Co., 1966), p. 77.
6. Cook, "Wittgenstein on Privacy," p. 291.
7. A. J. Ayer, "Privacy," in his *The Concept of a Person* (London: Macmillan & Co., 1963), p. 59.
8. See Ludwig Wittgenstein, *Philosophical Investigations*, trans. G. E. M. Anscombe (Oxford: Basil Blackwell, 1958), p. 243, and Hacker, *Insight and Illusion*, pp. 277–78.
9. David Pears, *Ludwig Wittgenstein* (New York: Viking Press, 1970), pp. 149 and 168.
10. Malcolm, "Wittgenstein's *Philosophical Investigations*," p. 66.
11. Don Locke, *Myself and Others* (Oxford: Clarendon Press, 1968), p. 72.
12. Anthony Kenny, "The Verification Principle and the Private Language Argument: (ii)," in *The Private Language Argument*, ed. O. R. Jones (London: Macmillan & Co., 1971), p. 205.
13. Cook, "Wittgenstein on Privacy," p. 287.
14. P. F. Strawson, "Critical Notice of Wittgenstein's *Philosophical Investigations*," in *Wittgenstein and the Problem of Other Minds*, ed. Harold Morick (New York: McGraw-Hill, 1967), p. 30.
15. George Pitcher, *The Philosophy of Wittgenstein* (Englewood Cliffs, N.J.: Prentice-Hall, 1964), p. 298.
16. John W. Cook, "Solipsism and Language," in *Ludwig Wittgenstein: Philosophy and Language*, ed. Alice Ambrose and Morris Lazerowitz (London: George Allen & Unwin, 1972), p. 44. See also, Kenny, "The Verification Principle and the Private Language Argument," p. 209.
17. See Cook, "Wittgenstein on Privacy," p. 322, for this point.
18. Norman Malcolm, *Problems of Mind* (New York: Harper & Row, 1971), p. 47.

266

19. Locke, *Myself and Others*, p. 74.
20. Saunders and Henze call this a lack of a distinction between objective and subjective reality. John Turk Saunders and Donald F. Henze, *The Private-Language Problem* (New York: Random House, 1967), p. 80.
21. Malcolm, "Wittgenstein's *Philosophical Investigations*," pp. 76 ff.
22. See ibid., p. 68.
23. See J. J. Thomson, "Private Languages," in *Philosophy of Mind*, ed. Stuart Hampshire (New York: Harper & Row, 1966), pp. 125–26, for examples of apparent rules in which the distinction between thinking one is following them and not following them does not apply. This seems to indicate that private rules could be rules after all.
24. Locke, *Myself and Others*, p. 77, tries to distinguish between meaning based on the possibility of verification and meaning based on the ability to check the propriety of one's use of terms. However, the latter principle rests meaning on knowing under what conditions a statement would be true, by Locke's own admission, and this seems indistinguishable from tying meaning to the logical possibility of verification. The latter, as well as the former, does not demand that a statement is meaningful only if one knows that it is true or even if one knows in any particular case that the conditions for truth have been satisfied.
25. Locke, ibid., pp. 96 ff., suggests a way of avoiding the force of the private-language argument that resembles mine, but he allows criteria to determine the meaning of sensation words. This seems to me to be false and to reduce the scope and interest of skepticism.
26. Pears, *Ludwig Wittgenstein*, p. 169.
27. Hacker, *Insight and Illusion*, p. 235.
28. See Alan Donagan, "Wittgenstein on Sensation," in *Wittgenstein: "The Philosophical Investigations*," ed. George Pitcher (Garden City, N.Y.: Doubleday & Co., 1966), p. 337.
29. Malcolm, *Problems of Mind*, p. 53.
30. Locke, *Myself and Others*, pp. 107–8, my emphasis.
31. Hacker, *Insight and Illusion*, p. 234.
32. Pears, *Ludwig Wittgenstein*, pp. 170–71.
33. A. J. Ayer, "Can There Be a Private Language?" in his *The Concept of a Person* (London: Macmillan & Co., 1963), p. 45.
34. For this point see A. Phillips Griffiths, "Ayer on Perception," *Mind*, n.s. 69 (October 1960): 498.
35. Hacker, *Insight and Illusion*, pp. 237–38.
36. Cook, "Wittgenstein on Privacy," p. 322.

37. Pitcher, *The Philosophy of Wittgenstein*, p. 293. See both Pears, *Ludwig Wittgenstein*, p. 158, and Cook, "Wittgenstein on Privacy," p. 322, for the same charge.
38. Saunders and Henze, *The Private-Language Problem*, p. 188.
39. Although this seems reasonable when one considers adult human beings, it is confusing when applied to children (in one sense of 'possible', self-consciousness is not possible for them at an early time), and downright disturbing when applied to animals.

CHAPTER 9

1. P. F. Strawson, *Individuals* (London: Methuen & Co., 1959), p. 39.
2. "Now the physical object of the framework of common-sense cannot in any literal sense be said to have micro-physical objects as their parts. Chairs do not have electrons as parts in the sense in which they have legs as parts." Wilfrid Sellars, *Science and Metaphysics* (New York: Humanities Press, 1968), pp. 171–72.
3. Both Barry Stroud, "Transcendental Arguments," in *The First Critique: Reflections on Kant's "Critique of Pure Reason,"* ed. Terence Penelhum and J. J. MacIntosh (Belmont, Calif.: Wadsworth Publishing Co., 1969), p. 59, and Alvin Plantinga, "Things and Persons," *Review of Metaphysics* 14 (March 1961): 498, make this point.
4. Plantinga, "Things and Persons," p. 504.
5. Strawson, *Individuals*, p. 35.
6. Richard Rorty, "Verificationism and Transcendental Arguments," *Nous* 5 (February 1971): 5. Referred to hereafter as *VTA*.
7. Rorty adds (p. 11) that there cannot even be a wholly general way of showing that *any* alternative conceptual framework *must* be parasitic on our common-sense framework. All that one can do is to show this piecemeal as alternatives are suggested. But if this is so, then even the parasitism argument against skepticism does not claim to have any necessity to it.
8. Richard Rorty, "Strawson's Objectivity Argument," *Review of Metaphysics* 24 (December 1970): 219. Referred to hereafter as *SOA*.
9. Rorty, *VTA*, p. 7.
10. And Rorty adds that the restriction of concepts to language-users is an essential step in any transcendental argument. See *SOA*, p. 224.
11. Clarence Irving Lewis, *Mind and the World-Order* (New York: Dover Publications, 1956), p. 53.

12. Moore asks, "If I am *not* directly seeing a bluish-white expanse which *has* some such relation to a wall which is *not* bluish-white, how can I possibly know that that wall *is* looking bluish-white to me?" G. E. Moore, "Visual Sense-Data," *Perceiving, Sensing, and Knowing*, ed. Robert J. Swartz (Garden City, N.Y.: Doubleday & Co., 1965), p. 134.

13. J. L. Austin, *Sense and Sensibilia* (Oxford: Clarendon Press, 1962), p. 137.

14. J. L. Austin, "A Plea for Excuses," in his *Philosophical Papers* (Oxford: Clarendon Press, 1961), p. 133.

15. Gilbert Ryle, "Sensation," in *Perceiving, Sensing, and Knowing*, ed. Robert J. Swartz (Garden City, N.Y.: Doubleday & Co., 1965), p. 199.

16. Gilbert Ryle, *The Concept of Mind* (New York: Barnes & Noble, 1959), p. 203. Referred to hereafter as *COM*.

17. Ryle's example is in ibid., p. 217.

18. A very nice statement of this argument, and of the case for sense data, can be found in Timothy S. Sprigge, *Facts, Words and Beliefs* (New York: Humanities Press, 1970), chap. 1.

19. Richard Rorty, "In Defense of Eliminative Materialism," *Review of Metaphysics* 24 (September 1970): 117.

20. Ibid.

21. Ibid., p. 118.

22. Rorty himself is unsure whether one should say that dogs are conscious or not. See "Strawson's Objectivity Argument," pp. 236–37 n.14. And the thesis of the conceptualizability of experience, plus the identification of language and concepts, means for Rorty that the prelinguistic child experiences nothing. *SOA*, p. 228.

23. See Richard Rorty, "Mind-Body Identity, Privacy, and Categories," in *Philosophy of Mind*, ed. Stuart Hampshire (New York: Harper & Row, 1966), secs. 5 and 6.

24. Ibid., p. 55.

25. Ibid., p. 56.

26. After all, so staunch a foe of Cartesian Privacy as Malcolm is forced to distinguish between the describable "experience content" of the headache itself and the lack of such a content in the cases of deciding, intending, etc. See Norman Malcolm, *Problems of Mind* (New York: Harper & Row, 1971), p. 37.

27. H. H. Price, *Thinking and Experience* (London: Hutchinson's University Library, 1953), p. 76.

28. J. O. Urmson, "Recognition," *Aristotelian Society Proceedings* 56 (1955–56): 271–72.

29. Ryle, "Sensation," p. 210–12.
30. Frank B. Ebersole, "How Philosophers See Stars," in his *Things We Know* (Eugene: University of Oregon Books, 1967), p. 62.
31. Richard G. Henson, "Ordinary Language, Common Sense, and the Time-Lag Argument," *Mind*, n.s. 76 (January 1967): 25.
32. Wilfrid Sellars, *Science, Perception and Reality* (New York: Humanities Press, 1963), p. 91.
33. Gilbert Ryle, *Dilemmas* (Cambridge, England: Cambridge University Press, 1966), p. 3.
34. See Sellars, *Science, Perception and Reality*, p. 7.

CHAPTER 10

1. Richard Rorty, "The World Well Lost," *Journal of Philosophy* 69 (26 October 1972): 655.
2. P. F. Strawson, *Individuals* (London: Methuen & Co., 1959), p. 57.
3. C. D. Broad, *Scientific Thought* (London, Kegan Paul, Trench, Trubner & Co., 1923), p. 54. He says, "By an event I am going to mean anything that endures at all."
4. Richard Rorty, "Cartesian Epistemology and Changes in Ontology," in *Contemporary American Philosophy*, ed. John E. Smith (New York: Humanities Press, 1970), p. 284.
5. Rorty, "The World Well Lost," p. 660.
6. See Richard Rorty, "Realism, Categories, and the 'Linguistic Turn'," *International Philosophical Quarterly* 2 (May 1962): 317.
7. Rorty, "The World Well Lost," p. 652.
8. For a more complete defense of this view of logic see my *Bradley's Metaphysics and the Self* (New Haven, Conn.: Yale University Press, 1970), chap. 9.
9. See Rorty, "The World Well Lost," pp. 654 and 657. See also, for this suggestion, the unpublished dissertation of Philip Kitcher, Princeton University, 1973, esp. pp. 385–87.
10. For example, see Rorty's reformulation of 'incorrigible' in "Cartesian Epistemology and Changes in Ontology," p. 292.
11. Ludwig Wittgenstein, *Philosophical Investigations* (Oxford: Basil Blackwell, 1958), § 109.
12. David Pears, *Ludwig Wittgenstein* (New York: Viking Press, 1970), p. 33. See also p. 189.
13. Rorty, "Realism, Categories, and the 'Linguistic Turn'," p. 312.
14. Richard Rorty, "Keeping Philosophy Pure," *Yale Review* 65 (Spring, 1976): 339.

15. Rorty has a wonderfully illuminating discussion of Pears's attempts to preserve both sides of Wittgenstein in his description of the latter's "extreme anthropocentrism" in "Keeping Philosophy Pure," pp. 339–43.
16. Richard Rorty, "Review of *Reason and Analysis*," *Journal of Philosophy* 60 (12 September 1963): 557.
17. F. H. Bradley, *Appearance and Reality* (Oxford: Clarendon Press, 1955), p. 136.

CHAPTER 11

1. J. L. Austin, *Philosophical Papers*, ed. J. O. Urmson and G. J. Warnock (Oxford: Clarendon Press, 1961), p. 133. Of course, only a few pages before this remark, Austin stated that "in examining all the ways in which each action may not be 'free', i.e. the cases in which it will not do to say simply 'X did A', we may hope to dispose of the problem of Freedom" (p. 128). Surely, this suggests a harder line than do his above remarks.
2. See Stanley Cavell, "The Availability of Wittgenstein's Later Philosophy," in *Wittgenstein: "The Philosophical Investigations,"* ed. George Pitcher (Garden City, N.Y.: Doubleday & Co., Inc.), p. 169.
3. G. E. Moore, "The Conception of Reality," in his *Philosophical Studies* (New York: Routledge & Kegan Paul, 1951), pp. 209–11.
4. Stanley Cavell, "Knowing and Acknowledging," in his *Must We Mean What We Say?* (New York: Charles Scribner's Sons [1969]), p. 240. Cavell adds that this ground is not a matter of opinion or belief; thus Wittgenstein can say that he is not of the opinion that another has a soul. This means that the appeal to ordinary language is not an appeal to ordinary belief. Rather, it displays or makes evident the ground of believing itself, a ground that is simply there and that, Cavell allows, can "crack."
5. "Knowing and Acknowledging" is a brilliant analysis of the weaknesses of such appeals.
6. David Pears, *Ludwig Wittgenstein* (New York: Viking Press, 1970), p. 29.
7. Cavell, "Knowing and Acknowledging," p. 241.
8. Pears, *Ludwig Wittgenstein*, p. 117, states that Wittgenstein tries to bring one "back to the existing structure of discourse, which after all is not sacrosanct. But it was from the existing structure that the other took off, and so the first thing to be done is always to bring him back to it. After that, he may be shown how to modify it, if he really wants to. . . ." As a first step, there is noth-

ing here to which the skeptic need object. It remains obscure to me why Pears can also say that "when the other is retrieved it is always to a fact about language that he is retrieved, and never to a theory" (p. 119). Why bother to make this effort of retrieval unless one has a theory that gives philosophical weight to the linguistic facts that one highlights? This dimension of Wittgenstein's method emerges more clearly in Cavell's characterization: "For Wittgenstein, philosophy comes to grief not in denying what we all know to be true, but in its effort to escape those human forms of life which alone provide the coherence of our expression. He wishes an acknowledgement of human limitation which does not leave us chafed by our own skin, by a sense of powerlessness to penetrate beyond the human conditions of knowledge. The limitations of knowledge are no longer barriers to a more perfect apprehension, but conditions of knowledge *überhaupt*, or anything we should call 'knowledge'." Stanley Cavell, "The Availability of Wittgenstein's Later Philosophy," p. 172. Of course, one is then faced with explaining how to make a place for such transcendental claims within a purely descriptive enterprise.

CHAPTER 12

1. See Keith Lehrer, "Why Not Scepticism?" *Philosophical Forum* 2 (Spring, 1971): 284; and Peter Unger, *Ignorance: A Case for Scepticism* (Oxford: Clarendon Press, 1975), p. 93.

2. For Unger, the grounds of one's hesitancy need not be available to us now or even be imaginable in any detail by humans. To show that we don't know anything, it is enough to point out that "we cannot properly be certain that we have given a complete accounting of every sort of experience, evidence, and information which might possibly exist" (*Ignorance*, p. 134).

3. Unger does show some sympathy for what he calls the "Conservative sceptic about knowledge" (*Ignorance*, p. 148). This person agrees with Unger except that he exempts a certain area from the corrosive power of skepticism. Yet, it is clear that this is *not* Unger's position; and he fails to explain how such a position could be tenable for him, given the standards that he has set for knowing.

4. I do think, however, that there is a difficulty in Unger's claims that his sense of 'know' is the ordinary sense and, yet, that ordinary usage is careless or loose. For if none of the ordinary uses of 'know' are sanctioned by Unger, then one cannot look to these uses to supply one with data from which one might determine

what the ordinary sense of this word is. But how is one to determine the ordinary sense of 'know' if one cannot use examples of its ordinary use?

INDEX